ON A CLEAR DAY
THEY COULD SEE
SEVENTH PLACE

ON A CLEAR DAY
THEY COULD SEE
SEVENTH PLACE

Baseball's Worst Teams

By George Robinson
and Charles Salzberg

A DELL TRADE PAPERBACK

All photos courtesy of the
National Baseball Library,
Cooperstown, New York

ON THE COVER:
Pictured left to right: Fresco Thompson, 2b, 1928 Philadelphia Phillies; Babe
Ruth, of, 1935 Boston Braves; Marv Throneberry, 1b, 1962 New York Mets

This book is dedicated to the poor guys
who had to play for these ten teams.

Acknowledgments

Any book is the product of many hands besides those of the author(s), and this one is no exception. We have many people to thank for making this an especially pleasant writing experience. Naturally, these folks are not responsible for any shortcomings to be found in these pages.

The Society for American Baseball Research (SABR) has contributed mightily to the quality of historical writing about the sport. Their members are astute, dedicated, and a delightful group of people to be around. The mere existence of an organization like SABR is an impetus to anyone writing on baseball history, including the authors of this volume. Indeed, the germ of the idea for this book came from an encounter with the St. Louis Browns Fan Club at the 1985 SABR convention. The BFC (as they call themselves) are hearty warriors on behalf of the diamond dreadfuls. It was with great difficulty that we omitted the Brownies from this book. John Phillips is another example of the dedication of SABRites; his ongoing work on the history of major league baseball in Cleveland was of great help in writing the chapter on the 1899 Spiders.

Any author worth a damn will tell you that librarians are the unsung heroes of the writing business. Without the staff of the National Baseball Library at the Baseball Hall of Fame in Cooperstown, it would be nearly impossible to write about baseball history. Tom Heitz, Bill Deane, and the other wonderful folks at the NBL made our stay there a highly productive one, and they gave freely of their time and expertise. (Michael Jerome of The Inn at Cooperstown made our stay in town a pleasant one in spite of subfreezing February temperatures.) Back home in New York, the staff of the New York Public Library's main research branch and the annex were unfailingly helpful, as was the microform room staff at Butler Library, Columbia University. George Robinson had a particularly delightful sojourn in the periodicals room of the Free Library of Philadelphia and extends a special thank-you to the patient staff of that facility.

Howard Siner of Newspaper Enterprise Association has been exceptionally generous with his time and advice. Rob Tobias of ESPN is a model of what a public relations man should be—always helpful, attentive, and funny. Jon Miller was generous with his time and his insights into the '88 Orioles and their '89 recovery; he brings to a conversation the same charm, intelligence, and wit that make him such a fine broadcaster. Thank you also to Jamie Katz, who pointed out Thomas Boswell's postmortem on the '88 team.

The Toronto Blue Jays' public relations department and Jerry Howarth helped us find several members of the '79 Jays. Rick Bosetti and Tom Buskey were kind enough to share reminiscences of a season that both would probably rather have forgotten.

Kevin Smith, our editor at Dell originally, has gone on to other things, but he leaves with our gratitude for his faith in this project and his friendship. Craig Schneider did an impressively diligent job of copyediting the manuscript. Jody Rein and John Newsom, who took over after Kevin's departure, have been invaluable in shepherding the book through the difficult publishing process.

The life of the working writer is a difficult one. A good agent makes it a lot easier, and Gail Ross deserves that accolade. A good union helps a lot too. The National Writers Union can claim both authors of this book as loyal members.

George Robinson has a few personal thank-yous to add to this list: It is hard to find words to thank Michael Kimmel. Besides being an irreplaceable sounding board for ideas and a dear friend, he is also an excellent shortstop. My family—my parents, my siblings, my in-laws—have been a constant source of strength. Finally, Margalit Fox has been my best friend, confidante, collaborator, and copyeditor for many years. Her patience during the writing of this book bordered on the saintly.

To anyone we've inadvertently forgotten, our sincerest apologies.

Contents

Introduction

> Losing, rather than winning, is what baseball is all about, and why, in the end, it is a game for adults.
>
> —ROGER ANGELL

IN SPITE OF what the metaphor mongers say, life is not like baseball. Life is too complex, the rules and playing surface too ill defined. Those of us who love baseball may kid ourselves by arguing to the contrary, but generally that is the case.

However, baseball and life do share certain thematic similarities. On a basic level baseball is really about futility, about failure. So is life. The best hitter in baseball fails nearly 70 percent of the time; the best team in baseball loses between 40 and 60 games during a season. At the end of the day, as Earl Weaver sagely observed, "We gotta go out and do this again tomorrow." And at the end of the season one team wins the World Series. The other 25 are, well, losers. Ultimately, it is the game itself that triumphs and survives, not the players. Life is like baseball at least this much: It isn't about winning, it's about learning to live with losing.

In spite of that less than startling commonplace few writers have examined carefully the role of the truly lousy baseball team. We don't mean a team that finishes out of the money, in third or fourth place. We mean a team that is eliminated from contention

---

♦ **Babe Ruth in 1935: Even the gods have their off days.** (Photo courtesy of the National Baseball Library, Cooperstown, NY)

by Memorial Day. A team that finishes so far out of first place that the pennant race is no more than a rumor. Mercifully, such teams only come along a few times a decade. Teams like that are closer to what most of us experience in daily life than the '27 Yankees are.

And yet . . .

The worst teams in baseball usually win at least 40 games a year. The worst hitter in baseball succeeds at least 20 percent of the time. (Although John Shelby and Mike Pagliarulo pushed that figure down a lot in 1989.) On a given day the worst team in either league may beat the best team. It happens, often.

The authors of this book are drawn to baseball's great losers. Not to individuals, but to entire teams. We prefer our calamities as the product of collective effort, a shared culpability not unlike Watergate. The 1962 Mets (40–120), of course, the 1916 Athletics (36–117), the 1935 Boston Braves (38–115), the 1904 Washington Senators (38–113), this is the stuff of poetry, just like the lower circles of Dante's hell. While Marv Throneberry and Boom Boom Beck have their indisputable charms, the daily crucifixion of a single misbegotten schmoe in knickers and sanitary hose is almost too painful to contemplate. Besides, to err is human, to screw up royally requires a team effort. Throneberry didn't lose 120 games by himself in 1962; he only played in 116 games with the Mets that year.

Recalling his halcyon days as second baseman for the dreadful Phillies aggregations of the late 1920s, Dodger executive Fresco Thompson remarked, "On a clear day they could see seventh place." Thompson's bemusement echoes our own, hence the title of this book. For your edification and amusement we present ten of the worst teams in the history of organized baseball: the 1899 Cleveland Spiders, the 1904 Washington Senators, the 1916 Philadelphia Athletics, the 1928 Philadelphia Phillies, the 1935 Boston Braves, the 1942 Philadelphia Phillies, the 1952 Pittsburgh Pirates, the 1962 New York Mets, the 1979 Toronto Blue Jays, and the 1988 Baltimore Orioles.

The process by which these teams were selected was simple

and arbitrary. If the mark of a good team is how often it wins, the mark of a bad team must be how often it loses. In the interest of historical continuity we decided to choose a team from each decade of baseball's modern era (i.e., post-1901, the year in which the American League is generally considered to have achieved major-league status), plus the 1899 Cleveland Spiders, the losingest team of all time.

Each of these teams logged the most losses for a season in its decade, with one very arbitrary exception. The 1941 Philadelphia Phillies actually had more losses than their 1942 counterparts, but the '42 team had a lower winning percentage (.278 to .279). Given that in 1942 the talent pool of major-league baseball was already being depleted by the war, we thought the latter team's achievement more distinctive.

Our selection is probably unfair on at least two counts. First, for reasons we will explore momentarily, the bad teams of the '70s and '80s aren't nearly as awful as the preexpansion horrors. The 1932 Boston Red Sox, 1939 St. Louis Browns, and 1941 Philadelphia Phillies, none of whom are in this book, were much worse than the 1979 Toronto Blue Jays. Indeed, the 1919 Philadelphia Athletics (36–104) had a worse winning percentage than all but five of the teams we chose. In the interest of morbid historical accuracy here is a list of the 13 post-1901 teams to have lost 110 or more games in a season.

1904 Washington Senators	38–113
1909 Washington Senators	42–110
1916 Philadelphia Athletics	36–117
1932 Boston Red Sox	43–111
1935 Boston Braves	38–115
1939 St. Louis Browns	43–111
1941 Philadelphia Phillies	43–111
1952 Pittsburgh Pirates	42–112
1962 New York Mets	40–120
1963 New York Mets	51–111
1965 New York Mets	50–112

| 1969 San Diego Padres | 52–110 |
| 1969 Montreal Expos | 52–110 |

Second, it could be argued with some justification that the number of losses a team sustains during a season is not the most reliable yardstick of its atrociousness. The most glaring example, we think, is our team from the 1980s: you could make a pretty good case that the 1988 Atlanta Braves (54–106) were a worse team than the Orioles (54–107) that year. The 1989 standings seem to support that thesis.

As we researched the book, we discovered a few things about bad baseball teams. Tolstoy wrote, "Happy families are all alike; every unhappy family is unhappy in its own way." By contrast there are many ways for a baseball team to succeed, but the truly egregious teams are all very similar. To be sure, they all find their own inventive ways of losing individual ball games, but over the course of a season they are more alike than not.

Our ten teams feature a strange mixture of elderly vets and green kids. The rosters are invariably enormous, as the revolving door to the minors—and some other unexpected locales—spins wildly. Fielding is a variable, but more often than not bad, and most of the teams have trouble scoring runs. However, the one constant that links all ten of these teams is pitching—or rather, the lack of it. Each of these teams finished with the worst ERA in the league for their year, usually as much as a run per game worse than the league average. We're talking about ERAs that look like a measure of the circumference of Donald Trump's ego. If pitching is 75 percent of baseball, these teams should be 100 percent awful.

And yet, they aren't, at least not a hundred percent. Great players may prosper under the unlikeliest of circumstances, providing a glimmer of sunshine during a typhoon of bad baseball. In 1972 Steve Carlton won 27 games and the Cy Young Award, pitching for a horrendous Phillies squad that won only 32 more games the entire year. In 1987 Andre Dawson won the NL Most Valuable Player award by hitting 49 homers and driving in 137 runs for a dismal last-place Cubs aggregation, prompting one rival manager to observe that without Dawson, Chicago would have finished in Triple-A.

Our ten teams are distinguished by the presence of some sterling performances among the mountains of dross. Wally Berger shone for several awful Braves teams, but he seldom gleamed brighter than in 1935 when the Braves were worst. Richie Ashburn and Frank Thomas turned in highly creditable performances for the 1962 Mets. Pitchers like Case Patten of the 1904 Senators and Murry Dickson of the '52 Pirates pitched skillfully while suffering from a lack of offense and defense. Indeed, one could argue that a fourteen-win season like Patten's in 1904 or Joe Bush's fifteen wins in 1916 is a greater achievement than Dave Stewart's three consecutive twenty-victory campaigns with the powerhouse Oakland A's of the late 1980s.

Among the names that you will encounter in the pages that follow are several Hall of Famers and near Hall of Famers. The 1916 Athletics were managed by Connie Mack and had Nap Lajoie at second. The 1928 Phils introduced a slugging rookie named Chuck Klein. The 1935 Braves, managed by Bill McKechnie, were the final stop for Babe Ruth. The 1952 Pirates sported Ralph Kiner. The 1962 Mets boasted such luminaries as Gil Hodges and Richie Ashburn, not to mention skipper Casey Stengel. The 1988 Orioles were led by two of the best players of the eighties, Cal Ripken and Eddie Murray.

It is comforting to know that so many of our subjects were graced by the presence of truly great ballplayers. We think that this book will serve as a nice cautionary tale, simultaneously offering counsel on the need for perseverance (witness the Pirates, Jays, and Orioles), and the sin of pride. A valuable lesson to contemplate: It would seem that everyone gets to play with a real dog at least once in his life.

Which of our dogs hunted the best? That is to say, what is the worst team in baseball history? Conversely, which is the best team of this very bad lot? Neither of us is a statistician, so our attempt to answer these questions will seem rudimentary to some. However, a few statistical realities assert themselves. It is meaningless, we believe, to compare these teams across eras. Although baseball is easily the least changed of our major sports, numbers culled across a century of time are not strictly comparable. Consequently, we have compared each of the ten teams not to the others but to its contemporaries.

Howard Siner, the sports editor of Newspaper Enterprise Association, has devised a simple but telling system for evaluating major-league teams. Siner lists how each team ranks in its league in each of several offensive, defensive, and pitching categories. We have borrowed his grid, adding a few more categories, to show you how our ten teams stack up.

What does this collection of numbers tell us? Obviously, a team can rack up extra-base hits and score runs and still be dreadful, although it's not easy. The 1928 Phillies, aided immeasurably by their home field, the minuscule Baker Bowl, actually finished sixth in the National League in runs scored, third in doubles, and fourth in homers. The 1916 A's were actually second in the league in home runs, albeit in the dead-ball era, when round-trippers were a rare and generally insignificant phenomenon. However, most of our teams suffered from a paucity of offense.

The importance of defensive prowess may be overrated. While most of our teams had the lowest fielding percentage in the league, several—most notably Fresco Thompson's silly Phillies and the '88 Orioles—were actually good enough to be called mediocre. Double-play totals may reflect more accurately the inordinate number of base runners that these ten infields saw, rather than the level of defensive skill. After all, none of these teams had the lowest DP total for its league and the '04 Senators actually *led* the AL in double plays.

Pitching is one area of baseball that has changed considerably over the last 90 years. With the rise of the relief specialist and the increased emphasis on strikeouts, the meaning of pitching stats has changed over time. For example, it is silly to note the 1904 Senators' first-place finish in saves as anything more than an oddity; in fact, it probably reflects a paucity of quality starters on the Nats staff. The fact that no post-30s team is better than last in that category is much more telling.

	Offense									Defense			Pitching						
	R	OR	2B	3B	HR	BA	SLG	OBP	SB	E	DP	FA	CG	BB	SO	ShO	SV	ERA	OBA
'99 Spiders [12]	12	12	12	12	12	12	12	12	12	7	5	8	2T	11	12	12	10T	12	12
'04 Senators (8)	8	8	6	7	7T	8	8	4T	4T	8	1	8	4T	6	8	8	1	8	8
'16 Athletics (8)	8	8	8	4	2	7T	6	3T	7	8	3	8	1	8	5	4T	8	8	7T
'28 Phillies (8)	6	8	3	7	4	7	5	7T	8	5	4	5	8	8	4	6T	5T	8	8
'35 Braves(8)	8	7	8	7	5	8	8	8	8	7	7	6	7	4	8	8	8	8	8
'42 Phillies (8)	8	8	7	5	8	7	8	8	8	8	4	8	8	8	6	8	8	8	5T
'52 Pirates (8)	8	8	8	8	8	8	8	8	5	8	3	8	8	8	8	8	8	8	7
'62 Mets (10)	9	10	10	6	6	10	9	8	7	10	5T	10	6	7	10	9T	10	10	10
'79 Blue Jays (14)	13	14	7	8T	13	13	13	13	11	12	2	12	5	12	13	8T	14	14	13
'88 Orioles (14)	14	14	14	13	7	14	14	13	13	6	3	7T	10	8	14	13	14	14	14

Key

Number in parentheses following team name is number of teams in league that year.

R = Runs scored   OR = Opponents runs   2B = Doubles   3B = Triples   IIR = Home Runs   BA = Batting Average
SLG = Slugging Percentage   OBP = On-Base Percentage   SB = Stolen Bases   E = Errors committed
DP = Double plays executed   FA = Fielding Average   CG = Complete Games   BB = Walks allowed   SO = Strikeouts
ShO = Shutouts   SV = Saves   ERA = Earned Run Average   OBA = Opponents Batting Average   T = Tied

The truly dominant bad team would appear to be a thing of the past. Neither the Jays nor the Orioles broke the magic 110-loss barrier, a milestone that was breached eight times before 1962, but only five times since. One might reply that with eight teams per league over sixty seasons, we are talking about 480 team-seasons and more opportunities to lose 110; the implication, of course, is that major-league baseball, since expansion, has nearly equaled that figure in half as many seasons with only a few more teams. However, three of those 110-loss seasons were logged by the Mets in their first four years of existence, and the other two were the product of the second NL expansion, with the Padres and Expos both losing exactly 110 in 1969, their first season of operation, clearly atypical situations. Take out the first-year teams and you're left with the 1963 and 1965 Mets. (What did the 1964 Mets do right?)

We believe that expansion has diluted the talent pool in both directions. If the good players are spread thinner, so are the bad ones. How else to explain the extra-base-hit prowess of the 1962 Mets, or the near mediocrity of some of the Jays' numbers? It is possible that the days of the truly miserable team are behind us. At least until the next expansion.

Who does that leave as the worst team in baseball history? It would be easy to pick on the poor, pathetic Cleveland Spiders, a misbegotten team born, as we shall see later, out of corruption and bad faith. Certainly no team will ever match their record of 134 losses. However, their situation is unique and 19th-century baseball is a somewhat different animal. In fairness, we should look elsewhere.

It is our considered opinion that the dubious distinction of being called the worst team of the modern baseball era falls on the 1952 Pittsburgh Pirates. After all those years of listening to Joe Garagiola make jokes about this crew, we can honestly say that he was, if anything, too kind. No other team in our survey was last in more significant statistical categories. On offense the Pirates were last in every category listed except stolen bases; in 1952 stolen bases were a pretty insignificant part of anybody's offense. On defense they were as bad as any of our ten teams, and their pitching bordered on the terminal. It was an impressive achievement, one that Garagiola can add to his talk-show routine with pride.

On the other hand, the 1942 Phillies finished 62^1/$_2$ games out of first, the worst of any of our teams. Then again, the 1916 Athletics finished 40 games out of seventh place, a then unheard-of feat, and logged the worst winning percentage of the modern era, .235. If you see a pattern emerging here, you are right. Philadelphia holds the record for most seasons with two cellar ball clubs; the Phils and the A's both finished last the same year nine times. No other two-team city comes close. If Philadelphia fans are the most noisily negative in baseball, as is often charged, they've had good reason.

Which of the teams is the best? This is a little like arguing the comparative merits of natural disasters. Did you prefer the 1906 San Francisco earthquake and fire, the Johnstown Flood, or Hurricane Hugo?

We suspect that if one could stage a baseball season involving these ten teams, the result would resemble Warren Brown's prediction for the 1945 World Series, the last and most talent-depleted of the World War II Fall Classics: "I don't think either team can win," opined the great Chicago sportswriter. However, the 1935 Braves and 1988 Orioles deserve a special mention. Each team improved itself considerably the following year, the Braves going from 38–115 to 71–83, the Orioles from 54–107 to an astounding 87–75 and second place in the AL East.

There is hope for the future.

Consider the case of two of major-league baseball's greatest avatars of long-term futility, the St. Louis Browns and the Boston Braves (also briefly known as the Bees). In the modern era these two franchises endured for a total of 105 seasons. Between them they won three pennants and one World Series in that time. They both have added incalculably to the losers' legends. It was as the Brownies' owner that Bill Veeck sent midget Eddie Gaedel to the plate, let the fans vote on team strategy, and put Satchel Paige in a rocking chair in his bullpen. It was while managing the Bees that

Casey Stengel reputedly told a barber, "Give me a shave but don't cut my throat. I may want to do it myself later."

These two franchises were so pitiful that even their best teams are remembered for their shortcomings. The Browns' most talented squad, the 1922 team, *lost* a pennant race to the Yankees. Their only pennant winner, the 1944 squad, a collection of 4-F's, kids, and oldsters, lost the World Series in six games to the Cardinals. The two Braves pennant winners are best remembered for their inadequacies: the "Miracle" Braves of 1914 and the pitching-shy 1948 team ("Spahn, Sain, and pray for rain"). Then, both teams moved to other cities (Baltimore and Milwaukee, respectively), and became juggernauts.

For a brief time. No one would characterize recent editions of these franchises as powerhouses, although both seemed to be on an upturn entering the '90s.

Which brings us to one of the most satisfying aspects of baseball: The mighty shall be brought low. It's downright biblical the way dynasties die out in this game, now more than ever. The one exception to the rule, until CBS and George Steinbrenner took their whacks, was the Yankees. And what have they won lately?

Finally, you ask yourself, who cares? These teams were lousy, why should anyone want to write about them?

A few years ago Stephen Pile, a British humor writer, published a hilarious volume, *The Incomplete Book of Failures.* When it was reprinted in an American mass-market paperback, it was retitled *The Book of Heroic Failures.* The change struck us as typical. This is a culture that valorizes success to a degree that we find, frankly, unhealthy. The trend became overwhelming in the nineteen eighties, the decade of Oliver North, Ivan Boesky, and the Trumps. For us baseball in the eighties is symbolized by former commissioner Peter Ueberroth, a man who cared only for results, without a thought for the justness of the process by which they were achieved, a man who would sell anybody anything if the price were right, a commissioner who loved marketing baseball but not baseball itself. We like to think of this book as an antidote to the departed '80s.

Our games mirror the society in which they are played. The

urgent need of the media—reflecting the cues they get from consumers, who, in turn, reflect the prompting they get from the media, and so on—to seek out and, if need be, manufacture heroes makes them complicitous in the cheapening of our games. It hardly constitutes a revelation that television has polluted virtually every sport with which it has come in contact, baseball included. The mad rush for television dollars has given us all sorts of ugly phenomena, from a World Series with seven night games to 3 1/2-hour-long NFL games to endless play-offs in every sport. At its nastiest this greed has given us truly corrosive situations like the rampant corruption in college football and basketball.

While *On a Clear Day They Could See Seventh Place* is hardly likely to change the social and political atmosphere of the United States, we thought it might be useful to recognize and acknowledge that most of us have more in common with Joe Quinn, the player-manager of the 1899 Cleveland Spiders, desperately juggling a completely untalented team that is doomed from Opening Day, than with the handsome, gifted, and wealthy Jose Canseco. Thoreau may have been exaggerating when he wrote that "the mass of men lead lives of quiet desperation," but we don't believe there would be as much concern with success and winning if everybody were getting enough of both.

We do not denigrate the achievements of the truly great players and truly great teams. It is their excellence that gives us a yardstick by which we can measure our own efforts. On the other hand, we are inclined to agree with Vince Lombardi, who was not happy being remembered for the line "Winning isn't everything; it's the only thing." Lombardi apparently felt that he had been misquoted and amended his famous encomium by saying, "Winning isn't everything. Trying to win is."

The players on these ten teams were trying.

In every sense of the word.

Chapter 1
The 1899 Cleveland Spiders

WON: **20**   LOST: **134**   GAMES OUT OF FIRST: **84**

DAYS IN FIRST: **NONE**

HOME RECORD: **9–32**

ROAD RECORD: **11–102**

LONGEST WINNING STREAK: **2**

LONGEST LOSING STREAK: **24**

THE PAST is a foreign country," writes L. P. Hartley in his novel *The Go-Between.* "They do things differently there." The same might be said of 19th-century baseball, viewed from our perspective. In his excellent monograph "Baseball in the Nineteenth Century: An Overview," Jack Selzer enumerates the basics of the evolution of the professional game:

> Once the games began, fans of the 1880s could count on seeing contests very similar to the ones later played by Mathewson, Medwick, and Mays. Basic rules affecting the number of players per side and the means for scoring runs and recording outs had been codified before professional teams formed. The basic uniform—

◆ **Joe Quinn recumbent: Is this a typical posed baseball-card photo of the 1880s or a harbinger of things to come?** (Photo courtesy of the National Baseball Library, Cooperstown, NY) knickers, stockings, shirt, cap—had become conventionalized by the early 1870s. Basic tactics like catcher's and coach's signs, pitchouts, brushbacks, relays, and cutoffs, were widely practiced before 1890. Pop-ups, passed balls, fungoes, grounders, assists, balks, walks, and whitewashes were all part of the game's lexicon. Hillerich began manufacturing customized bats in Louisville by 1884, and batters waited to hit in on-deck circles. The size, weight, and composition of the ball had been made relatively consistent with modern standards by Spalding's company, although "dead" and "live" versions of the ball were in circulation. Infielders stationed themselves as modern players do, shortstops and second basemen flanking second base, and first- and third-basemen away from their bags, after the "fair-foul hit" was outlawed in 1877. (Before that time any hit that touched fair ground even once was ruled fair no matter where it went, so fielders on the corners had to stick close to their bases where they could cover "foul" ground.) Bench jockeying was considered standard behavior, and everyone berated the umpires, one of whom typically supervised a game alone until the early eighteen eighties. . . .

Of course the game was also different in certain respects. Most fielders disdained the use of gloves until the 1880s, when they wore modest kid gloves. Catchers wisely stayed far behind the batter unless a runner was aboard because (a) it was safer there and (b) a foul ball caught on one bounce was an out before 1879. When that rule was discarded and the mask, chest protector, and overstuffed glove were developed (all by the late 1880s), catchers began to squat closer to the batter. The pitcher's box remained just 45 feet from home until 1881, when the distance was lengthened by five feet, and pitchers were given five to nine balls (depending on the specific season) before a walk was awarded. But they were also required to pitch underhand, and until 1887 a batter could request high or low pitches. Sidearm pitching began to encroach on professional play in the early 1870s and overhand pitching was permitted in the more innovative American Association [one of the NL's periodic competitors] in 1883 (National Leaguers were permitted to throw overhand in 1884). Clubs scheduled games two or three times a week: the National League played under 100 games a season until 1884, when competition among leagues forced them to seek additional revenues through expanding their schedules and cutting back on exhibitions with independent clubs. By 1888 the major leagues scheduled 140 games. Since one or two pitchers could cover the shorter schedules and since no substitutions were permitted once a game began, except in the case of injuries and illnesses certified by the opposition, rosters consisted of only a dozen or so players through the 1880s.

The 1890s saw the institutionalization of many of the key features of major-league baseball that we take for granted. It is in the 1890s, for instance, that four balls and three strikes finally and permanently made a walk and a strikeout, respectively. If we were to go back to the 1899 National League baseball season by time machine, the game we would see would be instantly recognizable to us, but there would be subtle differences. The uniforms were baggier, the wedding-cake hats would probably conjure up mental pictures of the 1979 Pittsburgh Pirates. Rosters were set at nineteen and many of the team's nicknames would be unfamiliar. Admission prices were considerably lower and the wooden grandstands would remind us more of high school than the majors. But the game was fundamentally the same.

Off the field, however, the game was substantially different, a reflection of the age of the Robber Barons of the decades before. There was only one major league functioning in 1899, a 12-team National League whose members were the Boston Beaneaters, Philadelphia Phillies, Baltimore Orioles, Brooklyn Superbas, Cincinnati Reds, Pittsburgh Pirates, Chicago Orphans (or Colts), New York Giants, Louisville Colonels, Washington Senators, St. Louis Perfectos (or Browns), and Cleveland Spiders. The last rival to the NL, the American Association, folded after the 1891 season. With no competition for players the magnates of the National League conducted themselves with a mixture of ruthlessness and stupidity that would be familiar to anyone who has lived through Charlie Finley and George Steinbrenner. They did so with the unique impunity of a monopoly.

The best example of ethical corruption of the team owners was also the most conspicuous difference between the NL of the monopoly-driven '90s and the NL of the modern era, the so-called syndicate system, a series of interlocking ownerships of teams. Although it existed before, the system reached its peak in 1899. In the winter prior to the start of the season, the owners of the Baltimore Orioles—also the owners of the Brooklyn Superbas—transferred most of the O's stars to Brooklyn, hoping to capitalize on a larger population base and the newly opened Washington Park in the Red Hook section of the borough. (Incidentally, the left-field wall and clubhouse of this ball yard are still standing.)

For the Cleveland Spiders the effects of syndicate baseball would be nightmarish. Cleveland would go from being a legitimate pennant contender to the losingest team in major-league history. To understand how they made that transition, we must go back to the end of the previous season and earlier.

Cleveland had been a strong team and a successful franchise only a few years before. Indeed, the Spiders had won the Temple Cup, a forerunner of the World Series, in 1895, defeating John McGraw and the Baltimore Orioles four games to one. By 1898, however, the club had slipped considerably. The talent on the Spiders was undeniable. The pitching staff was anchored by Cy Young. The infield was rated among the best in the league, featuring Hall of Fame shortstop Bobby Wallace. The outfield included another Cooperstown denizen, Jesse "The Crab" Burkett. But the team was aging and had fallen to fifth place, finishing the '98 campaign with a record of 81–68. More importantly, local support had diminished as the team's victory totals declined, much to the dismay of the team's owners, Frank deHaas Robison and his brother, M. Stanley Robison.

The Robisons were street railway magnates at a time when urban transit was usually privately owned and franchises were often acquired with some judicious greasing of palms. One may speculate that Frank and Stanley, who were held in some regard in league circles, were well equipped for the sharp business practices to which their hobby was about to lend itself.

By the 1898 season interest in the Spiders had declined to the point that, in spite of their winning record for the year, home attendance had fallen to 70,496, easily the worst in the league. Two factors contributed additionally to the poor gate. First, Cleveland was one of several cities in the NL that still had blue laws prohibiting Sunday baseball. (New York would not permit Sunday ball until 1916, Pennsylvania until 1934.) Second, Frank Robison, the real boss of the Cleveland outfit, had put the team on the road for the final two months of the 1898 season, in response to the poor attendance. In the late '90s schedule making was still a capricious thing in the National League; owners could transfer home dates to their opponents' ballparks, ostensibly with the approval of the league.

Thus, the Spiders became known in the sporting press as the Exiles, a nickname that would receive new currency in 1899. In fact, when Cleveland played a home game on August 24, 1898, a local paper would treat the event with sarcastic incredulity: "Cleveland people were treated to a decided novelty yesterday afternoon at the park at the corner of Dunham and Lexington avenues [sic] when a game known as 'base ball' was played by two teams. . . . The game, although practically unknown in this city, is not a new one." In his excellent history *American Baseball* David Voigt writes, "Robison defended his move by telling fans that baseball was a money-making proposition, not a public service." Cleveland fans would pay him back for that smug remark in 1899.

By contrast St. Louis was faced with an even more dismal prospect, another season of the Browns. Once a powerhouse, winners of the World Championship in 1884, 1885, and 1886, the Browns were coming off a dismal 39–111 season, finishing last, 63 1/2 games behind Boston, the 1898 pennant winner. To complicate matters the team was on the verge of bankruptcy, although they had drawn twice as many fans as Cleveland. The cause of their financial miseries was their owner, the controversial and colorful Chris von der Ahe.

Von der Ahe was a sort of a cross between Charles O. Finley, Bill Veeck, and Al Davis, although the unsympathetic sports press treated him like a baggy-pants dialect comic. In the 1880s he and a group of like-minded men had founded the American Association, a rival major league designed to give the NL some much-needed competition. The major attraction the AA added to the standard bill of diamond fare was that beer could be purchased at the ballpark. Needless to say, the high-minded WASPs who dominated the NL were outraged by the upstart immigrants and their profligate ways.

St. Louis had leavened the mix with a combination of cheap tickets, Sunday baseball, and fireworks displays, both on and off the field. Eventually, the NL owners conceived a merger and von der Ahe was reluctantly taken into the fold. The old guard couldn't have been too pleased to have him in their midst, and when his extravagant life-style caught up to him, there must have been secret smiles of joy around the league.

With their owner bankrupt the Browns team was placed in receivership. The league suspended the team for failure to pay dues and assessments. St. Louis was still an attractive city for a baseball team; it had Sunday baseball, a loyal fan base and a population of 575,000 (1900 census), nearly 200,000 more than Cleveland had at the time. The NL was damned if they weren't going to make sure who controlled it. The league declared that the actual franchise was not transferable by the bankruptcy court; with the legal right to participate in the league reverting to NL control, they could handpick the new owners. Their choice: Frank deHaas Robison.

Robison denied his interest in purchasing the Browns almost up to the date of the sale, although it is unclear why. After all, the league already had one "syndicate" operation, with the Orioles and Brooklyn both owned largely by Ned Hanlon. The growth of syndicate baseball, however, represented a trend so transparently sleazy that even a staunch defender of management like *The Sporting News* was put off. "The game would suffer" under syndicate owners, *TSN* wrote during the winter of '98. "With Brooklyn and Baltimore controlled and owned by the same individuals the [game's detractors] will be given a grand opportunity to throw great gobs of mud at the good name of the grand old sport."

Cynically, Robison offered the league an alternative to more syndicate baseball. At the beginning of the year *Sporting Life,* the other weekly sports paper of the time, was filled with talk that, threatened with a serious boycott of their Cleveland club, the Robisons would move the team elsewhere, i.e., St. Louis. The January 28 issue reported, "The faithful in Cleveland have reached the conclusion that if any championship games are played in this city this year, they will be played by a Western League [forerunner of the soon-to-be-major American League] club. . . . Not the slightest move [has been] made by President Robison that would in any manner whatever indicate his purpose of keeping the exiles of '98 in this city the coming season. . . . It is a moral certainty that Robison and [Reds owner and league powerhouse John T.] Brush expect to send the present Cleveland club to St. Louis."

In a roundabout way that is, in fact, what Robison did. On March 14, 1899, Frank deHaas Robison purchased the St. Louis Browns at the sheriff's auction, taking the presidency of the club himself. Stanley, his brother, took the reins of the Cleveland franchise, at least on paper. After a couple more weeks of suspense the Robisons transferred nearly all of Cleveland's players to St. Louis and vice versa. Spiders player-manager Patsy Tebeau was kept on at the helm of the St. Louis team, now renamed—so help us—the Perfectos. Lave Cross, the only regular to hit above .280 in 1898, took on the same job with the Spiders.

There is one final footnote to the wholesale transfer between the two teams. Over the winter Dick Harley, the Browns' Philadelphia-born outfielder, told one of his hometown papers, the *Inquirer,* that he wouldn't play for St. Louis anymore. Harley, one of the rare college-educated players of the era, later would coach the baseball teams at Villanova, Pitt, and Penn State. Right now, all the 26-year-old Georgetown alumnus wanted was to be traded from St. Louis. Rod Serling might have put it this way: "Dick Harley doesn't know it, but he's about to get his wish. He is going to be traded to a team playing baseball somewhere in the Twilight Zone."

Harley was one of nine ex-Browns who were transferred to Cleveland. Eleven of the Spiders—including Tebeau, Young, Burkett, Wallace, and 24-game winner Jake Powell—became Perfectos. The remainder of the Cleveland roster was filled out with rookies and unpromising journeymen.

For Lafayette Napoleon Cross the Spiders represented a first chance to manage at the major-league level. Also the only chance. Lave was a lifetime .292 hitter, a bowlegged ex-catcher whose career had begun in the late 1880s and would extend through the 1907 season. In addition to his duties behind the plate Cross had played short, second, the outfield, and third in recent years, but he would spend his brief time in Cleveland at the last of these positions.

With little help from the Robisons, Cross was still assembling his ragtag band with less than two weeks to Opening Day. In addition to the other ex-Browns he had a motley mix of has-beens and never-will-bes. The Cleveland *Plain Dealer* called the resulting aggregation the Misfits; the *Sporting News* would label them the Discards. Either name fits nicely.

Things began promisingly enough. The April 14 *Sporting News* reported, "The old Browns . . . have shown better form than was expected. They have defeated the strong Indianapolis team twice. The players are confident they will not be last in the pennant race." Of course, Indianapolis was a minor league team, so "strong" is a relative concept. A more realistic note was struck by the next paragraph of the article, a discussion of where various team members might go if the Cleveland franchise folded.

Cleveland was scheduled to open the season at home against the Perfectos, but the Robisons, their eye always on the main chance, transferred the game to St. Louis. If there were any justice, we could report that Cleveland hammered the Perfectos and humiliated the perfidious Robisons. Needless to say, that's not what happened.

Although the mid-April weather was still bitter, 15,200 turned out on April 15 to see the Perfectos pulverize the Spiders, 10–1. The Mound City–based *Sporting News* was not the most unbiased source of information on the home team at this early stage of the magazine's existence, but we can take them at their word when they report that the game "was not up to National League standards." Their correspondent added, "Young pitched good ball and was fairly well supported[!], but [Spiders hurler Wee Willie] Sudhoff was not so fortunate. The young St. Louisian started well and did his best to stem the tide when the team behind him went all to pieces." A harbinger of things to come, one might add. On the other hand, to say that Wee Willie pitched well is generous to a fault; he gave up thirteen hits, five of them doubles, walked four, and threw a wild pitch. As the *Plain Dealer* less charitably head-lined, THE FARCE HAS BEGUN.

Who were these guys? The Opening Day lineup reads as fol-lows:

Tommy Dowd, CF
Dick Harley, LF
Joe Quinn, 2B
Lave Cross, 3B
Jack Clements, C
Tommy Tucker, 1B
Suter Sullivan, SS
George Bristow, RF
Willie Sudhoff, P

Harley and Cross were introduced earlier, and Quinn will come onstage momentarily.

"Buttermilk" Tommy Dowd was one of the ex-Brownies. An eight-year veteran major leaguer with a lifetime batting average of .271, the 30-year-old Dowd had managed the Browns for parts of the 1896 and 1897 seasons, compiling a record of 30–63. It is no small surprise that he wasn't offered the helm of the Spiders.

Jack Clements is a mere footnote in the history of the Spiders; already in his mid-30s, he would play only four games with Cleve-land before being released in May. Clements is also a footnote of another sort, the last left-handed player to catch regularly in the majors, and one of the first catchers to wear a chest protector. He would return for a brief stint with the Beaneaters in 1900 before hanging up his spikes.

Tommy Tucker was a 12-year veteran of the NL wars, a four-time .300 hitter who would finish his career with the Spiders. In his obituary *The Sporting News* recalled the first baseman as a capa-ble pro with a loud mouth. "Tucker was renowned for his noise as well as his . . . antics on the coaching line," *TSN* recalled. "No less an authority than Clark Griffith [one of the era's great pitchers and later the owner and manager of the Washington Senators] . . . regarded Tucker as one of the greatest natural hitters." A singles hitter with little power, Foghorn Tommy was adept at getting hit by pitches and was a notably aggressive base runner. He was also an agile fielder who still utilized the small kid glove of an earlier baseball age. Unfortunately, Tucker was 35 in 1899 and his best days were well behind him.

Suter Sullivan and George Bristow would probably be totally forgotten were it not for the diligence of the people who keep baseball records. Bristow's entire career consists of three games and eight at bats with the Spiders. Sullivan played 42 games with St. Louis in 1898, hitting .222 with only three extra-base hits. He would manage to survive a full season with Cleveland but then disappears from *The Baseball Encyclopedia* utterly.

It was an era of small rosters. On Opening Day the Spiders carried only five pitchers: Kid Carsey, Still Bill Hill, Coldwater Jim Hughey, Harry Maupin, and Wee Willie Sudhoff. By the end of the season fourteen pitchers had appeared in Cleveland uniforms. None of them had won-lost records approaching .500. At a time when rosters of twenty or fewer were the norm, thirty-one players would appear for Cleveland.

Sudhoff, who had the dubious honor of pitching on Opening Day, was an oddity on the Cleveland roster, a young player of genuine promise. The Robisons rectified the error by sending him back to St. Louis a third of the way into the season. After going 3–8 for the Spiders, he would win thirteen games for the Perfectos against ten losses. Returning to his hometown obviously did Wee Willie good; he would play eight more seasons, all but one with either the Cards or the Browns, finishing with a 103–135 lifetime record that included a 21–15 mark for the 1903 Browns. Incidentally, he came by his nickname honestly; Sudhoff was only five-seven and weighed 165 pounds.

Wilfred "Kid" Carsey probably got his nickname the same way; he was also five-seven and weighed 168. However, he was at the end of his career when he came to Cleveland. Carsey, a junk baller of some repute, had begun his career with Spider-like numbers. In 1891, his first season in the majors, Carsey pitched for the American Association's Washington franchise, where he compiled a 14–37 record. When he went over to the National League the following year the results were considerably improved: in his next five full seasons, all with Philadelphia, Carsey strung together four winning seasons and a .500 season, notching double figures in victories each year. However, the Phillies guessed correctly that his workload—nearly 1500 innings pitched in five seasons—had taken its toll. By the time he reached Cleveland, Carsey was a spent bullet and would pitch in only ten games as a Spider, going 1–8 before being sent to the slightly less dismal Senators. He would appear in only six more games in the majors after leaving Cleveland.

However, Coldwater Jim Hughey is worthy of some consideration. In an age of colorful nicknames his is one of the liveliest. How disappointing to find that it was the name of his Michigan hometown. Hughey was a journeyman's journeyman, a player who spent seven seasons in the majors with six different teams. In 1898 he went 7–24 with the Brownies. Naturally, he was one of the players that the Robisons sent to Cleveland. For the Spiders he was a true workhorse. Give Jim Hughey the ball every fourth or fifth day and he would pitch. Generally he would lose, but he would pitch. At the end of the 1899 season, his penultimate as a major-league pitcher, Hughey would be one of only two Cleveland pitchers to win as many as four games. Indeed, his 4–30 record and 5.41 ERA qualify him as one of the aces of the Cleveland staff. Unbelievably, he would be back in St. Louis the following year, closing out his career with a 5–7 mark, his best performance since going 6–8 for Pittsburgh in 1896.

Still Bill Hill and Harry Maupin don't figure heavily in the saga of the 1899 Spiders, although Hill's 3–6 record makes him the third-winningest pitcher on the team that season.

To lose over 100 games in a single season a team must not only be untalented, it must be unlucky as well. The Spiders proved themselves well equipped in both categories as early as the second game of the year. This time they gave the Perfectos a tough battle, outhitting them 12–7. Kid Carsey held St. Louis to a single run over the first five innings, but the Perfectos tallied five more in the sixth, elating 18,000 cheering St. Louisians. Needless to say, the Spiders fell short in a comeback attempt, losing 6–5. To add injury to multiple insults Dick Harley was spiked on the hand when he overslid second on a steal attempt, and would be lost for several days.

For the next three days the schedule makers took pity on Cleveland, leaving them idle. The Spiders took the opportunity to reach back into their own past in search of help. In Cleveland Louis Sockalexis announced that he would return to the Forest City fold.

Sockalexis, a Penobscot Indian from Maine, was baseball's first Native American player of note. A star at Holy Cross (where he was expelled for drinking) and Notre Dame, he had signed with Cleveland in 1897 after walloping a home run off Amos "The Hoosier Thunderbolt" Rusie in an exhibition game against the New York Giants. (Rumor has it that Sockalexis was expelled from Notre Dame around the same time after another drunken escapade.) The first half of his rookie year Sockalexis, derisively nicknamed Chief and greeted with "war whoops" around the league, tore up NL pitching. By late July he was hitting .413, but at the end of the month he injured an ankle, sat out all of August and half of September, and began to drink heavily. By season's end his average had fallen to .338. For all intents and purposes his career was nearly over. He appeared in only 21 games in 1898, hitting .224.

Although he turned up in Cleveland to announce his signing on April 17, he would not appear in a Spider uniform until May 9. This comeback proved as ill fated as his 1898 campaign; Sockalexis was released on May 16, after seven games with the Spiders, apparently due to Cross's impatience with his renewed drinking. He drifted back into the low minors and then to semipro ball before returning to the Penobscot reservation, where he died at 42. Ironically, he was so popular among Cleveland fans that when the AL team looked for a new name in the early 1900s, they voted overwhelmingly for "Indians" in his memory.

While Sockalexis was announcing his intention of returning to the Spiders, the team was traveling to Louisville, where they dropped the first two games of a four-game series. Happy Jack Stivetts, an ex-pitcher of some note—his career record was 204–131—played right field for the injured Harley. Stivetts would eventually be pressed into service as a Cleveland hurler, going 0–4 in seven appearances. When the Robisons began to cut their losses by paring down the payroll, Stivetts was among the first veterans released, ending his playing career.

On the third and final day of their stay in Louisville, a near miracle befell the Spiders. They actually won a game, the first half of a doubleheader. In fact, of their twenty victories in 1899, twelve came in twin-bill splits. Kid Carsey got the victory in relief of Jim Hughey, and the split of the doubleheader catapulted the Spiders briefly into a tie for tenth place, the highest ranking they managed all season.

Three days of bad weather allowed them to savor the thrill a little longer. Then a loss to the Reds sent them back to Cleveland for the long-postponed home opener. However, Frank Robison's eldest daughter died, and he postponed the two scheduled home dates of April 28 and 29 again. The Perfectos played in Pittsburgh on both dates.

The Spiders finished the month of April with a dismal Sunday game in Cincinnati. The most interesting feature of the 9–0 drubbing is that no umpires showed up. Spider utility man Lew McAllister and Reds pitcher Frank Dwyer officiated. The first month of the season ended with the Spiders 1–7, firmly entrenched in last place. They hadn't played at home yet.

The Spiders finally opened in Cleveland on May Day, splitting a closely fought doubleheader with Louisville, 5–4 and 2–1. Willie Sudhoff won the opener in relief and Bill Hill lost the nightcap on a disputed play at home. The boycott was on in earnest from the start of the season, and only five hundred fans saw what seems, on paper, to be one of the few exciting afternoons of baseball in the entire Cleveland season. The following day another throng of five hundred watched the Spiders and the Colonels split another pair. Sudhoff, who had relieved the previous day, started and won again, raising his record to 2–3. It proved to be the last Cleveland victory of the home stand. The next three games were lost in front of gatherings of 500, 600, and 125.

Three days in Chicago meant two more losses and a rain-out for the Spiders, then it was home again, this time to face the Perfectos. Given a chance to see last year's heroes, Cleveland fans turned out in slightly greater numbers than before. Fifteen hundred saw a closely pitched 1–1 battle for seven innings before the Spiders reverted to true form and lost 8–1. The following day a mere 500 returned to see St. Louis beat them even more soundly, 12–2. After that the Perfectos added two more defeats to the growing Spider skein.

♦

Cleveland returned to the road with a nine-game losing streak for company. They added two more losses to that heavy load before beating Philadelphia 10–4 at home for their third win of the season. In the meantime heads were rolling. Jack Clements was released. Lou Sockalexis followed immediately. The cost cutting had begun.

The day after their May 20 victory the Spiders won again, beating Louisville on the road 4–3, behind Jim Hughey. (Where would the Spiders have been without Louisville?) It marked the first and only time that they would win consecutive games during the entire season. Unfortunately, a second scheduled game was rained out. The Spiders stayed hot, winning one of their next two games at home against the Senators, losing to the Senators, and then beating the Orioles. The 4–2 streak is by far the best stretch of baseball Cleveland would play all year, but they ended the home stand with a 12–0 loss to Baltimore and the steady downward slide began again. The Spiders finished the month with a 7–19 May record, better than Louisville's 7–21 for the same period, but not good enough to escape the NL basement.

Throughout the growing debacle the Spiders were blessed with few positive achievements. Although the pitching was unrelievedly awful, Tommy Dowd, Joe Quinn, and Lave Cross all hit respectably. In fact, player-manager Cross hit well enough that he and Willie Sudhoff, the best of the Spider hurlers, were transferred to St. Louis for pitcher Frank Bates and underworked catcher Ossee Schreckengost on June 5. In his useful volume *The '99 Spiders* Cleveland baseball historian John Phillips notes that even John T. Brush was outraged by the Robisons' blatant manipulation of their syndicate rosters. The Reds owner told a reporter, "It looks bad for a strong club to be made stronger at the expense of a weak club owned by the same parties. . . . Such things hurt the game."

The Spiders now had a new player-manager, second baseman Joe Quinn. Quinn is one of the more interesting characters in nineteenth-century baseball. Born on Christmas Day 1864 in Sydney, Australia, he and his parents migrated to Dubuque, Iowa, in the early 1880s. In Dubuque he played on a well-regarded amateur nine whose members included future Hall of Famer Charlie Comiskey. Quinn would be the only Australian to play in the majors until Craig Shipley came up with the Dodgers a century later. He was also the first Australian to manage in the big leagues, when Chris von der Ahe convinced him to briefly take the helm of the Browns in 1895; they went 11–28 under Quinn and he gladly returned to his playing duties.

What made Quinn uniquely well suited to manage the Spiders, however, was his off-season business. His father-in-law was a successful St. Louis undertaker and Quinn developed a serious interest in embalming. On road trips he would even visit other undertakers around the country to further his studies. Now he found himself in charge of some twenty stiffs, on a team that had lost its last five games in a row.

That losing streak would stretch to 12 before the Spiders would win again, notching their ninth victory of the season on June 15 before a hundred hometown diehards. For Still Bill Hill, who pitched the Spiders to the 6–2 triumph over the Pirates, it would be his third victory against six defeats. Inevitably, he was traded shortly thereafter to Baltimore. The Orioles-Superbas syndicate transferred him to Brooklyn at the end of the season, so Hill actually went from the basement to the pennant over the course of the year.

The Robisons had not been idle while the seemingly endless humiliations continued. Stanley further reduced the Spiders' payroll by giving ten days' notice to Jack Stivetts, who would return home to become a carpenter, Kid Carsey, who landed with the hapless Senators, and Chief Zimmer. Zimmer, who was best remembered as one of Cy Young's favorite catchers, was hitting .342

at the time; he signed with Louisville and hit .298 for them for the remainder of the season.

The remaining bright spots in this murky picture were few. Quinn himself played valiantly. As one leafs through John Phillips's book, a day-by-day account of the season, the eye repeatedly falls on the phrase "Joe Quinn had two hits." Quinn would end the season leading the team's regulars with a respectable .286 batting average. "Pirate," the *Sporting News* correspondent from Pittsburgh, offered this October encomium to Quinn: "I wish to go on record as saying that it is a shame to keep such a grand player as Joe Quinn tied up with such a combination. The 'old man' was very much the whole team."

The young catching prospect sent over from St. Louis, Ossee Schreckengost, would prove even more successful; in his forty-three games Ossee would hit .313, so the Robisons hurriedly shifted him back to the Perfectos later in the season. Schreckengost played a leading role in the Spiders' only victory over St. Louis, getting three hits in the June 25 contest, including the game winner. (The same day Louis Sockalexis was released by Hartford of the Connecticut League, once more a victim of his drinking problem.) Schreckengost was on the brink of a long and moderately successful career in baseball. An excellent defensive catcher who pioneered the one-handed style long before Johnny Bench, he would gain some notoriety as Rube Waddell's receiver and roommate. Connie Mack once called Schreckengost "the Harpo Marx of his time," perhaps recalling the time that Waddell insisted that his next contract with Mack include a clause barring Schreckengost from eating crackers in their shared bed on road trips.

The pitching situation, however, showed no signs of improvement. Frank Bates was apparently one of the Robisons' many miscalculations. He went 2–1 in 1898 with the Spiders, so when the wholesale transfer of rosters took place before the season began, they readily shifted him to St. Louis. At the beginning of the 1899 season he appeared twice with the Perfectos, pitched nine innings, and gave up seven hits and five walks. Clearly he was expendable in the Robisons' ledger, so he was sent back to Cleveland. Bates had trouble throwing strikes, averaging over six bases on balls per game for Cleveland; when he threw strikes, he was in worse trouble, giving up an average of 14.1 hits per game. He finished the year with a 1–18 record and a 7.24 ERA for the entire year.

Charlie Knepper was a minor leaguer from nearby Youngstown when he was signed to play for the Spiders in June. Knepper was a hard thrower, who some observers compared to Amos Rusie. He was also a workhorse, appearing in 27 games for Cleveland over the remainder of the season, going 4–22 with a 5.78 ERA. It would be his only season in the majors.

By the end of June, Cleveland was so desperate for pitching that strange things began to happen. On June 27 the Spiders signed Fred "Crazy" Schmit, a lefty whose checkered past included brief sojourns with three NL teams between 1890 and 1893 for a record of 5–17 and a barnstorming tour with a baseball comedy act. Schmit (whose name is often spelled Schmidt) was 33 when he joined the Spiders and hadn't pitched in the majors in six years.

A noted eccentric and an alcoholic, Schmit is the subject of numerous stories. On one occasion in the early nineties he was toiling for a Macon, Georgia, minor-league outfit when he became entangled with a local fan who took him to court, charging that the ballplayer had heaved a brick at him. Schmit pleaded not guilty, noting that he was a professional ballplayer and wouldn't have missed a target as big as a human being. "If I had thrown a brick at him, the guy would be dead," Schmit allegedly told the court. Not guilty, the judge ruled.

Late in July, Cleveland added a hurler from an even more unlikely source. Playing in Washington and hoping to hype the gate for a July 21 game between the two worst teams in the league, the Spiders used a local amateur and sometime minor-league player named Harry Colliflower. The 30-year-old Colliflower succeeded beyond anyone's wildest dreams. The lefty, whose last assignment was with the Eastern Athletic Club, would not only attract a nice showing of 2500 local fans, but he also pitched well, defeating the Senators 5–3 on a six-hitter and getting a pair of base hits. Of course, the Spiders signed him for the remainder of the season. Unfortunately, that game proved to be Colliflower's one moment of glory. He lost his remaining eleven decisions and was out of the majors at the end of the season, never to return.

All through the summer attendance in Cleveland dwindled. The nadir was reached on June 13 when 75 people paid to watch the Pirates beat Charlie Knepper with the help of seven Cleveland errors, 10–6. Rumors were beginning to fly. The Robisons were planning to move the team to Toronto. No, they were going to Detroit. The league would dissolve the weakest two franchises. No, they would dissolve the four weakest franchises. With Cleveland losing its franchise Tom Loftus would move the Columbus franchise of the upstart Western League to the Forest City. No, the NL would never allow that.

Although it had headlined early in the season that CLEVELAND CRANKS ARE WARMING UP TO EXILES, *The Sporting News* editorialized in its June 17 issue, "St. Louis shares fifth place with Baltimore and Cleveland is a hopeless tail-ender. The patronage of the St. Louis club is gratifyingly good, but the Exiles are not making expenses." The grumbling around the league was growing. The June 24 *TSN* reported that Pittsburgh received slightly more than $64 as its share of the gate from a three-game set in Cleveland, $75 less than the team's hotel bill. Frank Robison steadfastly denied rumors that Cleveland would transfer all its remaining home dates as late as the July 1 issue of *The Sporting News,* but on June 26 his brother announced that after the current home stand ended on July 1, the Spiders would become Exiles once more, taking to the road for the rest of the season. (Actually, the Spiders played six more games at home, late in August, a home stand that would include their ninety-ninth loss and penultimate victory.)

Cleveland finished June with a 3–21 mark for the month, 11–48 for the season. Common sense would dictate that the team couldn't do any worse. Common sense had long ceased to have anything to do with the Spiders. The worst was yet to come. A Fourth of July doubleheader in Pittsburgh is typical of what the Spiders were capable of in the second half of the season. Cleveland blew leads in both games, losing each contest in extra innings.

They would lose 13 in a row before a July 17 victory in Balti-

more. The first half of a doubleheader, of course, the win was Jim
Hughey's fourth and last of the season. John McGraw, the Orioles
manager, was so incensed that his hurler Jerry Nops had pitched
and lost while hung over that he suspended Nops for a month
without pay. The fiery manager must have blistered the clubhouse
with his tongue as well, because the O's won the nightcap 21–6,
with considerable help from Frank Bates, who hit five batters and
surrendered eighteen runs in the first four innings. The Spiders
helped with seven errors and Baltimore stole eleven bases. The
next day the Spiders split a pair with the eleventh-place Senators,
with Crazy Schmit in left field for the once-again injured Dick
Harley.

July closed with the Spiders going 4–26 and the Robinsons
shipping Ossee Schreckengost back to St. Louis. Even *The Sporting News* bridled at this latest act of larceny, writing, "The switching of players between the St. Louis and Cleveland clubs is censurable. It is unjust to Cleveland and unfair to the other clubs."

By August 1 it hardly mattered. Cleveland had embarked on a
seemingly endless journey into the abyss. After winning the front
end of a doubleheader with Chicago on August 6, abusing Colts
hurler Bill Phyle before 14,000 fans, the Spiders lost eleven
straight. During the next-to-the-last of these defeats Cleveland
pulled off a triple play in Brooklyn, but lost 4–2 anyway. The next
day, in Pittsburgh, the Spiders split a doubleheader with the Pirates, giving Charlie Knepper his third victory. A week later they
won again during their final home stand.

The worst had now arrived. From August 26 to October 15, the
remainder of the season, the Spiders would win one game and lose
forty. Between August 26 and September 18 they lost 24 contests in
a row, still a major-league record. Batting averages and won-lost
records plummeted; ERAs soared. The Spiders played well, they
played lousy. They lost close games, they got routed. It didn't matter. On August 31 they notched their hundredth loss of the year
when Schmit blew a three-run lead to Brooklyn. A few days later
Frank Bates blew his entire career, losing to the Reds 19–3. Shortly
after, Stanley Robison gave the hapless Bates and Tommy Tucker
ten days' notice.

By now the Spiders would try anybody on the mound. On September 13 Howard "Highball" Wilson, fresh from the minors, started for Cleveland. He gave up five runs in the first inning and didn't pitch for them again, but he did resurface with the 1904 Senators and will turn up briefly in the next chapter.

On September 18 another rookie went to the hill for Cleveland, twenty-one-year-old Jack Harper. This time youth prevailed as the Spiders defeated Washington in the first game of a doubleheader to snap the losing streak at 24. Although Harper ended the season 1–4 with the Spiders, he was a pitcher of some promise and would win 23 for the Cardinals in 1901 (proving that even the Robisons couldn't be wrong all the time), and again in 1904 for the Reds.

During their road trip to hell the Spiders missed several paydays. In the October 7 issue *The Sporting News* reported that several players had contemplated a strike after the October 1 game in St. Louis. Stanley Robison's reply is certainly in character. *TSN* wrote, "When M. Stanley Robison was told that the boys wanted money, he said that he would speak to his brother Frank about the matter. The Robisons left for New York the next morning, but before their departure Secretary Heilbronner was instructed to allow the players to draw $25 each."

The September 18 victory was Cleveland's last of the season. They finished the campaign with a 16-game losing streak. In Cincinnati for the last weekend, Quinn selected as his final starter in a season-ending doubleheader a cigar-store clerk from the local hotel at which the Spiders were housed. Nineteen-year-old Eddie Kolb was a local sandlot player who had been bugging the Spiders manager for a chance to pitch. The undertaker obliged him and Kolb went the distance, giving up nineteen runs, eighteen hits, and five walks, a fitting ending to the season.

J. Ed Grillo, the *Sporting News* correspondent in Cincinnati, reported that the Spiders looked on the end of the season as a veritable liberation. "I saw the Cleveland players after Sunday's games and I don't think I ever met a happier bunch of players," he wrote. "Had they won the pennant, they could not have expressed more joy. The fact that their season's work had ended made them happy. Every man on the team was thoroughly disgusted with the season's work. If the Cleveland Club has offered these players contracts for the next season at an increase of money I doubt whether they would have signed. Not one of them wants to put in another season like the one just closed."

John Phillips, in *The '99 Spiders*, adds that after that final game was completed, the Spiders met in a hotel for a few drinks and a presentation. Phillips writes, "The present [is] a diamond locket to George W. Muir, their secretary. One of the Spiders tells Muir: 'We are doing this for you because you deserve it. You are the only person in the world who had the misfortune to watch us in all of our games."

The Spiders finished 84 games out of first at 20–134, 35 games behind the eleventh-place Senators. They scored 529 runs, 275 below the league average; they gave up 1,252 runs, 448 above the league average. Cleveland's opponents scored ten or more runs fifty times in 1899; by contrast the Spiders managed to score in double figures only seven times and lost four of those games.

Cleveland played only 41 games at home, going 9–32 in their infrequent stops there. On the road they were 11–102. The only teams they beat as many as four times were Louisville and Washington. Brooklyn and Cincinnati swept their season series with the Spiders, each winning all fourteen games.

For the Robisons syndicate baseball had been a satisfying arrangement. Granted, the Perfectos finished a disappointing fifth. However, the team turned a tidy $40,000 profit (according to *TSN* —Phillips gives the figure as $45,000). Given the payroll juggling and date transferring, it is unlikely that Cleveland lost money; John Phillips says they broke even. The highest-paid Spider received a pitiful $2500 for the season and the Robisons left Cleveland without issuing the final paychecks to the team.

The icing on the cake for Frank and Stanley came the following year when the National League cut back to eight teams; The Robisons were paid $25,000 for their interests in Cleveland.

Many of the former Spiders stayed in the majors. Jack Harper and Willie Sudhoff pitched through the 1906 season. Lave Cross was still playing in 1907, Ossee Schreckengost in 1908. Utility player Charlie Hemphill was the last Spider in the majors, finishing his career in 1911. Dick Harley ended the 1899 season swearing that he'd quit baseball before he'd play for Cleveland again. He got his wish again, playing for Cincinnati the next two seasons, the Tigers and the Cubs the two years after that. Joe Quinn played into the 1901 season but never managed again. After he left baseball, he opened a very successful funeral parlor in St. Louis.

The Perfectos became the Cardinals. They never finished higher than fourth place for the Robison brothers, and when Frank died in 1910, his daughter took over the team and really ran it into the ground. St. Louis would not win its first NL pennant of the twentieth century until 1926, long after both the 1899 Cleveland Spiders and their owners were forgotten.

1899 Cleveland Spiders Roster

Player	POS	G	AB	R	H	2B	3B	HR	RBI	SB	BA
George Bristow	OF	3	8	0	1	1	0	0	0	0	.125
Jack Clements	C	4	12	1	3	0	0	0	0	0	.250
Lave Cross	3B	38	154	15	44	5	0	1	20	2	.286
Tommy Dowd	OF	147	605	81	168	17	6	2	35	28	.278
Jim Duncan	1B-C	31	105	9	24	2	3	2	9	0	.229
Dick Harley	OF	142	567	70	142	15	7	1	50	15	.250
Charlie Hemphill	OF	55	202	23	56	3	5	2	23	3	.277
Otto Krueger	IF	13	44	4	10	1	0	0	2	1	.227
Harry Lochhead	SS-2B	148	541	52	129	7	1	1	43	23	.238
Lew McAllister	Ut	113	418	29	99	6	8	1	31	5	.237
Joe Quinn	2B	147	615	73	176	24	6	0	72	22	.286
Ossee Schreckengost	C	43	150	15	47	8	3	0	10	4	.313
Lou Sockalexis	OF	7	22	0	6	1	0	0	3	0	.273
Jack Stivetts	Ut	18	39	8	8	1	1	0	2	0	.205
Joe Sudgen	C	76	250	19	69	5	1	0	14	2	.276
Suter Sullivan	Ut	127	473	37	116	16	3	0	55	16	.245
Tommy Tucker	1B	127	456	40	110	19	3	0	40	3	.241
Charlie Ziegler	SS-2B	2	8	2	2	0	0	0	0	0	.250
Chief Zimmer	C	20	73	9	25	2	1	2	14	1	.342

Figures include games played with Cleveland only.

Pitcher	G	IP	H	ERA	ShO	SO	BB	W	L
Frank Bates	20	153	239	7.24	0	13	105	1	18
Kid Carsey	10	78	109	5.77	0	11	24	1	8
Harry Colliflower	14	98	152	8.17	0	8	41	1	11
Jack Harper	5	37	44	3.80	0	14	12	1	4
Bill Hill	11	72	96	7.00	0	26	39	3	6
Jim Hughey	36	283	403	5.41	0	54	88	4	30
Charlie Knepper	27	220	307	5.78	0	43	77	4	22
Eddie Kolb	1	8	18	10.13	0	1	5	0	1
Harry Maupin	5	25	55	12.60	0	3	7	0	3
Lew McAllister	3	16	29	9.56	0	2	10	0	1
Crazy Schmit	20	138	197	5.86	0	24	62	2	17

Pitcher	G	IP	H	ERA	ShO	SO	BB	W	L
Jack Stivetts	7	38	48	5.68	0	5	25	0	4
Willie Sudhoff	11	86	131	6.98	0	10	25	3	8
Howard Wilson	1	8	12	9.00	0	1	5	0	1

Figures include games played with Cleveland only.

Chapter 2
The 1904 Washington Senators

WON: **38**   LOST: **113**   GAMES OUT OF FIRST: **55¹/₂**

DAYS IN FIRST: **NONE**

HOME RECORD: **23–52**

ROAD RECORD: **15–61**

LONGEST WINNING STREAK: **3**

LONGEST LOSING STREAK: **13**

5¢

LIFE

DEVOTED TO

BASE BALL, TRAP SHOOTING AND GENERAL SPORTS.

Volume 44—No. 19.   Philadelphia, January 21, 1905.   Price, Five Cents.

WILSON, P.

JACOBSEN, P.   PATTEN, P.

TOWNSEND, P.

HUGHES, P.

KITTRIDGE, C.

W. WOLFE, P.

CLARK, C.

WASHINGTON
BASE BALL CLUB
AMERICAN
LEAGUE
P. J. DONOVAN, OF & MGR.
1904

J. STAHL, 1ST B.

McCORMICK, 2ND B.

HILL, 3RD B.

J. CASSIDY, S.S.

Sporting Life
Phila.

HUELSMAN, O.F.

J. O'NEIL, O.F.

> You can learn little from victory.
> You can learn everything from defeat.
>
> —CHRISTY MATHEWSON

IN 1900 major league baseball, which, at the time, consisted solely of the National League, reflected the booming economy of the nation. The majority of clubs made money, and sensing there was even more money to be made, Byron "Ban" Johnson, president of the Western League, a Midwest-based minor league, decided the timing was right to fulfill his longtime dream of establishing another major league. Taking advantage of the NL's decision to trim back the number of its teams to eight, Johnson defiantly proclaimed the formation of the rival American League.

Backed by men like Charles Comiskey, who moved his White Stockings team to Chicago where they would go head to head with the Cubs, and Connie Mack of the Philadelphia Athletics, the league began by stocking its teams with surplus National Leaguers. They also brazenly raided several National League clubs for star players like Cy Young, Jimmy Collins, and Nap Lajoie.

That first year, 111 of the AL's 182 players had jumped from the National League. Unfortunately, the Washington Senators

---

♦ **The 1904 Washington Senators: Wanted for impersonating a major-league baseball team.** (Photo courtesy of the National Baseball Library, Cooperstown, NY)

were one of the economically poorer teams in the league, consequently they were unable to lure away top-caliber players.

In 1903, after two years of sniping at each other, an agreement was finally reached between the rival leagues. They would operate as separate but equal major leagues, with common playing rules, playing schedules that would not conflict within common cities, and mutually recognized territories and player contracts. Hence, the reserve clause was reestablished and player raids between the leagues ceased.

Replacing the old National League team (their last campaign was in 1899), which also played footsie with the lower depths, the Washington Senators were one of the original eight teams established by Johnson for his new league. In 1901, the team's first year in the league, it was primarily staffed with players from Johnson's own disbanded Kansas City franchise.

It didn't take long for the Senators to establish a pattern of mediocrity, which soon tumbled into downright despair. After finishing in sixth place their first two seasons, the Senators succumbed to the immutable law of gravity, wallowing in either seventh or eighth place for the next nine years.

But no year was quite as bad as 1904, when the team won only 38 games while losing 113, a dismal .314 percentage. To put this into perspective, that same year, Jack Chesbro, pitching for the second-place New York team (which, incidentally, lost the pennant on the last day to Boston), won 41 games. Downright embarrassing, isn't it, when one man wins more games than your entire team?

The overall picture in Washington that year was not a pretty one. Consider the following:

- They wound up 55$\frac{1}{2}$ games out of first place, 23$\frac{1}{2}$ games behind the seventh-place Detroit team.
- They managed to drop the season series with every other club in the league.
- They were last in fielding with a percentage of .951.

- They had two one-hit games pitched against them; six two-hit games pitched against them; and three three-hit games pitched against them.
- They were shut out 25 times (in contrast the New York Highlanders were shut out only eight times).
- Their pitching staff, such as it was, boasted three twenty-game losers: Albert ("Beany") Jacobson, 6–23, Case Patten, 14–23, and John Townsend, 5–26.
- John "Happy" Townsend's record of 5–26 was the worst record in the league. (How in the world he could have obtained that particular nickname is well beyond us.)
- The team ERA was 3.62, almost a full run more than the seventh-place Detroit's 2.77 mark (the league ERA that year was 2.60).
- Senator pitchers gave up 1,487 hits, 142 more than the seventh-place Detroit team.
- They had a team batting average of .227, 17 points below the league average.
- The Senators did lead the league in one category, double plays, with 97. But this makes complete sense, since, when you include the 347 free passes issued by Washington pitchers, over 1800 men reached base that season, an average of nearly 12 a game.
- They drew a mere 131,744 fans, while the pennant-winning Boston club drew 623,295.

Just as it takes years to build a baseball dynasty, it also takes some time to construct a complete disaster. No team as bad as the Senators were in 1904 exists without some serious preparation. And so, we must return to the previous year wherein the seeds of ignominy were sown, to see just how the Washington club managed to stake out such an inglorious place in baseball history.

One could justifiably argue that the Senators' horrendous last-place 1904 finish was sealed with a splash that occurred the night of July 2, 1903, when their best player, "Big Ed" Delahanty, took a long walk off a short bridge.

"Big Ed," who wasn't really all that big, at six–one, 170 pounds, played for the Phillies from 1891 to 1901. Between 1893 and 1901 he batted .368, .400, .404, .397, .377, .334, .410, .323, and .357. In 1902 he played his first year for the Senators and led the league in hitting with a .376 average.

The best of five baseball-playing Delahanty brothers, he was a genuine superstar who would be voted into the Hall of Fame in 1945. But he was also a man who appreciated a drink or two, or three. Every so often, perhaps as a result of a particularly tough bout with demon rum, he would grant himself an unscheduled vacation from the team. But he always returned.

This time, however, he did not.

"Big Ed" was not enjoying his stint with the Senators, so he asked to be traded to the New York team. The Senators, however, were not about to let the one jewel in their crown of thorns go. This was not what Ed wanted to hear, and taking matters into his own hands, he decided to jump the club. It was neither the only nor the most momentous leap he was to make that season.

It was July 2 and Delahanty, at 35 years of age, still had his batting eye. At the time he was hitting .333, second only to Nap Lajoie for the league's best average. That night Delahanty left the Detroit Hotel Oriental (which, by the way, was owned and operated by one of the supposed owners of the Senators) and purchased a one-way ticket, bound for Buffalo aboard Michigan Central train No. 6.

It was a long trip, and no doubt to break the boredom, "Big Ed" had a few, or maybe more than a few. Evidently, these drinks brought out the beast in "Big Ed," and according to a conductor he began brandishing an open razor, terrifying his fellow passengers. The conductor promptly and unceremoniously eighty-sixed "Big Ed" from the train. From that moment on "Big Ed" was to be counted among the mysteriously missing.

A week or so later Tom Loftus, the manager of the Senators, received a letter from a railroad official. It stated, in part, that "a passenger in one of our cars July 2 had some altercation with the Michigan Central train conductor, and he was ejected from the train at Fort Erie, Ontario. Later, according to reports, a bridge tender found a man on the International Bridge, who had succeeded in evading the guard. . . . The International Bridge is a bridge for foot passengers. In putting his lantern into the passenger's face, the passenger was angered, and I understand they had some words, and this bridge tender states when his attention was attracted in another direction he heard a splash and the man was gone. . . . A dress suitcase and black leather bag were found on our train afterward . . . and I find in the suitcase a complimentary pass, No. 26, for your club."

A few days later Delahanty's hat was found floating below Niagara Falls, leaving little doubt that "Big Ed" had obtained his final release and would henceforth be batting in that big ballpark in the sky. It also left the lowly Senators with little hope of bettering their place in the league standings in the 1904 season.

But the loss of Ed Delahanty was not the sole reason the team stank that next year.

There were, to put it mildly, severe front-office problems, which stemmed from an absentee ownership and the fact that Washingtonians didn't particularly relish shelling out their hard-earned money to see a team that had the annoying habit of winning less than a third of their games.

In August of 1903 club president Postal was threatening to resign while the manager, Tom Loftus, was complaining because the front office wouldn't put up any money to buy talent. Seeking to smooth things over, Ban Johnson hurried to Washington and met with Postal and team vice-president Charles Jacobson. At first Wilton J. Lambert, an attorney representing a group of Washington businessmen, offered to buy Postal out for $12,000 and assume the $6,000 worth of debt. But when he looked into the matter he found that the club was not six thousand but $12,000 in the hole, and to make matters a little more bizarre, Postal didn't own *any* stock in the club at all. In fact, Postal was merely a dummy owner for the American League, which, translated, meant none other than Ban Johnson.

When this deal fell through, Johnson quickly announced, without offering any proof or further explanation, that "local interests" had purchased the Senators and that Mr. Postal had returned to Detroit to see to his hotel interests—which, the way it sounded, probably meant making up beds in the Hotel Oriental.

Having hometown owners didn't seem to help the club's morale much. But then, morale doesn't win ball games, players do. By August 20, 1903, the team was mired in last place by eight games and one sportswriter, trying to put as good a flavor as he could on a team that had become a perennial loser, wrote:

> The Washington baseball team in the West continues to give its opponents an interesting argument in every game played, but when the smoke of battle has blown away the Loftus band is invariably found on the losing side.

By season's end, however, the kid gloves were off as a writer in *The Washington Post* summed up the 1903 campaign in terms no one, especially manager Tom Loftus, could possibly mistake:

> There was a breach between Mr. Postal and some of the stockholders which included Manager Loftus. Loftus was brought here as a capable and careful team manager. He has done as much as he could, but that he has signally failed there is not the least question.
>
> He lacks the knack of infusing ginger into his players, and his good nature forbids that he shall use a strong hand on the players who are not doing their utmost.
>
> It is difficult to see the value of a manager who sits in the rear of the grandstand and reads the morning paper when his players are practicing. It is apparent that the club lacks a head.
>
> Jimmy Ryan was spilled at home plate Saturday because there was no one coaching third.
>
> Washington has been surfeited with promises of a good ball team. These promises have covered thirteen years and here we are today with a club that occupies the last position in the League, and the percentage of games won is lower than any previous club the city ever gave its name to.

Washington, you ain't seen nothin' yet.

◆

The new year dawned with a sense of hope for Washington fans when Henry J. Killea, owner of the Boston Red Sox, sent a young catcher named Jake Stahl to the Senators. This addition to the lineup, along with the fact that everyone in town, except perhaps for Tom Loftus himself, knew that the Senators would have a new manager by the time the season opened, gave rise to cautious optimism.

But before the season was to open there were more behind-the-scenes machinations. In mid-February, Wilton Lambert was dispatched to Chicago to purchase the ball club for a syndicate headed by William J. Dwyer, a former Associated Press baseball writer turned promoter who was co-owner of a single-sheeter that carried last-minute news up to seven o'clock and could be purchased solely in drugstores, saloons, and restaurants; John R. McLean, owner of *The Washington Post* and the Washington Gas Light Company; and millionaire congressman William W. Wadsworth.

The deal looked done, when suddenly it fell apart, apparently because the consortium balked at paying Johnson's price. So, with the start of the season only a couple of months away, the Senators were back where they'd started from, which was nowhere.

In the second week in March, Ban Johnson arrived in Washington to discuss a new manager with the dummy directors and officials of the club. At the same time the signing of four new players was announced. They were young shortstop Joe Cassidy, first baseman Jake Stahl, and a pair of famous Princeton athletes, the Hillebrand brothers.

At the same time Johnson issued the following statement:

"I have promised the Washington people a good club for the coming season and I will keep my word. Every club in the American League has from four to twelve extra men they cannot use, and if Washington needs additional players they will get the first call."

This proclamation was supposed to allay the fears of Washington fans, but how secure can you feel about your team's chances when the president of the league has just admitted that your beloved team will be stocked by players that no other team wants?

◆

Spring training began on March 21 and two days later the team was purchased by William Dwyer and his two partners, Thomas C. Noyes, whose family owned the Washington *Evening Star,* and John J. Walsh. Wilton Lambert was installed as president and Dwyer was appointed vice-president and business manager. Dwyer, however, did not last long. In the middle of the season he was set adrift by the owners, who didn't approve of the way he was running the club.

Hope, along with the cherry blossoms, was springing eternal in Washington that March. Concerning the sale, *Sporting Life* remarked of the new owners, "Both gentlemen are of means, ability, good repute, and public spirit, to which fact we can testify from personal knowledge of both."

The first thing the new owners did was send manager Tom Loftus packing (one wonders whether he read the news in the local paper while ensconced in the grandstand during a training session).

The hot rumor about town was that the new owners wanted St. Louis Cardinal star P. J. "Patsy" Donovan to become the new manager, but there were problems getting St. Louis to release him. And so, while the team waited for Donovan to become available, they named veteran catcher Malachi Kittridge as interim manager.

Kittridge had a reputation for being a good fielder, with an accurate arm and a good baseball mind. Alas, at the plate, he seemed lost. After playing 16 years in the major leagues his lifetime average was a meager .219.

New owners, new manager, so how about a new stadium to complete the face-lift? Perhaps the thinking went something like this: *Maybe we can con the fans into thinking the Senators of 1904 are an entirely different entity from the bumblers they saw out on the field a year earlier?*

And so, plans were set in motion for the Senators to move into the old, somewhat renovated National Park. *Sporting Life,* obviously caught up in the optimistic spirit which abounded along the Potomac that spring, applauded the move: "The status and prospects of the Washington Club under the new regime are further vastly improved by the leasing of the grounds at Seventh Street and Florida Avenue, formerly occupied by the National League Club, the very best spot, geographically and historically, for base ball in Washington."

As it turned out, the Senators played their home games at this stadium, known as National Park, only until March 1911, when the edifice burned down during spring training, the result of a fire caused by an errant spark from a plumber's blow lamp. After the performance of the 1904 team it's somewhat amazing to us that the stadium lasted that long.

By the time the season opened the Senators were already 2–0, having easily won their only two preseason games. But perhaps we should mention that those two games were against Georgetown University. But hey, what the heck, a win's a win, isn't it?

The season opened with, according to *Sporting Life,* "a rattling good snow storm," which caused the team to dispense with the usual street parade. Nevertheless, several thousand fans braved the weather and showed up to cheer the home team.

The opening lineup was as follows:

Charles Moran, SS: He played his rookie year for the Senators in 1903, batting .225. He was traded in the middle of the 1904 season to St. Louis, where he played one more year in the major leagues, batting .195, leaving him with a lifetime average of .207.

William Coughlin, 3B: In 1903 Coughlin batted .251 for the Senators. He improved that mark to a career-high .275 in 1904.

Kip Selbach, LF: Although built somewhat like a bowling ball, at five seven, 190 pounds, Selbach was a speedy outfielder who stole 334 bases in his career. In 1895, playing for Washington in the National League, he led the NL in triples with 22. He batted .250 for the Senators in 1903, but had a lifetime average of .293 for his 13-year career. More about Selbach later.

Jake Stahl, 1B: Stahl was both college educated (a rarity), and independently wealthy. Although he managed to lead the AL in home runs with ten in 1910, he had the reputation of being a rather indifferent hitter. Playing for Boston in 1903, his rookie year, he batted .239 in forty games. He would finish his nine-year career as a lifetime .260 hitter.

William (Barry) McCormick, 2B: A utility infielder, McCormick came over in the middle of the 1903 season from St. Louis, where he batted .217. Playing the second half of the season with the Senators he actually managed to lower his average by a point.

John Thoney, RF: Playing for Cleveland in 1903, Thoney hit .205. He was to play only 17 games for the Senators before he was traded to New York. At the time he was traded, he was hitting .300. Does this make any sense? Does anything concerning the 1904 Washington Senators make sense?

Harry (Izzy) Hoffman, CF: 1904 was his rookie season. He played only ten games, during which time he hit .100, before he was sent down. He didn't return to the major leagues until 1907, when he played 19 games with the NL's Boston team, after which he retired from the game.

Malachi Kittridge, C: After jumping from the NL's Boston franchise in the middle of the 1903 season, Kittridge batted .214 for the Senators. Now he was doing double duty, not only catching but managing the team.

Howard Wilson, P: In a perfect world it makes perfect sense that the starting pitcher for the 1904 Senators should be Howard "Highball" Wilson, whose rookie year in the major leagues was spent—where else?—hurling for one of the other ten worst teams of the century, the Cleveland Spiders. In Cleveland that year "Highball" got into one game, pitched eight innings, gave up twelve hits, and had an ERA of 9.00. Pitching for the Senators in 1903, he won seven games and lost eighteen, though he did lower his ERA considerably to 3.31. He only lasted three games into the 1904 season (he was 0–3, naturally, with an ERA of 4.68) before he disappeared from the game forever.

The Pitching Staff:

The real thoroughbred on the 1904 Senator staff was Case Patten, who might rightfully be nominated as Hardluck Pitcher of the Decade. From 1901 to 1907 he averaged fifteen wins and nearly 300 innings per season. At the same time he managed to string together three 20-game-loss seasons in a row (1903–1905). In 1903, when he went 11–22, he lost seven shutouts. A lot, you say? In 1904 he topped that, losing nine shutouts. The most amazing thing is that spending almost his entire eight-year career with the Senators (he was 0–1 with Boston in 1908, the year he retired), he came remarkably close to being a .500 pitcher, winning 105 and losing 127. An astounding feat when you consider the team he was playing for.

The Senator staff that year also boasted Al "The Curveless Wonder" Orth, who won 202 games (he lost 188), without ever throwing a curveball. Instead, he relied solely on change of speeds. With the 1899 Phillies he led the NL with a 2.49 ERA. He was a control pitcher who, with the 1902 Senators, only allowed forty walks in 324 innings. In 1903 his record fell to 10–22 (remember, this was with the Senators, so it isn't half as bad as it sounds).

One of the earmarks of a bad team is that the front office is a poor judge of talent. The Washington team was no exception: Starting the 1904 season with the Senators, Orth was 3–4. Obviously, he was far too close to a winning record, so the Washington brain trust shipped him to the New York Highlanders. He went 11–6 with the Highlanders for the rest of the year, learned the spitball from Jack Chesbro, then proceeded to lead the league in 1906 with twenty-seven wins against seventeen losses.

The staff was rounded off with "Long Tom" Hughes, who spent the 1903 season with Boston and had an impressive 20–7 record, with a 2.57 ERA. He started the 1904 season with the New York team, where he was 7–11, before being sent to Washington, where he went 2–13; Albert "Beany" Jacobson, a rookie, who wound up losing 23 games for the Senators that year, while winning only six; Del Mason, another rookie who went 0–3 that year; Wilbert "Barney" Wolfe, who started the season with New York, where he was 0–3, before being shipped to the Senators (he pitched his way to six victories and nine defeats with the Washington team); and Jack "Happy" Townsend, 2–11 with the 1903 Senators.

♦

You might have noticed that the much heralded Hillebrand brothers failed to make the starting lineup. That's because they failed to show up for the start of the season. But the promise that came from the front office was that they were simply temporarily detained. Suspicious minds might think instead that they'd seen the writing on the wall, and perhaps, since they were, after all, Ivy Leaguers, they were actually able to read it.

The team took the field with new white uniforms with red stockings and lettering and two horizontal red stripes around old-style flat-top caps.

Hopes in Washington had never been higher, many of them riding on the acquisition of Jake Stahl. As *Sporting Life* pointed out:

> Jake Stahl will get a thorough try-out at the near corner, as the wise ones consider him a likely proposition. He has the physical make up of an ideal first baseman. He has the stature and reach of a giant and sheds base runners as easily as a dog does fleas. He goes as fast as money won on the races—a hundred yards in 10 1/2. His is an unusual combination of weight and speed, and he hits the ball with terrific force for long drives, although he got in wrong with the stick last year.

It didn't take long for Stahl to make a lasting impression. In fact, he got himself into the record books rather early when, on April 15, he was hit *three* times by a pitched ball in one game. This record stood for 65 years, until Ron Hunt, playing for the Giants, tied it in 1969 (since then, Craig Kusick in 1975 and Glenn Davis, in 1990, have also joined Stahl in this record of dubious distinction.)

On paper there were some adequate, if not good, players on the team. Pitcher Case Patten was a solid workhorse who'd won eighteen games in 1901, though he'd fallen to 11–22 with an ERA of 3.60 in 1903. With any other team he might have been a Hall of Famer, but with the Senators he was just another losing pitcher. Kip Selbach was a solid veteran, if not a spectacular ballplayer. Still, it should be pointed out that Selbach was not a particular favorite of the fans, as one sportswriter from *The Washington Post* referred to him in 1903 as "the fat fielder," who he hoped would "be in better form next season," as "this year he could not cover as much ground as a man on stilts." Third baseman Bill Coughlin was a reliable journeyman. And the book on Stahl was that he was a comer.

And then there was always the hope that hurler John "Happy" Townsend would live up to his potential. Townsend, who broke into the major leagues with the Phillies in 1901, had learned how to pitch by throwing stones at apple trees on a farm near his hometown, Townsend, Delaware, and was the possessor of a blazing fastball. Unfortunately, Townsend had a slight control problem. That is, if you consider walking as many as fifteen to seventeen batters in a game a slight problem.

Even with new ownership, new manager, new players, and a new field, they were still the same old Senators on Opening Day. They lost to Philadelphia, 8–3.

In the second game of the season they managed to come away with a tie, and, so the fans thought, they were headed in the right direction. Unfortunately, they didn't actually win a ball game until May 5.

In fact, the team lost their first thirteen games, while collectively batting an anemic .214. Jake Stahl, the man with weight, speed, the reach of a giant, and possessor of "terrific force for long drives," was batting .088, just a few points above the temperature. Even so, he was, as reported in *Sporting Life*, evidently able to keep his cool, if not his feet, in the field.

"A spectator who has closely followed the game for many years declared that the greatest catch he ever saw was Jake Stahl's capture of a foul fly close to the stand, in the fifth inning [against Boston]. Just as the fly, which was a cloud-scraper, was about to be gathered in, Stahl, who was still running, slipped in the mud and fell flat on his back. He kept his eye on the ball, which must have been caught when he was falling, and near the earth."

Well, at least that gave Senator rooters *something* to cheer about. They had precious little else. The fans, those of whom bothered to show up at the ballpark, were grumbling, and the front office, still waiting for those fabulous Hillebrand brothers to show up, was casting about for something to do, some sacrificial lamb to be thrown to slaughter. That lamb's name was Malachi Kittridge. William Dwyer, the business manager, ordered Kittridge to "doff his uniform" while playing a series in Philadelphia. As *Sporting Life* remarked, "It is reported that Kittridge has not kept himself in condition to give the club his best services. . . ." What condition that might have been, considering what he had to work with, is beyond us. It should be pointed out that Kittridge's managerial career began and ended after 18 games with the Washington Senators that year. His record: one win, 16 losses, and one tie. Obviously, here was a man who knew when enough was enough.

By this time Patsy Donovan had finally been released by St. Louis and he was signed to play right field and manage the team. Donovan's credentials for the job were impeccable: he was fresh from managing the Cardinals to a last-place finish. Obviously, the Washington brain trust felt that they might as well find a manager who was used to looking at the rest of the league from the bottom of the standings.

Donovan, sensing that the task in front of him was not an easy one, immediately expressed his desire to add three or four new players to the team. But he was having a slight problem arranging "the details." What this really meant was that the team owners were too cheap to come up with the necessary cash.

Born in County Cork, Ireland, Donovan began his playing career with Boston in the National League. In 1892 he joined the Pittsburgh team, where he starred for eight years, during which time he hit over .300 for six consecutive seasons. He served as player-manager in 1897 and 1899. The next year he was traded to the St. Louis team, where he was the player-manager from 1901 to 1903. Besides being a good hitter, he was an expert base stealer, leading the NL in 1900 with 45, while amassing 518 during his 17-year career.

When Donovan entered his first game in a Senators uniform the crowd gave him a rousing ovation, which, seeing as the Washington fans had little practice in executing such a maneuver, is a wonder in itself. Donovan appeared as a pinch hitter for pitcher Edward "Fats" Dunkle, who a year earlier had been released by the White Sox after literally eating himself out of major-league baseball. Naturally, he was immediately signed by the Senators.

Donovan's first appearance as a player was an auspicious one. As *Sporting Life* reported, the new manager "cut loose" with a slow grounder and raced to first "under such a press of sail that" Frank "Bald Eagle" Isbell "became alarmed" (who wouldn't?). As a result "Izzy got busy in his error department and threw the ball into the bleachers, and Donovan went the entire route."

On May 5, the Senators finally defeated another major-league team, the New York Highlanders, by the score of nine to four. Still, Senator fans didn't get too excited, since in large part the team owed their victory to the fact that the New Yorkers committed eight errors.

The game was even more significant, however, in that the Senators also discovered a budding star in Joe Cassidy, who, replacing Charles Moran at shortstop, banged a triple and a single.

Cassidy, who earned the reputation as being a fine, agile fielder, was one of the first to play in the majors with no minor-league experience. As bad as the Senators were that year, Cassidy, who had an auspicious rookie season, was a bright spot. His nineteen triples tied him for the league lead and set a record for rookies that still stands. The next year he led AL shortstops with 520 assists and 66 errors.

Unfortunately, as Senator luck would have it, Cassidy only lived another two years, tragically falling victim to typhoid fever at the age of 23.

When things aren't going so well on the field, the temptation is to do something to take the fans' minds off the game. Today we have promotional games, where teams give away bats, balls, cushions, hats, anything to bring the fans in. In this case the owners of the Senators, who were probably too cheap to give anything away even if they'd thought of it, decided to tinker with the playing field. For one thing, "the invisible scoreboard" was taken down and "planted somewhere so that the naked eye can figure out the scores" (maybe this wasn't such a good idea); and for another, they moved the back fence in seventy feet.

It didn't do any good. The Senators still managed to lose

games (and, much worse, now the fans could *see* the score). In fact, during the final week of July *Sporting Life* wryly observed that "last week the Senators dispensed with the usual formality of winning a game."

During this week, which turned out to be a rather momentous one, the usually reliable Kip Selbach had what could be charitably called a nightmare game.

Albert Karl "Kip" Selbach was one of the few good ballplayers on the team. Born in 1872 in Columbus, Ohio, he first played five years for the National League Washington club, batting over .300 every season. He then moved on to Cincinnati, where he batted .296, then spent two years in New York, where he batted .337 and .289. Finally, he played for Baltimore, batting .320, before moving on to the Senators.

During the off-season he toured the country as captain of an ace bowling team and, with his partner, Herm Collin, won the ABC doubles title with a record-breaking three-game score of 1,227.

He had the reputation as "a crack outfielder," albeit an idiosyncratic one. While he was playing in Cincinnati one sportswriter wrote that "Selbach's strongest point is making his toilet while standing at the plate." The complaint was that he dallied at bat too long. An early avatar of Mike "The Human Rain Delay" Hargrove, it was reported that "he hitches his trousers, kneels and dusts off, pulls his cap. . . ." And he often chewed gum and stuck the wad on the button of his cap while he batted.

These odd habits earned Selbach the derision of many fans, and when he was playing for New York, *Sporting Life* reported that "Al Selbach wants to get away from New York, [where he is] under the ban of the bleacherites."

And so, when he moved back to Washington, he was a known quantity and already the brunt of fan abuse.

In this particular game against the New York Highlanders, Selbach began the inning by throwing the ball away after fielding a single. Then, "a minute later, the usually reliable" Selbach dropped an easy fly ball and two runs scored. One more error by

Selbach added up to three for the inning and resulted in five High-lander runs, at least four of which were gifts of the Senators.

Unfortunately, Selbach's performance did not go unnoticed by Ban Johnson, who, irate at the outfielder's disgraceful perfor-mance, suspended him for "indifferent play." This, added to the fine Johnson had levied on Selbach a day earlier for "drinking one bottle of beer" during the team's western trip, meant Selbach's days as a Senator were numbered. Lucky Kip.

A week later Selbach was an ex-Senator, shipped to Boston for a journeyman named Bill O'Neill. This provided frustrated Washington fans one more thing to gripe about. As one sports-writer observed, "The whole affair, stripped of the large amount of language that has been expended upon it, to no effect so far as influencing intelligent opinion is concerned, was merely a gift of a very valuable player to a club that was already too strong, and the deprivation of a weak club of one of its few first-class men."

And this pigeon did, indeed, come home to roost the very next week when the Senators faced Boston.

"The Senators," reported the *Sporting Life* sportswriter, who was obviously developing a sense of humor concerning the hap-less team, "were not at bat long enough for their friends to recog-nize them, but when the visitors were up there were happenings and occurrences. . . . The loss of Selbach blew a hole in this Sen-atorial ship of state, such as are made by war vessels in the Ori-ent, and the Bostons, who had a losing streak before, have won almost every game since he joined them, including three with New York [their rival for the league pennant]. One of their number said while here that Selbach's work in his first game in Boston was the most marvelous he ever saw."

Thanks.

It was now near the midpoint of the season. The losing contin-ued. The Hillebrand brothers were nowhere in sight. Something had to be done. When you're desperate you'll try just about any-thing, which is exactly what the Senators did. They were so des-perate, in fact, that they appeared to take leave of what little senses they had left when they drafted one Hy "Lefty" Herring to play the outfield.

"Lefty" Herring? Minor league phenom? New secret weapon located by Senator scouts combing the boondocks? Not quite. Try poolroom operator at the Ebbitt Hotel where he was friend and confidant of several Senator ballplayers who stayed there. "Lefty" was an amateur outfielder who evidently talked a great game of baseball. So great a game, in fact, that he was actually able to convince several of the ballplayers into putting in a good word for him with Patsy Donovan. Donovan, who, though certainly inured to losing, was probably pretty much at his wit's end, was willing to try almost anything to turn things around. Consequently, he gave Herring a fifteen-game tryout in center field.

"Lefty" repaid the manager's confidence and largesse by hitting a lofty .174 during that period, considerably lower than the already pathetic team average. This put an end to "Lefty's" professional baseball career, as he was given a friendly pat on the back and sent packing back to the poolroom of the Ebbitt Hotel.

It is an immutable law of nature, and baseball, that when things are going bad, there is always room for them to get worse. Even what under normal circumstances is a good play can, on a losing team, lead to disaster. Take, for instance, a game in which the Senators were playing St. Louis. Al "The Curveless Wonder" Orth, under normal circumstances a pitcher (but then, in Washington that year, only losing could be considered normal), was, for some inexplicable reason, playing center field (perhaps because "Lefty" Herring had miserably flunked his tryout and a careful search of local bars and pool halls hadn't yet resulted in a replacement being found). Hunter Hill, the Cardinal third baseman, was on second when pitcher Fred Glade drove a high fly to center. The ball was over Orth's head, but gamely he went after it. Somehow, he managed to catch up to it and he made an astonishing over-the-shoulder catch. Obviously much impressed with his heretofore unknown fielding prowess, Orth, in true showboat style, just kept trotting until he reached the fence.

In the meantime a somewhat amazed yet alert Hill raced toward third, then kept going and scored standing up.

The next day Orth was traded to New York for two pitchers. And the same day Hunter Hill, yes, the very same third baseman

Hunter Hill who'd scored on Orth's superb catch, was purchased from St. Louis and, with a logic that only losers can understand, was appointed to patrol right field. But then, maybe the Senators knew what they were doing, since Hill, who spent the first month of the season in bed with the mumps, was leading AL third basemen in errors.

By this time, with the Hillebrand brothers but a fond memory, the team was fifteen games deep in last place. And it was only mid-July.

But perhaps the most insulting blow was yet to come. So poor and amateurish was the play of the team that many fans began referring to them as Sunday School Leaguers. These same fans even offered to wager good American greenbacks that a team from the Sunday School League, a local amateur circuit, could beat the Senators.

Surprisingly, and perhaps because he really needed a win, manager Donovan accepted the challenge and a game with an All-Star team from the Washington Sunday School League was promptly scheduled. It was played before 6000 paying customers, several thousand more than usually showed up for a Senators game.

The Senators gave those Sunday School punks a real good drubbing, winning 17–0, proving once and for all that they were every bit as good as a bunch of amateurs.

After sending Selbach to Boston, the Senators had precious few truly major-league players on the team. One of them was third baseman Bill Coughlin, who was hitting a respectable .260. Much to the dismay of the few diehard Senator fans that remained, rumors were rampant that Coughlin was going to be set free. Naturally, these rumors set off a hue and cry in Washington.

"The Detroit people are hot after Coughlin," a horrified *Sporting Life* reported, "but his sale would finally convince the local fans that they have nothing to hope for in the future. The long suffering public had fallen off in their attendance to an extent unknown before, previously to the recent changes, and it is evident that they will pass up tail-enders in the future, preferring to be wiped off the base ball map."

The public be damned. Bill Coughlin was history. He was shipped to Detroit for $8000 and Hunter Hill was shifted from right field to his more familiar position of third base.

By the end of August the Senators were nineteen games behind the seventh-place Detroit team and there were rumors that the club was going to be bought by a Rhode Island millionaire who was going to move the team out of Washington and install it in Providence. Surprisingly, this did not sit well with Senator fans, who had their ire reflected in local various daily newspapers and weekly periodicals like *Sporting Life.*

> The writer knows scores, if not hundreds, of fans here who would go to nearly all the games if a fairly good club was located here, and every one of them says that he knows "hundreds" who feel the same way; but, as things are going now, they never attend the games. They cannot be blamed for the biggest sucker living is the man who will pay, day after day, to see a club that stands no chance to win half of its games at home. . . . The club has been deprived of all these men [like Selbach and Coughlin] and made a dumping ground for what other clubs considered their refuse. . . .

The Senators' season mercifully ended (and without the Hillebrand brothers to witness the occasion) on October 10 with the Senators "safe in last place," 24 games behind seventh-place Detroit. The final indignity was a doubleheader split against the Athletics. In keeping with the rest of this nightmare season, *Sporting Life* reported that the Senators should have won both games, "but an error let the visitors score three additional runs in the fourth inning of the first game, after the side should have been out with only two tallies."

♦

When the dust of the season had lifted, the Senators were, of course, in last place, 55$\frac{1}{2}$ games behind the pennant-winning Boston team. Yet there was at least some cause for optimism. For one thing, they'd won eighteen games more than the 1899 Cleveland Spiders, and that was something, wasn't it?

And then there was Jake Stahl. After a horrendous start Stahl had managed to move his average up to a respectable .262. It should be pointed out that he was not the team leader in this category. That honor went to Kip Selbach with a .275 average, who, unfortunately, had left the team way back in July. Stahl, in fact, had made such a name for himself that, to make him happy and keep him on the team, the club actually named him as manager for the 1905 season. (Under his leadership the Senators moved up to seventh place in 1905, winning a whopping 64 games, almost twice as many as they'd won in 1904. In 1912 he managed the AL Boston team to a record of 105–47, good enough to win the pennant.)

The Senators never quite equaled the depths to which they fell in 1904, a year that certainly justified the wisecrack "Washington —first in war, first in peace, and last in the American League."

1904 Washington Senators Roster

Player	POS	G	AB	R	H	2B	3B	HR	RBI	SB	BA
Joseph Cassidy	SS	152	581	63	140	12	19	1	33	17	.241
William Clarke	C	85	275	23	58	8	1	0	17	5	.211
William Coughlin	3B	65	265	28	73	15	4	0	17	10	.275
Patrick Donovan	OF	125	436	30	100	6	0	0	19	17	.229
Lewis Drill	C	46	142	17	38	7	2	1	11	3	.268
Silas Herring	OF-1B	15	46	3	8	1	0	0	2	0	.174
Hunter Hill	3B-OF	77	290	18	57	6	1	0	17	10	.197
Harry Hoffman	OF	10	30	1	3	1	0	0	1	0	.100
Frank Huelsman	OF	84	303	21	75	19	4	2	30	6	.248
Malachi Kittridge	C	81	265	11	64	7	0	0	24	2	.242
William McCormick	2B	113	404	36	88	11	1	0	39	9	.218
Charles Moran	SS-3B	62	243	27	54	10	0	0	7	7	.222
James Mullin	OF	27	102	10	19	2	2	0	4	3	.186
George Nill	2B	15	48	4	8	0	1	0	3	0	.167
William O'Neill	OF/2B	95	365	33	89	10	1	1	16	22	.244
Albert Selbach	OF	48	178	15	49	8	4	0	14	9	.275
Garland Stahl	1B	142	520	54	136	29	12	3	50	25	.262
John Thoney	OF	17	70	6	21	3	0	0	6	2	.300

Figures include games played with Washington only.

Pitcher	G	IP	H	ERA	ShO	SV	SO	BB	W	L
Edward Dunkle	12	74	95	4.96	0	0	23	23	2	9
Thomas Hughes	16	124	133	3.48	0	1	48	34	2	13
Albert Jacobson	33	254	276	3.55	1	0	75	57	6	23
Adelbert Mason	5	33	45	6.00	0	0	16	13	0	3
Albert Orth	10	74	88	4.74	0	0	23	15	3	4
Case Patten	45	358	367	3.07	2	3	150	79	14	23
John Townsend	36	291	319	3.58	2	0	143	100	5	26
Howard Wilson	3	25	33	4.68	0	0	11	4	0	3
Wilbert Wolfe	17	127	131	3.26	2	0	52	22	6	9

Figures include games played with Washington only.

Chapter 3
The 1916 Philadelphia Athletics

WON: **36**   LOST: **117**   GAMES OUT OF FIRST: **54½**

DAYS IN FIRST: **NONE**

HOME RECORD: **23–53**

ROAD RECORD: **13–64**

LONGEST WINNING STREAK: **2**

LONGEST LOSING STREAK: **20**

CONNIE MACK

There is a man in Quakertown
    And he is wondrous wise.
Each year he jumps into the bush
    And gathers bush league guys.
And after he has sold his stars,
    With all his might and main
He tries with every trick he knows
    To make new stars again.

—W. R. HOEFER,
Baseball Magazine, *May 1916*

NO OTHER TEAM in this book fell as far as fast as the 1916 Athletics. It is almost inconceivable that a team could go from being American League pennant winners in 1914 to the worst won-lost percentage in AL history in 1916, even harder to believe that the 1914 flag bearers were coming off three World Championships in four years. One could argue with some justification that from 1910 to 1914 the A's were the greatest dynasty of the first quarter of this century, a team constructed by one of the great baseball minds, Connie Mack. The team was built around one of the best infields of the modern era, the fabled "$100,000 infield" of John "Stuffy" McInnis, Eddie Collins, Jack Barry, and Frank "Home Run" Baker, and a pitching staff that was anchored by the likes of Chief Bender, Eddie Plank, and Jack Coombs.

♦ **Joe Bush in the off-season: After a year like he had in 1916, it was kill or be killed.** (Photo courtesy of the National Baseball Library, Cooperstown, NY)

There is no gainsaying Connie Mack's brilliance as a manager and owner. Coming into the 1915 season he had won five pennants in ten years and three World Series. Over that decade no Mack-managed team had finished lower than fourth. But Mack, one of the few baseball men worthy of the word *genius,* tore that team apart. Granted, they were humiliated by the "Miracle Braves" in the World Series, getting swept in four games, but how could such a team descend so quickly, as if they had stepped into an empty elevator shaft?

The answer, as is so often the case, is money.

While the newspapers were filled with the news of the growing war in Europe on their front pages, the sports pages were full of the war that was breaking out in baseball between the upstart Federal League and the forces of "Organized Baseball," as the American and National leagues and their minor-league junior partners liked to call themselves. As usually happens when an interleague war erupts in sports, bidding for the services of star players escalated rapidly. The Federal Leaguers, spearheaded by oil magnate Harry Sinclair, appeared to have some big bankrolls to flash.

The Federal League money must have looked pretty good to some of Mack's star players. While tight with a buck, he was not as penurious as Branch Rickey or football's George Halas (of whom Mike Ditka once said, "He throws nickels around like they were manhole covers"); but baseball was Mack's only business and the Athletics were not drawing that well, in spite of their considerable on-field success.

For some reason Mack always claimed that money was not the primary motivation for the dismantling of the 1914 team. In the July 24, 1915, issue of *The Literary Digest,* Mack denied that he was motivated by financial considerations in selling off Jack Barry and Eddie Collins to the Red Sox and White Sox, respectively, and the outright release of Bender, Coombs, and Plank. The magazine's unnamed correspondent writes, "He did not break up 'the greatest baseball machine ever put together' for money, but because he foresaw the end of that machine and knew it was already time to build a new one."

Joe Williams, the great baseball writer of the *New York World-Telegram,* chatted with Mack during spring training in 1932. He quotes the Athletics owner on the aftermath of the 1914 Series, "I wasn't surprised that we were beaten. In fact, I don't know whether you know it or not, but I quit on my team in August." Mack goes on to explain that virtually the entire A's roster was considering offers from the Federal League, with half ready to jump and the other half prepared to stay. The result, Mack told Williams, was a shattering of the team's morale. "The fact is that . . . I broke it up solely because the boys had shown me that they could not get along together." That motivation would come as a shock to the A's of the early 1970s, a dynasty that was distinguished by the fact that they couldn't get along together either.

Finally, in his 1950 autobiography, *My 66 Years in the Big Leagues,* Mack repeats the internal-dissension theme but reluctantly admits that he was unwilling (and probably unable) to try to match the dollar offers of the Federal League. He closes the discussion with a bizarre explanation for the nearly total dismantling of the franchise:

> "Why didn't you hang on to the half of your team that was loyal and start to build again?" This question has often been asked me.
> My answer is that when a team starts to disintegrate it is like trying to plug the hole in the dam to stop the flood. The boys who are left have lost their high spirits, and they want to go where they think the future looks brighter.

If the World Series of 1914 was a flood for Mack, then the 1915 and 1916 seasons must have left him feeling like Noah at the Deluge. Even though the Federal League folded after its 1915 season, the damage had already been done in Philadelphia.

Why does Mack adamantly reject the economic interpretation of his decision to break up the team? Perhaps the petty mercenary concerns such a decision bespeaks were beneath the dignity of the Grand Old Man of the Game. Certainly, his financial troubles were no secret. Billy Evans, an American League umpire who dabbled in sportswriting, comments at some length on the poor attendance the A's suffered even during their winning seasons in his preview of the 1915 season in *Harper's Weekly*. In the *Literary Digest* article Mack admitted that he was pretty near broke, all the while voicing his determination to rebuild the team. Maybe he really believed all the prepsychobabble stuff about "a house divided."

Whatever the reasons the 1915 Athletics were pretty bad. The year began with the death in Philadelphia of Louie Van Zelst, the team's much-beloved mascot, just before the end of spring training. It was an inauspicious omen. Collins had been sold to the White Sox for the then considerable sum of $50,000. Bender, Plank, and Coombs had been released. Frank Baker had resolved to sit out the entire season, hoping either to be traded or given a new contract. In July Jack Barry would be sold to the Red Sox for a paltry $8000. Eddie Murphy, Herb Pennock, and Bob Shawkey would depart over the course of the remainder of the season.

The A's opened the season impressively, with Pennock holding the Bosox to a single hit in a 2–0 victory, and for the first couple of weeks of the season they looked like the Athletics of old; but by May they were in seventh place, en route to the basement.

One of the few marquee players to be added to the Athletics' fading roster that year was an aging Napoleon Lajoie. One could make a pretty good case for "Larry" Lajoie as the greatest second baseman of all time. He was one of the most consistently deadly righty hitters of the dead-ball era and was judged one of the most graceful of fielders by his contemporaries. However, Nap would turn forty just before the 1915 season ended. He was grateful to return to the town in which he had enjoyed some of his early successes, but he was clearly reaching the end of the line. In late September 1915 Billy Evans wrote of Lajoie's hitting, "It is possible that the batting eye . . . of Lajoie . . . [has] been slightly dimmed by age and continued use. It is possible that [he has] slowed up some, and every now and then [loses]a hit that years ago might have gone to [his] credit." That he had lost something of his old grace in the field was proven on April 22, when he made a record five errors in one game. Years later Lajoie was able to look back on that day with amusement, but it couldn't have been too funny then, especially when the A's lost the contest by a single run. Lajoie had the small consolation of hitting .280, third highest among the A's regulars that season, but a far cry from his lifetime average of .338.

Rubbing more salt in Mack's wounds, 1915 was the year in which the Phillies won what would prove to be their only pennant until 1950. The Athletics, 99–53 in 1914, finished the 1915 campaign with a dismal 43–109 record. After 1916 they would look back on even that mark with nostalgia.

As the 1916 season approached, Mack was outwardly confident of his ability to mold a new dynasty from the odd collection of veterans, cast-offs, and college players that he was assembling. His penchant for signing college boys was often remarked upon in the baseball press, usually derisively. He told *Literary Digest:*

> Some people say, "Why doesn't Connie Mack go out and get some good minor leaguers?" But I don't work on those lines. Except in some very rare instances players of the higher class minor leagues do not appeal to me, because I have my own ideas of how to develop players. That we have had success is due, I think, to the fact that we handle them differently. I want youngsters with the qualifications, and, when I see them, I will bring them out myself.

He wasn't kidding about the last part; at one set of tryouts, Mack, then 53, could be seen putting on his old catcher's mitt to test some of the would-be hurlers in camp.

Interestingly, the reasoning behind Mack's preference for college players, that he could mold them into his system more completely than he could minor leaguers, is the exact reasoning that leads many major-league organizations today to draft high-school amateurs ahead of college players. Of course, in Mack's day college baseball was more informal than it is today, while the minor leagues were still largely independent of the majors. Mack had enjoyed considerable success with college players like Eddie Collins (Columbia) and Eddie Plank (Gettysburg). However, in 1916, his luck with the denizens of higher education ran a little thin.

The winter of 1915–6 was an eventful one for Mack and his White Elephants. (The nickname predated this team, but Connie finally had one worthy of the nickname.) The city series between the Phils and A's was in jeopardy, largely due to lack of fan interest. Rube Oldring retired in November to run his farm in New Jersey; he would unretire before spring training. One completed deal was apparently a mark of the generous side of Mack's nature: Jack Lapp was sent to the White Sox in exchange for an agreement that the stingy Chisox owner, Charlie Comiskey, not cut his salary, Philadelphia receiving no other compensation in the transaction. Frank Baker wasn't, then was, then wasn't, then finally really and truly was sold to the Yankees for $37,500. Rumors abounded that Mack would unload the team itself; American League president Ban Johnson had to squelch the persistent gossip. In fact, Mack would run the ball club through the 1950 season, and his heirs would not sell until 1954.

One thing was certain, as William Weart would report in *The Sporting News:* the 1916 A's "will be almost a new team." Not good, just new.

How complete a housecleaning Mack was planning could be judged by the report in December that he planned to take 39 players to Jacksonville for spring training, a large number in those days. Eighteen of those players were pitchers. After all, wasn't it Connie Mack who said that pitching was 75 percent of baseball?

The main topic of conversation in baseball circles that winter was the peace treaty signed between the major leagues and the Federals. *Baseball Magazine,* in the purple prose of the period, would offer, "The sun of peace has risen full orbed with the promise of a new and better day in baseball and the shadows of doubt and uncertainty have evaporated." Except in Philadelphia.

Although many Federal League players would return to the two surviving leagues, Mack would eschew signing any of them for Philadelphia, preferring to rely on his scouting instincts and the cheaper college talent he had stockpiled. Late in January, Weart complained that, while every other American League club had been strengthening itself, Mack was content to continue his youth movement.

As in 1915, the new season began with a troubling omen involving the Athletics' off-field personnel, when longtime A's grounds keeper Joe Schroeder died in January. The trip south had a dire beginning as well; bad weather and steamship troubles cost them two days, delaying the start of spring training.

When they finally arrived down south, the Athletics received a series of beatings from National League teams. From March 23 through April 1 the Philadelphia regulars lost to the Braves and Dodgers nine consecutive games, usually by scores like 8–0 and 13–3. They managed to score five runs in only one of these games and were shut out three times, another harbinger of the season to come.

Of course, spring-training games are meaningless, except as testing grounds for young and untried players, of whom the A's had many. Mack was slowly crafting the lineup with which he would begin the season in mid-April. And he had a lot of crafting to do. Although he finally settled on a much smaller spring-training group than the 39 announced in December, Mack went to Jacksonville with a lot of untested kids.

Nobody could say he didn't make his players work hard. William Weart observed, "Never before has Manager Mack driven a squad as hard as he is working the men this year. . . . [W]ith the problem of building a new team before him, the leader seems to be a different man." Even so, Weart would report that as the season drew nigh, "there is a lot of gloom in the camp of the Athletics."

When finally assembled, Mack's Opening Day roster was well stocked with kids, some of them collegians, but several drafted or purchased from the minors. The initial starting eight was an uneasy blend of too old and too new, particularly in the infield, where two rookies were present.

Charlie Pick, acquired from Jack Dunn's Baltimore Orioles (the source of Babe Ruth and Lefty Grove, among others), would replace Frank Baker at third. Pick led AL third basemen in errors as a rookie in 1916. In fact, his .898 fielding average would be the last sub-.900 FA recorded by a regular until Butch Hobson equaled that figure in 1978. Hobson's errors were largely the product of bone chips in his throwing elbow. Pick had no doctor's excuse; he just couldn't field. Even Mack could only stand so much. He would sell Pick back to the minors, but Pick would reemerge in 1918 as a second baseman with the Cubs, and hit .389 in the World Series that year. On May 1, 1920, he would earn a small niche in baseball history with the Boston Braves when he and Ivy Olson, the Dodgers second baseman, played all 26 innings of the longest game (by innings) in major league history.

Sam Crane, who had been up and down with the A's for parts of two previous seasons, was the Opening Day shortstop, but he would suffer a charley horse and be sent to Baltimore, replaced at short by Whitey Witt. After his playing career ended, Crane killed his girlfriend and another man and was sent to prison. With typical loyalty Mack helped him achieve parole; after serving fourteen years of his sentence Crane came out of prison to work at Shibe Park for Connie.

Lawton "Whitey" Witt, a nineteen-year-old whom Mack had signed out of the Goddard Seminary, would replace him. "I signed with the A's right out of high school for $300 a month," he would recall on his ninetieth birthday. "I got $500 raises each year through 1921, and when I signed with the Yankees, I got $9000." Witt was a little guy (five-seven, 150 pounds), an excellent bunter who drew a lot of walks, an ideal leadoff hitter. After suffering through five years of Mack's small salaries and bad ball clubs (and one year in the Army), Witt went to the Yankees, where he played center field and led off. In the latter role he is the answer to a trivia question, the first man in pinstripes to bat in Yankee Stadium.

The right side of the infield was held down by two great ballplayers, Lajoie and Stuffy McInnis. Throughout spring training there had been rumors that one of the kids would displace the nearly 41-year-old Nap, but an aging Lajoie would be better than a young Lew Malone, both on the field and at the gate. Besides, reported *Philadelphia Inquirer* reporter Jim Nasium (and the man who made up that pseudonym ought to have been shot), "the biggest surprise that has been sprung on the Athletics' camp . . . is the vast improvement and rejuvenation of Lajoie."

McInnis was the last survivor of the "$100,000 infield," another one of Mack's schoolboys, who had signed as a teenaged shortstop out of the New England League (where he played for

Sliding Billy Hamilton, the man whose career stolen-base record Lou Brock surpassed). Mack converted him into a first baseman. The switch was a huge success; McInnis became one of the finest fielding first basemen of all time. In 1921, as a member of the Red Sox, McInnis would go through an entire season making only one error. In fact, he went 163 consecutive games without a miscue.

The outfield starters were all veterans, but not all veterans are created equal. Amos Strunk in right and Rube Oldring in left had played on the Mack's pennant winners. Interestingly, Amos was a Philadelphia native and had grown up in Mack's own neighborhood, but, as J. C. Kofoed wrote in *Baseball Magazine,* "[T]ill the tall outfielder began to burn up the grass in the Atlantic League old Connie never knew that Mrs. Strunk had a son." A highly regarded defensive outfielder, Strunk would enjoy one of his better years in 1916, hitting .316 and finishing fourth among AL batters. He would get one more World Series ring with the Bosox in 1918 before returning to Mack to finish his career.

Oldring, on the other hand, was showing signs of wear after eleven years in the majors; clearly, his waning enthusiasm led him to announce his brief off-season retirement. He would retire again in the middle of the year, only to return in a Yankee uniform for another brief stint. After missing the 1917 season he would finish his major-league career back with Mack for another 49 games in 1918.

The center fielder was Jimmy Walsh, a light-hitting speedster. Born in Ireland, Walsh is probably best remembered for pulling off two double-squeeze plays (a play you don't see anymore) in one game with Eddie Collins bunting. His anemic career batting average of .231 suggests an Omar Moreno–type player, a guy who never learned to take advantage of his speed.

The catching situation should have been one of the few stable ones on the team. Wally Schang was a good hitter, one of the few backstops to steal more than one hundred bases in his career and one of the game's great defensive catchers. Oddly, Schang was a converted shortstop. Playing with his brother Bob on a semipro team based in Buffalo, he was pressed into service behind the plate when his sibling broke a finger on a foul tip. Although both

Schangs would make it to the majors as catchers, it was Wally, the ex-infielder, who would become a star. With the inexplicable logic of a genius in the throes of creativity, Mack would play him more in left field than behind the plate over the course of the season.

All the preseason pundits pointed to Schang's backups, Mike Murphy and Bill Meyer, as a source of real depth on the Mackmen's roster. "Murphy and Meyers [sic] are finished performers behind the bat," wrote Nasium in the *Inquirer*. Unfortunately, Murphy hit .111 in only fourteen games with the A's that year, and Meyer went down with appendicitis in July (he was hitting .232 at the time). Finished performers indeed. After that, as pitcher Tom Sheehan would recall, "Everybody caught."

Sheehan told Jack Orr a story that sums up the futility of the Athletics' catching situation:

> Once we were playing the Yankees at the Polo Grounds and I'm pitching. [Val] Picinich warms me up, but as the first hitter gets in, Val goes back to the bench and takes off the tools.
>
> Another guy comes out, a guy I've never seen. He comes out to the mound and says, "My name is Carroll. I'm the catcher. What are your signs?" I tell him not to confuse me and get the heck back there and catch. He stuck around for about a week and nobody ever saw him again.

Picinich was an oddity, a career backup catcher who lasted eighteen years in the majors. A rookie out of prep school when Mack brought him up in 1916, Picinich would catch no-hitters for the A's' Joe Bush, the Senators' Walter Johnson, and the Red Sox's Howard Ehmke. Carroll was Ralph Carroll, who caught ten games with the 1916 Mack squad while hitting .091. (Billy Meyer, incidentally, went on to considerable success managing in the Yankees farm system and was actually offered the job of managing the Bombers in 1946, but turned it down for medical reasons. He would manage the Pirates to a fourth-place finish in 1948, winning *TSN*'s Manager of the Year honors for his efforts. Unfortunately, Meyer would stick around as Pirates skipper until 1952, thereby qualifying for another chapter in this book.)

Whatever else one could say of Mack's bench in 1916, there was certainly a lot of it. Over the course of the season 47 players would wear Athletics uniform, including 19 pitchers. It was a marginal improvement over the previous year, when 59 players had paraded through the Philadelphia clubhouse.

The pitching staff would seem to be the logical place to put most of the blame for the A's' dismal showing. After all, when your team loses 117 games, the pitching must be pretty bad. Some of the disapprobation heaped on Athletics hurlers in 1916 was justified; the team ERA was a full run higher than the league average. But the best of the Philadelphia pitchers, Joe Bush and Elmer Myers, pitched considerably better than their respective records of 15–24 and 14–23 would indicate.

Leslie Ambrose (Bullet Joe) Bush learned his hard-throwing ways, legend has it, as a young boy tossing rotten apples through the crescent cut in the door of a neighbor's outhouse in his native Brainerd, Minnesota. Bush had been brought up by Mack as a green kid in 1913 when Jack Coombs missed the entire season with illness and injuries. The 20-year-old Bush acquitted himself admirably, going 14–6 and pitching a five-hitter against the Giants in the World Series, the youngest hurler ever to start and win a Series game at that time. Bush came by his nickname naturally. As Mack once observed, "Except for Walter Johnson and maybe Amos Rusie, Bush had the fastest pitch I've ever seen."

When the Federal League war broke out, the Minnesota native had passed up a two-year contract with the St. Louis Federals worth $18,000, staying with Mack at $3500 a year. In the late sixties he would explain, "True I'd have had the $18,000 in my possession, but I believed the American League to be on more solid ground than the Federal League. It turned out to be the right decision." Although he didn't collect any more World Series checks in Philadelphia, Bush wouldn't have been any better off in the Mound City; when the peace treaty was signed, St. Louis Federal League owner Phil Ball was allowed to buy the Browns, who wouldn't win a pennant until 1944. As Bush noted with amusement, "That was a little too late to do me any good."

Bush would even find his way back to the World Series three

more times in the '20s, with the Red Sox and Yankees. By that time he had lost something off the fastball that earned him his nickname. His response was to invent the forkball, a pitch that enabled him to go 26–7 for New York in 1922. An excellent hitter, he would end his career playing the outfield in the Pacific Coast League.

Coming off a dreadful 5–15 mark the previous year, Bush entered the 1916 season with new resolve. William Weart noted, "He is showing an earnestness that was lacking before." That new determination was apparent in the results he achieved, even with a club as bad as the A's. Given his 2.57 ERA and eight shutouts (second in the league to Babe Ruth, who had nine), one could make a case for Bush as one of the best pitchers in the American League in 1916.

Bush needed those shutouts. The 1916 A's seldom scored runs. On most pitching staffs there is one hard-luck guy who never gets enough offensive support, but on the Athletics almost every pitcher could make that complaint. The team scored only 447 runs the entire year, an average of 3.25 runs per game. Even the seventh-place Senators scored 536 runs, a quarter run per game higher.

Elmer Myers was a fair pitcher who had the misfortune to be part of Mack's great transition to oblivion. On October 6, 1915, in his first major-league game, Myers hurled a four-hit shutout. The following season he became one of the workhorses of the Philadelphia staff, pitching 315 innings. He would suffer through three more seasons with the tail-ending A's before Mack finally allowed him to escape in 1920 to Cleveland, where he just missed playing in the Indians' first World Series, getting traded to Boston in midseason.

The hurler who was most consistently victimized by lack of support was Jack Nabors. The Alabama native had been a star in local circles, pitching a 13-inning no-hitter in the Georgia-Alabama League in 1914. Mack purchased his contract the following year and Nabors took his 12–1 minor-league record to Philadelphia. He appeared briefly in an A's uniform in 1915, going 0–5 in ten appearances. The following year Nabors would experience the worst nightmare any pitcher ever had. In 1916 he would go 1–20, losing nineteen straight decisions to tie the major-league record set in 1909 by the Senators' Bob Groom. Five of the games were lost by one run, another five by two. On fourteen separate occasions the A's would score two or fewer runs for him; in five of those games they were shut out.

His roommate, Tom Sheehan, who would go 1–16 that year, told Jack Orr a story that encapsulates Nabors's season and the team's:

"Once we go to Boston for a series. I pitch the opener and give up one hit, by Doc Hoblitzell. But it happens to follow a walk and an error by Witt [one of the 78 he would make that year] and I lose, 1–0.

"Now Nabors pitches the second game and he is leading, 1–0, going into the ninth. He gets the first man. Witt boots one and the next guy walks. Hooper is up next, I think, and he singles to left and the man on second tries to score.

"Well, Schang has a good arm and he throws one in that had the runner cold by fifteen feet. But we have one of those green catchers. (Never forget his name, Mike Murphy.) The ball bounces out of his glove, the run scores, the other runner takes third, and it is 1–1.

"Nabors winds up and throws the next pitch 20 feet over the hitter's head into the grandstand, the man on third scores, and we lose another, 2–1.

"Later I asked Nabors why he threw that one away.

" 'Look,' he said, 'I knew those guys wouldn't get me another run, and if you think I'm going to throw nine more innings on a hot day like this, you're crazy.' "

Nabors's fate after the 1916 season was even more cruel. He sojourned briefly with the A's in 1917, logging no decisions in two appearances and only three innings, before Mack sold him to Indianapolis of the American Association. He finished the year with Denver in the Western League, where he started to show signs of life, throwing a no-hitter against Sioux City in July. After another year in the WL, this time with Sioux City, he enlisted in the Army. While stationed in Iowa he fell victim to the Spanish influenza epidemic that ravaged virtually the entire world in 1919. Nabors spent the remaining three years of his life bedridden with tuberculosis. His brother, a doctor, told a reporter, "The tissues around his heart began to wear down and finally he just went to sleep." His one victory in 1916 would be his only win in the major leagues.

Tom Sheehan made out much better, finishing his days in baseball as a superscout for the Giants, even getting a brief stint as their manager in 1960. Sheehan was a gifted raconteur whose scouting prowess and storytelling abilities earned him more ink than his pitching record of 17–39 scattered over six seasons and four teams. Asked about rooming with Nabors, he told Bob Broeg, "Man, you never saw two guys celebrate when they won a ball game." Maybe it's just as well they were a combined 2–36 that year. (By the way, didn't anybody suggest that they split up that roommate combination? Or were they all afraid that whatever those two had might be contagious?)

It would be unfair for the hitters to take all the blame for the A's' woeful performance, though. The pitching staff did its share of damage. The previous year Athletics pitchers had been extremely generous to opposing batters, surrendering a league-high 827 walks, 5.4 passes a game. While their control was better in 1916, the A's hurlers still surrendered 715 passes, again the worst in the AL. Ring Lardner, tongue firmly planted in cheek, suggested that such openhandedness would bring the Athletics the pennant in 1916: "Connie Mack has a staff of simply unhittable pitchers, unhittable, that is, unless the opposing batsmen are permitted to take ladders up to the plate with them."

Other pundits were equally unkind in their preseason assessment of the Athletics' prospects. The most generous prediction came from *Baseball Magazine*'s W. A. Phelon, who picked the Mackmen to finish seventh. His colleague, W. R. Hoefer, was closer to the mark when he wrote that Mack should give thanks, "because there are only eight clubs in the American League and the misfits he commanded couldn't finish twenty-seventh." Another wag noted, "You can't do anything to make an eighth-place club worse." In a subsequent issue the editors gave the odds on Philadelphia finishing first as 100 to one, second 50 to one, third 25 to one, and fourth ten to one. That descending scale would prove overly charitable.

♦

It didn't take long for the A's to stumble. They lost the season opener to the defending champion Red Sox, 2–1. Babe Ruth pitched well against the Mackmen, but the inability of the A's to convert scoring opportunities in the late innings proved their real undoing. Jack Nabors pitched as well as Ruth, holding the Sox to two hits over four shutout innings. Bush, who relieved him, gave up unearned runs in the sixth and seventh innings, thanks to his own error and one by Charlie Pick (who would make 43 more over the season). Wally Schang injured his right hand while catching and would miss a couple of weeks. The A's were establishing a pattern for the remaining 153 games.

After a rainout the A's dropped another game in Boston. Crane was replaced by Witt, who also was installed as the leadoff man. Mack reputedly told Boston reporters that he was "satisfied" with what he had seen in their town and was certain that the team would finish in the first division. He must have been eating tainted seafood.

The Athletics—or, as *Baseball Magazine* had taken to calling them, the Pathetics—moved on to New York, where old friend Home Run Baker did them in in the first of two Yankee victories. Joe Vila, *TSN*'s New York correspondent, reported that Mack told New York reporters that the team would finish last. Obviously, he had recovered, even if the team hadn't.

Then it was on to Philadelphia for the home opener against Boston, which of course they lost. In fact, the A's lost their first six games of the season. Finally, Elmer "Hap" Myers rescued them with a 3–1 two-hitter. Remarkably, they repeated the feat the following day, staking Jack Nabors to an improbable 5–1 lead in the first three innings against the defending champs. Nabors hung on to win 6–2, little suspecting that it would be his only victory in the majors.

In spite of the bizarre pronouncement from Boston, Mack was a realist. Two consecutive victories against the mighty Red Sox didn't dissuade him from shuffling the Athletic deck some more. He sold two rookies to the minors, one of them Sammy McConnell, another collegian, while the team continued on to Washington. In D.C. the A's took but one of three games to begin a long road trip. Although J. Ed Grillo reported that the team had impressed Senator owner-manager Clark Griffith, Griff's gaunt Philadelphia counterpart was not happy. With the school year drawing to a close Mack was gearing up for a steady influx of college boys seeking tryouts, and his right-hand man, Harry Davis, was expected to spend a lot of mornings at Shibe Park inspecting the would-be diamond stars. "Almost every college ball player of any prominence is said to have been signed for the Athletics," wrote William Weart.

By May 1 the A's were seemingly mired in last place for the duration with a record of 4–10. But over the next two weeks the impossible happened: Philadelphia went 6–5 and climbed over the prostrate Browns into seventh place. For a brief stretch the bats heated up and the A's knocked both Boston and Washington out of first place, taking two out of three in each series. On consecutive days home runs by Strunk, Schang, and Lajoie led to a trio of Athletics victories. For Schang, back from his hand injury, it was a satisfying return to action. Witt benefited from coaching by Lajoie, and Pick was beginning to hit as well.

When the western teams arrived in Philadelphia the following week, a strange sort of reality asserted itself spasmodically. May 9, the day after Philadelphia defeated Walter Johnson and the Senators, the Tigers came to town. The A's celebrated their arrival by losing 16–2 in a game in which thirty bases on balls were issued, eighteen by three A's hurlers and a dozen by two Tiger pitchers. Over the four-game series with Detroit, A's hurlers would issue 49 walks in a dismaying reversion to 1915's freehandedness. Detroit's mound staff added 36 of their own, in addition to hitting two batsmen. Both teams seemed to have trouble plating all those runners; over the four contests 92 runners were stranded. In the finale, an 11-inning debacle, the A's left 20 on base, the Tigers eighteen.

On the other hand, St. Louis was stymied by Elmer Myers in their only game in Philadelphia that week, as Myers notched his third win in a week. The win moved the Browns into the cellar and the A's into seventh, but the best was yet to come. Into town came the White Sox, who proceeded to drop a pair of games, one of them an eleven-inning three-hit shutout by Bush. Chicago fell into seventh as the Athletics reached the zenith of their 1916 campaign, sixth place. At this point in the season Myers had won five in a row, Bush six. Rookie outfielder Bill Stellbauer showed flashes of hitting ability and sportswriters around the league were murmuring that they might owe Connie an apology.

Then the A's went back on the road. After a fruitless series with the Senators, Rube Oldring enjoyed his one hot spell of the season in New York, going 12 for 19 in five games against the Yanks, and Bush and Myers won two, but the Yanks took the other three contests. The slippage had begun.

In St. Louis the A's seemed lifeless, losing to the doormat Browns. The *Sporting News* correspondent who saw the games wrote that the veterans were guilty of lackadaisical play and the defense was inept. Even Myers looked bad against the Browns. A series of rainouts kept the team idle in Chicago, the bats went cold, the pitchers went sour.

Mack celebrated the team's return home in June by sending several players back to the minors. Former Brown University hurler Minot Crowell, Lew Malone, and Bill Stellbauer were all shipped off for more seasoning. None of them would be back in A's uniforms and only Malone would make it back to the majors, albeit briefly, with Brooklyn in 1917 and 1918. By June 15 the A's were back in the basement to stay.

Mack began to experiment with his newly arrived college kids. Lester Lanning pitched and played the outfield; in 19 games, nine in the outfield, six on the mound, he went 0–3 and hit .182. Harland Rowe, a third baseman from the University of Maine, got a brief look but hit only .139. Ed King and Otis Lawry, two more New England schoolboys, were tried in right and at second, respectively. Lawry was recovering from tonsilitis when he made his debut, pressed into service when Lajoie came up with an infected toe at the end of June. Although he fielded adequately, he hit only .203. King was even worse, hitting .188.

The pitchers were suffering the torments of hell. Against the Senators, Bush and Nabors combined on a three-hitter and lost.

Sheehan pitched a two-hitter against the Red Sox and lost 1–0 on a walk, a pair of fielder's choices, and a wild pitch. On June 30 the A's lost their eleventh straight game. Rube Oldring retired again.

The college-boy pitchers became sacrificial lambs. While an entire generation of Europe's youth was being decimated in the trenches of France, an entire generation of college baseball players seemed to be parading across the pitching mounds of the American League, wearing Athletics uniforms and giving up walks. Russell "Jingling" Johnson, a research biochemist from Ursinus, Marshall Williams of South Carolina, George Hesselbacher, Michael Driscoll, they were just so many names, so much raw meat for AL hitters to feast on.

On July 1 the A's were 17–41. When the month ended, they were in the midst of one of the most ignominious stretches in the history of the franchise, a twenty-game losing streak that stretched on through the heat of the summer and threatened to go on even longer. "I had a haunting feeling we'd never win another," said Tom Sheehan. They wouldn't win a game until August 9, tying what was then the AL record for consecutive defeats.

Murphy's Law reigned supreme: everything that could go wrong did. Charlie Pick was spiked by a base runner in St. Louis and would miss nearly a month of the season. McInnis suffered a charley horse and missed a couple of weeks. Wally Schang fell over a cement wall chasing a foul and broke his jaw. After three weeks' retirement Rube Oldring showed up as a Yankee. Jimmy Walsh was suspended after a mammoth argument with an ump. Billy Meyer had an attack of appendicitis. The only victories the team could muster in July were shutouts pitched by Joe Bush against the Browns and Indians.

The Athletics were humiliated by other teams in the unlikeliest ways imaginable. When the Indians arrived in Philadelphia in late July, they found the infield grass had been left long to slow down ground balls. Lee Fohl, the Cleveland skipper, filed a protest with the league office. Indians first baseman Chick Gandil (later one of the Black Sox conspirators) took a more practical approach, hiding a ball in the long grass in front of first. At an opportune moment he asked umpire Billy Evans for time, scooped the ball out of its hiding place, and tossed it to the arbiter. The grass was cut the next day.

There were faint glimmers of hope. Bush proved indomitable. Pick's replacement, a Bowdoin College grad with the unlikely name of Leland Stanford McElwee, actually hit .265 (which was 24 points higher than Pick would manage). But it was clear that the great collegian experiment was a disastrous failure, and Mack and his staff began to search for minor leaguers to shore up the collapsing structure that was the Athletics.

On August 9 the Athletics lost their twentieth game in a row, a 9–0 drubbing at the hands of the Detroit Tigers. Jack Nabors was pounded for sixteen hits in the effort as the A's sank to 20–80.

The next day, with the record on the line, Joe Bush finally prevailed, defeating the Tigers 7–1. Jimmy Walsh's misplaying a fly into a triple in the ninth was the only thing that prevented Bush from registering a shutout. Otherwise, he was masterful, allowing only four hits, two of them scratch singles. *The Philadelphia Record* offered a cartoon the next day that was adorned with, among other things, a drawing of Bush in the stocks, with a sign around his neck reading FOR SALE, JOE BUSH, referring to him as "the Benedict Arnold." Mack was similarly derided by some sportwriters for pitching the dependable Bush instead of one of his potted collegians and thereby sacrificing a chance at the record.

The victory was only their third in the last 42 games, and it was Bush who had stopped each losing streak. A few days later they would actually win consecutive games from the Yankees.

In one respect the A's' hopeless ineptitude was contributing mightily to one of the best pennant races in AL history. At some point in the season each of seven teams occupied first place. By season's end all but two teams were over .500 and the seventh-place Senators fell but one game short of the break-even point. Clearly every team in the league was fattening up on Mack's Pathetics.

By mid-August even Mack had to laugh ruefully at the state of affairs. H. G. Salsinger, the Detroit correspondent of *The Sporting News,* quoted the manager at length:

"You'll have to give the Athletics credit for one thing," says Mack. "We are making it a good race. When we went into St. Louis to start our western trip I told them in St. Louis they had a great ball club. They looked incredulous. Then the Browns beat us five straight and everybody perked up. And you know what the Browns have done since trimming us those five.

"We swung over to Chicago for eight games. The Sox did not expect to take them all, of course. But they did. They gained the league lead, and Chicago is now convinced that the White Sox will surely cop the flag this year.

"Cleveland was about resigned to drop into the second division when we reached that city. They took all of the games we played and that gave them a fresh start and new hope. Now they are going pretty well again.

"We are the race makers, although this is not doing us any particular good. But we are the little tonic team of baseball. We come along when any other club is sick and get it back to health."

For all the joking Mack's players were still giving good effort. For example, when the Browns came into Philadelphia in late August, they took two out of three from the Athletics, but each of the games was a one-run affair, and two of the three went to extra innings. Nabors, pitching in hard luck as usual, lost a two-hitter when the Browns strung together two walks, two singles, and a sacrifice for three runs.

On August 26 a double milestone occurred in Shibe Park. Joe Bush pitched a no-hitter against the Indians, allowing only one base runner, outfielder Jack Graney, who led off the first with a walk. Bush retired the next 27 batters. The A's even managed to get Bush five runs to work with. Bush fanned seven and finished the game by inducing Graney to fly out to McInnis, after which he was mobbed by Athletics fans on his way to the dugout. For Bush it was sweet revenge; the day before he had been knocked out by the Indians in the third inning and he had begged Mack for a second chance at the Tribe.

The other milestone was not recognized as such at the time, but this would turn out to be Napoleon Lajoie's last major-league game. The next day, during batting practice, he injured himself and was through for the season. His final hit was a triple over Tris

Speaker's head off Indians pitcher Fritz Coumbe. His final at bat was a deep fly to right. Like Ernie Banks he never did get to play in a World Series.

As August drew to a close, the Athletics were 28–95. Ironically, as William Weart pointed out, the end of the 20-game losing streak had signaled a faint turning of the A's' fortunes. "The team is doing steadily better and there is a noticeable improvement in various departments," he opined. "Since [the losing streak] the Mackmen have won one or more games in each of their last seven series." On the other hand the Athletics notched their hundredth loss on September 6, Tom Sheehan being charged with the debit.

On their third and final Western swing the A's knocked both Detroit and Chicago out of the pennant race, largely on the strength of the pitching of Myers and Bush and late addition Socks Seibold, a converted outfielder. Each of the three victories was a shutout.

The season was winding down and Mack was beginning to make moves with an eye toward the 1917 season. He had two excellent right-handed pitchers in Myers and Bush. The outfield was well stocked, although Strunk was the only reliable player. He would add minor-leaguer Frank "Buck" Thrasher (a wonderful name for a power hitter; unfortunately, he was neither wonderful nor a power hitter) and Ping Bodie. The infield was more uncertain than ever with Lajoie gone. Pick wouldn't be back in 1917, either, although Mack hadn't decided that yet. At least Witt was set, both at short and as the leadoff hitter. Searching for infielders, Mack would also plunge into the minor-league draft with fervor, bidding for a dozen players, only to withdraw bids on most of them.

The campaign ended with the A's playing to dwindling crowds at home and on the road. They limped through the last two weeks of the season with an indifferent 6–9 mark to finish at 36–117.

♦

As always seemed the case when the A's didn't win a pennant, rumors began to circulate that Mack would take a managerial job elsewhere. This time it was the Red Sox that supposedly beckoned, but Mack demurred as usual, saying that Philadelphia was his home. It is no small tribute to his standing in the baseball community that after compiling the worst winning percentage in AL history (.235), somebody wanted to hire him to run a pennant winner.

How bad were the 1916 Philadelphia Athletics? They finished 54 1/2 games out of first, not the worst in history by any means. On the other hand, they were 40 games out of seventh, which probably is a record. Their .235 W-L percentage is the modern record, surpassed only by the .130 of the 1899 Cleveland Spiders. The 2–28 record they logged in July set a still-unmatched mark for lowest percentage (.067) for a single month. Their 64 losses on the road is still the record for American League teams, even after the circuit added eight games to the schedule. Although their 20-loss skein has since been surpassed by the 1988 Orioles, their AL record 19 consecutive road losses still stands.

No other team in the American League that year would fail to score at least 500 runs. The A's 447 runs was 128 below the league average that year. No other team had an ERA over 3.00; the A's was 3.84. Only one other team allowed as many as 600 runs; the A's gave up 776, 201 over the league average. The team had three 20-game losers and only one regular hitting over .300, Amos Strunk. They made over 300 errors, *averaging* over two a game. In short, they were pretty bad.

Mack would run another pennant winner. In fact, he would rebuild his ball club as he promised, although not on the schedule he envisioned. Although he had promised another winning team within two or three years after the dismantling of the great team of the 1910–14 period, Mack would have to get used to the basement. The Athletics would occupy the AL cellar for seven years, from 1915 to 1921, still a record. They would never again suffer through a season as bad as 1916—to date no one has—but it would take until 1925 for the A's to get back over the .500 mark.

The team that would finally win another pennant for Mack— three of them in a row and back-to-back World Series victories as well—would be an even greater collection of talent than his first dynasty. From 1929 to 1931 the Athletics would halt the Yankee domination of the American League, powered by the bats of

Jimmy Foxx, Mickey Cochrane, Al Simmons, Bing Miller, and Mule Haas, and the pitching arms of Lefty Grove, George Earnshaw, and Rube Walberg. Then the Depression would strike and Connie would have to dismantle another great team in order to survive financially. This time he would not be able to rebuild, and from 1934 to 1968 the A's would finish no higher than fourth. They would finish above .500 only five times in that 35-year stretch. Happily, Mack would live to see three of those five winning seasons, all of them consecutive, 1947-9, at the very end of his stewardship of the club.

1916 Philadelphia Athletics Roster

Player	POS	G	AB	R	H	2B	3B	HR	RBI	SB	BA
Don Brown	OF	14	42	6	10	2	1	1	5	0	.238
Ralph Carroll	C	10	22	1	2	0	0	0	0	0	.091
Sam Crane	SS	2	4	1	1	0	0	0	0	0	.250
Harry Davis	PH	1	0	0	0	0	0	0	0	0	–
Charlie Grimm	OF	12	22	0	2	0	0	0	0	0	.091
Roy Grover	2B	20	77	8	21	1	2	0	7	5	.273
Ray Haley	C	34	108	8	25	5	0	0	4	0	.231
Thomas Healey	3B	6	23	4	6	1	1	0	2	1	.261
Bill Johnson	OF	4	15	1	4	1	0	0	1	0	.267
Ed King	Ut	42	144	13	27	1	2	0	8	4	.188
Nap Lajoie	2B	113	426	33	105	14	4	2	35	15	.246
Lester Lanning	P-OF	19	33	5	6	2	0	0	1	0	.182
Otis Lawry	2B-OF	41	123	10	25	0	0	0	4	4	.203
Lew Malone	SS	5	4	1	0	0	0	0	0	0	.000
Lee McElwee	Ut	54	155	9	41	3	0	0	10	0	.265
Stuffy McInnis	1B	140	512	42	151	25	3	1	60	7	.295
Billy Meyer	C	50	138	6	32	2	2	1	12	3	.232
Ralph Mitterling	OF	13	39	1	6	0	0	0	2	0	.154
Mike Murphy	C	14	27	0	3	0	0	0	1	0	.111
Rube Oldring	OF	40	146	10	36	8	3	0	14	1	.247
Val Picinich	C	40	118	8	23	3	1	0	5	1	.195
Charlie Pick	3B	121	398	29	96	10	3	0	20	25	.241
Harland Rowe	3B-OF	17	36	2	5	1	0	0	3	0	.139
Wally Schang	C-OF	110	338	41	90	15	8	7	38	14	.266
Bill Stellbauer	OF	25	48	2	13	2	1	0	5	2	.271
Amos Strunk	OF	150	544	71	172	30	9	3	49	21	.316
Shag Thompson	OF	15	17	4	0	0	0	0	0	1	.000
Buck Thrasher	OF	7	29	4	9	2	1	0	4	0	.310
Jimmy Walsh	OF	114	390	42	91	13	6	1	27	27	.233
Whitey Witt	SS	143	563	64	138	16	15	2	36	19	.245

Figures include games played with Philadelphia only.

Pitcher	G	IP	H	ERA	ShO	SO	BB	W	L
Rube Bressler	4	15	16	6.60	0	8	14	0	2
Joe Bush	40	287	222	2.57	8	157	130	15	24
Minot Crowell	9	40	43	4.76	0	15	34	0	5
Michael Driscoll	1	5	6	5.40	0	0	2	0	1
George Hesselbacher	6	26	37	7.27	0	6	22	0	4
Russell Johnson	12	84	90	3.75	0	25	39	2	8
Lester Lanning	6	24	38	8.14	0	9	17	0	3
Axel Lindstrom	1	4	2	4.50	0	1	0	0	0
Bill Morrisette	1	4	6	6.75	0	2	5	0	0
Elmer Myers	44	315	280	3.66	2	182	168	14	23
Jack Nabors	40	213	206	3.47	0	74	95	1	20
Rube Parnham	4	25	27	3.96	0	8	13	2	1
Carl Ray	3	9	9	4.82	0	5	14	0	1
Jack Richardson	1	1	2	40.50	0	1	1	0	0
Socks Seibold	3	22	22	4.15	1	5	9	1	2
Tom Sheehan	38	188	197	3.69	0	54	94	1	16
Harry Weaver	3	8	14	10.13	0	2	5	0	0
Marshall Williams	10	51	71	7.89	0	17	31	0	6
John Wyckoff	7	21	20	5.57	0	4	20	0	1

Figures include games played with Philadelphia only.

Chapter 4
The 1928 Philadelphia Phillies

WON: **43**   LOST: **109**   GAMES OUT OF FIRST: **51**

DAYS IN FIRST: **2**   LAST DAY IN FIRST: **April 12**

HOME RECORD: **26–49**

ROAD RECORD: **17–60**

LONGEST WINNING STREAK: **4**

LONGEST LOSING STREAK: **12**

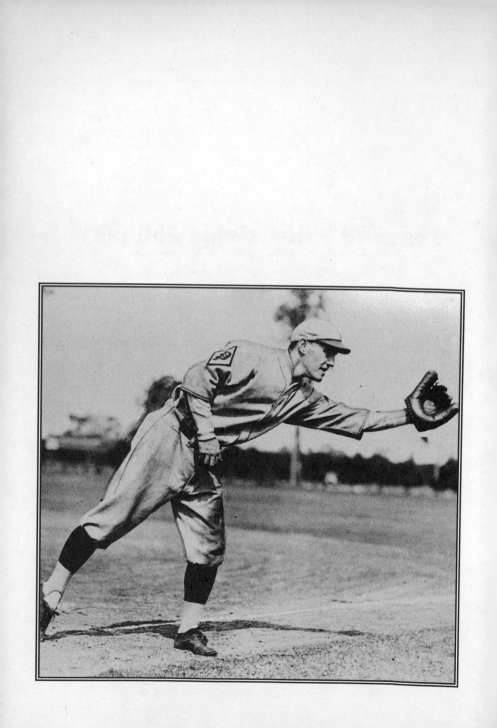

While always aiming for the highest place, our
players, proud of their past reputation, prefer to
sacrifice both championship and place rather than
win either by trickery, rudeness, or other conduct
unworthy [of] their good name or the approval of
the ladies and gentlemen whose refining presence
honors their contest for supremacy on the ball
field.

—*Dedication of Baker Bowl, 1895*

In my day you had to be humble if you played
for the Phillies.

—Pinky Whitney,
Phillies third baseman, 1928–33, 1936–39

THE PRINCIPAL CHARACTER in the farce that
was the 1928 Philadelphia Phillies is both hero and villain, an aging derelict whose presence in Philadelphia dictated the character
of one of the most peculiar teams in baseball history. The decrepit
hulk was the Baker Bowl, home of Philadelphia's National League
franchise from May 2, 1895, to June 30, 1938.

Ballparks were not built to last that long in the 1890s, as is

---

♦ Fresco Thompson afield: His glove kept him in the majors, his wit
bounced him out. (Photo courtesy of the National Baseball Library,
Cooperstown, NY)

readily apparent if one considers the nature of the two interruptions in the Phillies' tenure in the Bowl. The first occurred on August 8, 1903, when the second game of a doubleheader with the Boston Braves was canceled because the right-field stands had collapsed onto Fifteenth Street, causing 12 deaths and finishing the Phillies' home schedule for the remainder of the season. The second occurred on May 14, 1927, when ten rows of those troublesome right-field stands collapsed again, with less deadly results. In short, the Baker Bowl was an aging pile of junk.

More important, for our purposes, it was a small pile of junk. For all the talk of the "cozy confines" of Wrigley Field and the imposing presence of the Green Monster in Fenway Park, these two stadia are wide-open spaces compared to the field that Philadelphia sportswriters called "the Bandbox." (It was also called the Hump because it was built on an elevated piece of ground over a railroad tunnel that ran under the outfield.) The salient feature of the Baker Bowl was its right-field wall. Imagine the Green Monster, on the other side of the park, 40 feet high (two and a half feet higher than in Fenway) and made out of corrugated tin. Now move it 35 feet closer to home.

That's right. The right-field fence at the Baker Bowl was 280.5 feet from home plate. The right-center power alley was only 300 feet deep. Moving across the field toward the left-field foul line the dimensions become slightly more realistic: 408 in straightaway center, 341.5 to the left-field foul line. The left-field fence was only four feet high.

It could have been worse and, in fact, had been. In 1925 home plate had been moved back a foot; prior to that it was 279.5 feet to the right-field foul pole.

How close was that wall? In one of his most famous bons mots, Red Smith wrote, "It may be exaggerating to say the outfield wall cast a shadow across the infield, but if the right fielder had eaten onions at lunch the second baseman knew it." Longtime Phils pitcher Ray Benge said that it felt like "you could reach right out and thump" the wall.

A lot of batters certainly thumped it.

Balls would rattle off the tin like pistol shots. The noise resounded so loudly that Philly pitcher Walter Beck, who gave up a lot of liners off the tin, acquired the unhappy nickname "Boom-Boom," one boom off the bat, the next off the wall.

High up the right-field wall was a sign extolling the virtues of Lifebuoy soap. THE PHILLIES USE LIFEBUOY SOAP, it trumpeted. A wag replied, "And they still stink."

When New Englanders moan about "the Greek tragedy which is Red Sox history," when George Will talks of the "long-suffering Cubs fans," veteran Phillies fans snicker. From 1901, the beginning of the modern era of baseball, to 1975, the year before the Phillies emerged (temporarily) from the dank cave in which they resided, the team won exactly two pennants and one World Series game. They finished below .400 26 times in that 75-year stretch, and occupied the NL basement 20 times before divisional play was instituted in 1969, three times after. From 1919 to 1930 the Phils were last eight times, seventh twice, tied for sixth once, and fifth once. From 1936 to 1945 they were last eight times, including a string of five consecutive cellar finishes between 1938 and 1942. It is no accident that the Philadelphia Phillies have two chapters in this book, the only team so honored.

James Michener, the best-selling novelist and a lifelong Phillies fan, wrote of his favorite team, "Year after year they wallowed in last place, and I remember my friend Marvin saying in October with real hope, 'Next year's gotta look up,' and a listener said, 'There ain't no up.' "

It was true. With the Phillies of the '20s, '30s, and '40s there were only degrees of down.

The crazy thing about the Phillies is that the team had good hitters, scored runs, hit homers. That's where the Baker Bowl comes in. In 1928, their worst season in the '20s, the Phils were fourth in the league in home runs and doubles and fifth in slugging percentage, but lost 109 games. The major sources of this paradox are twofold. First, Philly hit 54 home runs at home and only 31 on the road, scored 360 runs at home and only 300 on the road. Second, they surrendered a league-worst 67 home runs and 521 runs at home, but also a seventh-place 42 home runs and a league-worst 436 runs on the road.

In other words the Phillies had constructed an everyday lineup that was so tailored to the dimensions of the Baker Bowl that they couldn't hit anywhere else, and a pitching staff that would have had trouble getting their mothers out in the Grand Canyon.

The source of the Phillies' troubles was—here's that word again—money. First, Pennsylvania was the last holdout against Sunday baseball. The Pennsylvania Supreme Court ruled, yet again, in July of 1927 that the state's stringent "blue" laws prohibited "worldly employment" and "business" and that professional baseball definitely fell under this stricture, even as played by the Phillies. Pennsylvania would not have legal Sunday baseball until 1934.

Second, the Phillies were a losing team in a two-team town. During the 1928 season the Athletics, long since rebounded from the debacle of the late '10s, were in a heated pennant race with the Ruth-Gehrig era Yankees. Who would come to see the Phillies get their brains beat out yet again?

The story is told of a home game against the Cubs during which Chicago sportswriter Warren Brown, to stifle his ennui, began throwing peanuts at the Cubs traveling secretary, a man whose ears provided an ample target. Needless to say, Brown's aim was not perfect and many of his projectiles fell beyond the press box (which was pretty small anyway) and into the stands below. Gerry Nugent, then assistant to Phils owner William F. Baker, later the owner himself, came charging up from the stands to berate Brown. "Stop that," Nugent demanded. "Don't you know we have patrons down there?" Brown grabbed his notebook and peered over the railing. "Gosh, no. You really mean that?" bubbled Brown. "What a story!"

Even if the stands had been filled to overflowing, an unlikely happenstance, the Phils would still have been run on a shoestring. For one thing, the Baker Bowl only held 18,800. More important, William F. Baker, whose name the ballpark bore, was about as tight as any owner in major league history.

Baker would do a great deal to save a buck, even more to make one. When the Phillies won their first pennant in 1915, Baker quickly hired carpenters to install seats on top of the clubhouse, which was in center field, and to extend the bleachers around the front of the clubhouse to the flagpole in right center, thereby reducing the distance from home plate to center. Those seats led directly to the Phils' losing the final game of the 1915 Series when Red Sox star Harry Hooper bounced a pair of shots into the shortened porch for what were then ground-rule homers.

The seats were removed after the Series; why make it easier to hit home runs, thereby adding to someone's production? If you put up numbers like Ruth you may want to pull down a Ruthian salary. Baker added twenty feet to the tin fence in right after the 1928 season for the same reason. As the "lively ball" explosion began to reach its apex, the Phils added Chuck Klein, the most explosive left-handed hitter in their history; not even Klein could belt one over a sixty-foot wall every time he came to the plate.

One of the Baker Bowl's oddities was another testament to Baker's tightfisted ways, the presence between games of three sheep grazing in the outfield. This *au naturel* lawn-mowing equipment was kept on hand until the ram charged the club's president, Billy Shettsline.

Baker made numerous trades that were motivated solely by financial considerations, a practice that Gerry Nugent would raise to an art form when he took over the helm after Baker's death in December 1930. For example, on July 25, 1921, Baker sold Irish Emil Meusel to the Giants for $30,000 and three nonentities, claiming that Meusel was guilty of "indifferent performance." He was hitting .353 at the time. As William Curran writes in his excellent book *Big Sticks*, "In the new ["lively" ball] era, it appeared that if you had even one home-run hero in your lineup, you could run a shoestring baseball operation indefinitely. For the remainder of his tenure Baker made sure that without compromising his coolie wage scale, the Phils' batting order included one or more muscular left-handed swingers." (Curran makes an extremely convincing case, by the way, that the ball was not, in fact, livened in the twenties, as has always been assumed by baseball writers and historians.)

The 1927 season had been a typical one for the Phillies. They finished last in the National League with a dismal 51–103 record, hit .280 as a team with a .370 slugging percentage, fielded adequately, and sported a 5.35 ERA. Stuffy McInnis, who had suffered through several years of cellar dwelling with the dismantled Athletics of the late '10s, was the Phils manager in 1927, a job he held, mercifully, for only that one campaign.

Stuffy had a year to go on his contract, but like Art Fletcher the year before he was given his walking papers over the winter. Because he was listed as a player-manager, McInnis had to clear waivers from all major-league clubs before the Phils could dispense with his services. It was an arrangement that must have given Stuffy some laughs; he made exactly one appearance at first base as a defensive replacement that season and never even registered an at bat.

His replacement, Burt Shotton, was the seventh Phillies manager in eight seasons. Shotton was a Branch Rickey protégé, a fleet outfielder who had achieved considerable acclaim with the Browns in the tens. Shotton had enjoyed some success as skipper of the Syracuse Stars in the International League. When he took over the club, it was a chronic tail-ender, but by the time he left two years later, the Stars had finished second with what one contemporary news account described as "only a fair team." Equally important, Syracuse had developed a loyal fan following.

Shotton had a reputation as a good judge and developer of young talent, having sent the Cardinals such talented players as Tommy Thevenow (who would eventually end up with him on the Phils), and pitchers Fred Frankhouse and Art Reinhart. At the time Shotton was hired by the Phils, baseball historian Ernest Lanigan wrote of the skipper's minor-league tenure, "he was a wonder with youngsters. He never lost his patience with any of them and he could have done so without even Job criticizing him." Lanigan tells of an incident in which some of the younger players on the team appeared "about three minutes before" game time one afternoon. "[H]e suggested to them that if they could do so without inconveniencing themselves, he would like to have them there by batting practice time. And he said it with a smile."

Fresco Thompson, who was the Phils second baseman in 1928,

would recall 25 years later, "Of all the managers I played for, Burt Shotton came closer to trying to give instructions than any of the others. Burt was trained by Branch Rickey and a lot of Mr. Rickey's technique rubbed off on him."

Shotton could even boast of some major-league managerial experience; he had run the Cards for Rickey on Sundays when he was assistant to the Sabbath-observing Mahatma. Lanigan, for one, was enthusiastic about the appointment. "If anybody can pull the Phillies out of the slough of despond he ought to be able to."

The team that Shotton inherited from McInnis was generously characterized by another local paper as "a fair ball club." The reporter opined that "while they did not get anywhere, nevertheless they looked good in many games." In fact, the team was rebuilding the pitching staff around young talent and, on paper at least, appeared to have some possibilities.

Actually, the 1928 Phillies would be a perfect team on which the 43-year-old Shotton could practice his fatherly skills with younger players. Although Heinie Sand, the Phils' shortstop, Jimmie Wilson, their starting catcher on Opening Day, and Fred "Cy" Williams, the slugging outfielder, by now reduced to pinch hitting, were all veterans, most of the team would be rookies or in their first two or three seasons in the majors. As one headline in June would optimistically phrase it, PHILS' MANAGER, BUILDING FOR THE FUTURE, IS GIVING YOUTHS CHANCE TO MAKE GOOD.

Some sportswriters were a bit cynical about the source of all this youth. Bill Dooly of *The Philadelphia Record* speculated that the Shotton-Rickey connection might work to the advantage of the Phils, given the well-stocked Cardinal farm system, the first of its kind in baseball. "It is argued that the Cardinals can't possibly use all of these young men that are ready for steps upward," wrote Dooly. "Therefore they could keep the youngsters satisfied by selling them to a club that won't bother the home office too much in the pennant race."

James Isaminger, another Philadelphia sportswriter, who also served as the city's correspondent for *The Sporting News,* added fuel to the fire shortly after Shotton was hired. "The rumor is around that Branch Rickey of the Cards will help out Shotton, who was a faithful lieutenant for many years," Isaminger reported in December 1927. "There is also a report that the Phils may close a deal with the Cards. Certainly the Phils are not averse to making trades." Not when President Baker can save a few bucks.

Sure enough, within two weeks the Cards and Phils consummated a trade, Philadelphia sending outfielder Johnny Mokan, catcher Clarence Jonnard, and shortstop Jimmy Cooney to St. Louis in exchange for former Phils hurler Jimmy Ring and catcher John Schulte, both a little long in the tooth, and catcher Walt Wheat. Rumors abounded that the Cards would eventually sweeten the deal with some kids from the farm system.

Ring was a relic of a recently departed era, an era nobody would miss. In the 1919 World Series he had beaten Black Sox pitcher Eddie Cicotte, 2–0, in a game the fixers may have actually been trying to win, then lost to honest Dickie Kerr in relief, in spite of pitching well. More to the point, Ring was involved in a fixing scandal of his own in 1918 when he allegedly took $25 from the infamously corrupt Hal Chase after a loss. No charges were ever brought and he stayed in baseball. In his first stint with the Phils, Ring led the NL in walks four consecutive years from 1922–25, not a good habit for a pitcher in the Baker Bowl. He was a workhorse pitcher, the kind of guy you would expect to finish in double figures in wins and losses year after year, but by 1928 he was running out of gas. After going 4–17 for the Phils this year, he would hang up his spikes.

Schulte, who would be the Phils backup catcher, was delighted to be reunited with Shotton. "I learned a lot of baseball from Shotton while we were at Syracuse," he told Isaminger. He also drooled at the prospect of the tin fence in right and expected to hit a lot of "over the fence she goes" four-baggers. There's many a slip . . . Schulte would hit .248 with four dingers in 113 at bats during the 1928 season.

The Phils would be inaugurating a new spring-training facility in Winter Haven in 1928 and expected to take at least fourteen new players, six of them pitchers, south. Augie Walsh, a pickup from the New England League (where Stuffy McInnis would end up managing) and Bob McGraw, another Cardinals cast-off, would play important roles in the Phils' 1928 campaign.

The most promising of the newcomers was Ray Benge, a right-hander acquired from the Indians during the winter. Although the former Texas League star would go 8–18 in 1928 (with a 4.55 ERA, which was dazzling for this staff), Benge would log double figures in victories six times with a series of second-division clubs.

The new Phils pitcher who constructed the most memorable record for himself in 1928 was actually an ex–Syracuse Star who had gone 1–1 for the Phils at the end of the '27 season, Russell Miller. Miller, whose brother Walter pitched for the Indians in the twenties, was a lanky right-hander, a three-sport athlete at Ohio State who would become an agricultural agent after leaving baseball. Judging from his 1928 numbers a lot of National League teams planted and harvested him on the Baker Bowl mound; in 1928 Russ Miller would go 0–12 with a 5.42 ERA, allowing 137 hits in 108 innings pitched.

The mainstays of the Phillies pitching staff, however, were two veterans, 27-year-old Les (Sugar) Sweetland and 29-year-old Claude Willoughby. These two hurlers had so much work in the late '20s that George E. Phair, a New York baseball writer, used to stand before every Phillies game he covered and sing, "My country, 'tis of thee/Sweetland and Willoughby/Of thee I sing."

Sweetland was entering his second season in the majors, a lefty sinkerballer with control problems. Willoughby had been with the Phils since 1925 and would last in the Baker Bowl through the epochal 1930 season, during which he would register an extraordinary 7.59 ERA. Each of them would finish his career in a slightly more spacious ball yard, Willoughby in Forbes Field with the 1931 Pirates (although his 6.31 ERA would indicate that it didn't help) and Sweetland at Wrigley Field with the Cubs the same year. Poor Sugar, he would go 8–7 for the Cubbies with a five-game winning streak but couldn't get along with curmudgeonly manager Rogers Hornsby and soon found himself toiling in the minors.

A few other intriguing veterans were lurking around the Baker Bowl mound. Alex Ferguson, who would go 5–10 with the '28 Phils, had been a key acquisition down the stretch for the 1925 Senators and had pitched well in the World Series. Clarence Mitchell was the NL's only legal spitballer under the grandfather clause that allowed a few practitioners of the moist delivery to continue to practice their craft after the pitch was outlawed in 1920; he also had a memorable day in the 1920 World Series, hitting into Bill Wambsganss's unassisted triple play and a more conventional double play on successive at bats. Hub "Shucks" Pruett was best known for his mysterious mastery over Babe Ruth; when he came up as a rookie the screwballer struck the Babe out ten of the first thirteen times they met. Unfortunately, Pruett couldn't get anyone else out with any consistency. By 1932 he would be out of baseball; having put himself through medical school during the winters, Dr. Pruett would go on to a successful medical practice in St. Louis.

The Phils went south with their pitching essentially set, which is pretty frightening considering who the pitchers were. In addition to Benge, Willoughby, Sweetland, Walsh, McGraw, Ferguson, Pruett, and Miller, Shotton would take a look at minor leaguers June Greene, Ed Baecht, Ed "Lefty" Taber and veteran Art Decatur, none of whom would contribute much in '28.

Righty Frank Ulrich wouldn't contribute much, either, but he had a splendid excuse: he contracted pneumonia just before spring training and nearly died in Baltimore's Franklin Square Hospital. Over the previous three seasons Ulrich had gone 19–27 with a 3.48 ERA, pretty good numbers for a Phillie hurler, and Shotton was counting on having the 29-year-old on his staff. However, throughout the season the Philadelphia papers would be full of periodic updates on his condition, as he promised repeatedly that he would be back in Phils garb on the mound before the season ended. He wouldn't make it back that season and would die from the after-effects of his illness in February of the following year.

By contrast, although no one knew it, the everyday lineup would be in a state of flux for the first month of the season, as the Phils wheeled and dealed their way to the abyss. Heading for Winter Haven, Philadelphia had most of its players signed to contracts, but a lot of the guys they signed wouldn't be around by midseason.

The infield would have been in a state of flux anyway. Shotton was looking for someone to take the third baseman's job away from Barney Friberg. The 29-year-old Friberg was a valuable utility man, so valuable that in the thirties the Phils would toy with and then scrap an attempt to make him a pitcher because they needed him to plug too many other holes. However, when he registered a .961 fielding average in 103 games at third in 1927, it was apparent that he was creating rather than filling a gap at that spot. Rookie Arthur Carter Whitney, who went by the much less dignified handle of Pinky, was expected to take over at third; Whitney had been acquired from New Orleans in the minor-league draft. Pinky had hit .336 at New Orleans and would prove an instant success in his rookie year with the Phillies.

As spring training approached, the first-base situation was similar. Russell Wrightstone had been the starting first baseman the previous year and had hit .306, but he would be 35 on Opening Day and Shotton was looking to replace him. A good-field, no-hit player, Wrightstone also played the outfield, where he once explained that he had missed a fly ball "because it was too damned high." To replace him at first the Phils acquired Bill Kelly from the Minneapolis Millers. Kelly had apparently been out of shape in 1927, so his .230 batting average was thought to be deceptive.

By contrast the double-play combination was set, and it was a good one. Shortstop John "Heinie" Sand was a thirty-one-year-old San Franciscan who had already been the Phillies starting shortstop for five years. He had never been a great stickman, but his .299 average in 1927 was a hopeful portent. Sand was an adequate fielder who could turn a double play and, unlike his new teammate Jimmy Ring, a resoundingly honest man. In September of 1924 Sand was approached by Giants outfielder Jimmy O'Connell and told that he could make $500 if he didn't bear down too hard in a game that the Giants needed in their tight pennant race with Brooklyn. Given that the Phils were in seventh place at the time and the fact that Sand made 34 errors that season, it is likely that no one would have noticed if Heinie had taken the offer. (Goodness knows, anyone who played for the Phils could have used an extra five hundred.) Sand reported the conversation to the commissioner's office. O'Connell and Cozy Dolan, the Giants coach who supposedly instigated the offer, were both suspended from baseball for life.

Sand's partner on the double play was Fresco Thompson, one of the wittiest men ever to play in the majors and a pretty fair second baseman as well. Thompson, who went to Columbia University for two years but quit to play pro ball, had broken in with the Pirates in 1925. Thirty-eight years later he recalled that his first contract was for $425 a month. "I returned the contract to the club owner, Barney Dreyfuss," Thompson said. "I wrote that I was tickled to death to be with the Pirates, and I wanted to look and dress like a big leaguer, but I couldn't do it on $425 a month." Dreyfuss offered to solve the problem by sending Thompson back to the minors, "so I signed, naturally," he conceded.

Thompson's stay in Pittsburgh was brief, encompassing fourteen games of active duty and a lot of pine time. The Giants acquired him in the off-season and had settled on him to be their new second baseman when Rogers Hornsby became available. Fresco got into two games in 1926 as a Giant and was exiled to Philadelphia.

At least he got to play second base regularly. In both 1927, his rookie year, and 1928 he would be tied for second in the league in chances per game. He led the NL in putouts in '27 and in 1928 would put together a string of 136 consecutive chances without an error, although he led the league in errors that year. As a DP combination he and Sand were effective, especially given the number of base runners that Phillies pitching allowed.

However, as baseball historian Lee Allen aptly observed, Thompson was "destin[ed] to be remembered mostly . . . for his drollery." Late in his career he would land with the Dodgers, who were not much better than Philadelphia in the early thirties. On that club his primary responsibilities were bench jockeying and pinch running. Waite Hoyt once found Thompson at a sink in the Ebbets Field clubhouse, gargling with great enthusiasm. When Hoyt inquired what Thompson was doing, he cheerfully replied,

"Just getting in shape for the game!" On another occasion, being sent to relieve a pinch hitter who had reached first after batting for one of the lesser lights of the Dodger staff, Thompson shouted to the Dodger dugout, "How do you like that! From captain of the Phillies to a pinch runner for a pinch hitter for a pinch pitcher!"

In fact it was Thompson's mouth that got him bounced out of the majors. In 1934 he found himself back with the Giants, managed by Bill Terry. When the future Hall of Famer asked Thompson to pinch-run one day early in the season, Thompson responded, "I'd like to, but I just shined my shoes." That remark was a one-way ticket back to the minors, where he would spend the rest of his playing days. "No basketball ever bounced around more than I did after my stint as a player with the Dodgers ended in 1932," he would write in his autobiography. "After logging fifteen years of playing time in the minors, the majors, and back to the minors again, I managed Hartford, Williamsport, Reading, Montreal, and New Orleans." It was an itinerary that left him well suited to become a Dodger scout and front-office man. Five months before his death in 1968 he was made general manager of the Dodgers, a post he had coveted but would not get to enjoy for long.

The outfield seemed to be set in late January, as well, anchored by Cy Williams, Fred Leach, and Dick Spalding.

Cy Williams had been one of the leading home-run hitters in the NL since the days of Ruthian power had begun in the teens. An architecture student at Notre Dame, he had played football for Rockne, been a star hurdler and sprinter, and played baseball as well for the Fighting Irish. Between 1915 and 1927 he led the NL in homers four times and was in the top three eleven times. After he experienced a slump in 1917, the Cubs—in the tradition of Brock-for-Broglio—sent him to Philadelphia for 30-year-old outfielder Dode Paskert. A dead pull-hitting lefty like Williams—he was the object of the original "Williams shift," long before Teddy Ball Game was in the majors—was born for the Baker Bowl, and the trade gave him a new lease on life. Williams, who had played for a different manager each of the first dozen years of his career, including Tinker, Evers and Chance, shared the 1927 home-run title with Hack Wilson of the Cubs, so the Phils figured they could just pencil him in on the lineup card in 1928, even though the architect-to-be was 41. At the end of the season he would sign on for another campaign, but eventually Williams would settle down in a successful career as an architect.

Leach had gotten his start in the game playing for railroad teams in the Ozarks while employed as a telegrapher. He finally decided that pro ball held more promise than the telegraph and broke into the minors in 1922. His success was almost instantaneous, and by 1923 he was playing for the Phils. After the 1928 season he would be traded to the Giants for Lefty O'Doul, an ill-fated trade for New York that hastened John McGraw's departure from the Giant dugout. Leach was a better than adequate fielder, with a strong arm, and he hit decently, but O'Doul would hit a league-leading .398 in 1929, adding fuel to the rumors that the game had passed McGraw by.

When the Phils went south for spring training, it was assumed that Dick Spalding would once again be the third starter in the Phillie outfield, but he was cut before Opening Day, to the surprise of all concerned. In his place was Denny Sothern, a speedy young player who had been up briefly in '26, had gone to spring training with the club in '27 only to be returned to Pittsfield, and would finally stick for one year as a regular in 1928. Like Leach he was a good glove man with an excellent arm.

Finally, the catching situation seemed stable as the season approached. Jimmie Wilson was one of the finest defensive catchers in baseball in the '20s and '30s. He had finally won the starting job in 1927, hitting .275 and handling the woebegone pitching staff as well as could be expected. Schulte seemed the most likely second-string backstop.

In spite of the daunting news of Frank Ulrich's life-threatening illness, the Phils were sanguine in the South. Spring training was dotted with the usual stories of holdouts and signings, phenoms, and vets looking for a last chance. James Isaminger plumped for the new infield as "big-league stuff." Whitney showed real ability at third, but it was unclear if Kelly could hit major-league pitching, even in the Baker Bowl. Leach missed a chunk of spring training in a contract dispute, which gave Shotton a chance to try Wrightstone in the outfield. With Spalding and Sothern nursing charley horses for much of the spring, Shotton would try a lot of people in the outfield. In spring-training games the Phils got the worst of it, even losing to a minor-league team from Reading. With the seventh-place Braves adding Rogers Hornsby and Les Bell, the Phils would have to work hard to escape the cellar, Isaminger opined.

Back in Philadelphia the A's and Phils held their annual city series to tune up for the coming season. (The tradition had been restored since the dismal days of 1916.) The A's, who would chase the Yankees all through 1928 and would finally go on to win their first pennant since 1914 the following year, made quick work of the Phils, winning five games out of six, even though Al Simmons was laid up with rheumatism. Isaminger's conclusion after the exhibition games were concluded was that "Burt Shotton's Phillies need better pitching to make much of a race."

Just before the season opened, Shotton made his final roster moves. Reserve infielder Bill Dietrick would be one of his outfielders for the time being. Walter Wheat, acquired in the Jimmy Ring deal, was released. Eddie Taber and reserves Bill Holman and Harry O'Donnell were sent to New Haven in exchange for catcher Walter "Peck" Lerian. Lerian would be the Phils starting catcher by 1929, but his career would be cut short after that season when an out-of-control automobile climbed a sidewalk and killed him. For now, he would alternate backup catching and pinch-hitting duties with Schulte, or so it seemed on Opening Day.

The biggest surprise, however, was the release of Dick Spalding. The previous year, his first in the majors although he was 34 in 1927, Spalding had been among the league's leading outfielders in fielding average and had hit .296, but in the final game of the season he had busted up his ankle sliding into a base. The injury hadn't healed properly and even the Phillies had little room for a gimpy 35-year-old outfielder.

♦

The Phillies opened the season in Brooklyn, where it was cold and raw on April 11. Apparently the awful weather agreed with the Phils, because they won the first game of the year, 4–3, behind

Jimmy Ring. It was Ring's first victory since 1926. When the Robins, as they were then called, after manager Wilbert Robinson, threatened in the late innings, Sand started a 6-2-5 double play to stifle the rally. The only gloomy note in this picture was an ankle injury to Bill Dietrick that prevented him from making his first start in the outfield and would keep him out of the lineup for a month.

The newspapers of the day would feature something new in their baseball coverage this year. For the first time in memory box scores would include a record of runs batted in. It was a feature that was, as *TSN*'s Thomas Rice would note, "extremely interesting and useful."

April 12 dawned with the Philadelphia Phillies in first place. They wouldn't have long to savor the rarefied air of the first division. Although they won five games out of thirteen in the month of April, they would be in the basement by April 29 and would not emerge for the rest of the year.

April, however, was still a time of hope. Cy Williams would win a game against the hated McGraw and the Giants on April 16 with a three-run pinch-hit homer. It was the first loss the Giants suffered that season and one of 11 pinch-hit home runs Williams would hit in his career.

The home opener on April 19 was even more satisfying. The much-touted A's had not been able to win a game at home yet, but the Phillies, the butt of everyone's jokes, began their Baker Bowl doings with a 9–5 drubbing of the Robins, built around a seven-run explosion in the sixth, capped by a three-run homer by Fred Leach. The victory went to Jimmy Ring, who now was 2–0, a nice reversal of 1927's 0–4 mark. For the moment the Phils were at .500 3–3 and in fourth place.

Of course, it couldn't last. As *Record* reporter Tom Shriver noted, "The Phils have learned how to win ball games, but they have not learned yet how to win two in a row." They already knew how to lose ball games, and their second home game of the season showed that they hadn't forgotten. Four Philly errors, including two by Barney Friberg, who was subbing at short for the day, helped the Dodgers to an 8–6 victory over Alex Ferguson. The

Phils must have been tired from the previous day's offensive labors, because they could only muster five hits.

May dawned with the Phillies comfortably ensconced in the familiar confines of the National League basement, a position they would occupy alone for 155 of the season's 173 days. Whatever hopes they had for a successful season would be irretrievably dashed in May, when they would go 2–23. On June 1 Philadelphia would be 7–31, 8½ games behind the seventh-place Braves.

The month began with a western road trip and the release of Art Decatur and the exile to the minors of the unfortunately named June Greene. Shotton had taken it into his head that Greene was a slugger—he had gone three-for-six in his brief stay in Philly—and should be converted into an outfielder. He would return briefly to the Phils the following year, ostensibly still a pitcher, although his ERA of 10.76 in five appearances seems to belie that description.

The western trip began with a sweep of the Phils by the Cubs, who would be in the thick of a heated pennant race all summer. Philadelphia found all sorts of interesting ways to lose in Wrigley. One game ended when Les Sweetland gave up a sacrifice fly to Hack Wilson in the eleventh, Sugar having worked the entire game with virtually no offensive support. Another game was virtually gift wrapped as Fresco Thompson made three errors and Augie Walsh walked seven Cubs and hit another.

From Chicago it was on to St. Louis, where the Phils pitchers got their ears pinned back in the largest one-inning rally of the NL season. Ray Benge had pitched adequately for five innings before being lifted for a pinch hitter in the visiting half of the sixth. With Benge gone the Cards went wild, scoring nine runs in the sixth. As the *Record*'s correspondent observed, "McGraw, Willoughby, Ferguson, Sweetland, and Miller appeared on the hill after Benge was removed and it was hard to tell which looked the worst."

The next day brought more glad tidings. While Walter Hagen was winning his third British Open title in Sandwich, England, the Phils were losing to the Cards 3–2 and experiencing another example of the infamous Branch Rickey largesse. During the first inning the Phils traded Jimmie Wilson to St. Louis for first baseman Don

Hurst, catcher Spud Davis, and outfielder Homer Peel. The Phils immediately sent Bill Kelly, a flop at first, and pitcher Art Decatur to Rochester.

It was a trade with some weird sidelights. As the Philadelphia *Record* noted, "Jimmie Wilson . . . is the only man in baseball history, so far as known, who ever changed club uniforms during a game." Informed of the trade after the second inning, Wilson dashed over to the Redbirds clubhouse, changed into a Cardinal uniform, and sat on their bench for the remainder of the contest.

On the surface this looked like another Cards-Phils sweetheart deal, combining Baker's tightfistedness with Rickey's ingenuity and his relationship with Shotton to fleece the Phils. After all, as Isaminger wrote, "Wilson [is] the incontestable star of the team." For the Cards his acquisition would be the difference that put them over the top in 1928, allowing them to win the NL pennant and get their brains beat out by the Yankees in the World Series. Moreover, Wilson would be among the league's top catchers for several years to come, playing on two more pennant winners in 1930 and '31. He would return to the Phils as a player-manager in 1934, then go on to coach with the Reds. In Cincinnati he would be pressed into service as a catcher once more in 1940 after Willard Hershberger, the Reds' young backstop, committed suicide in midseason. Although he played in only 16 regular-season games, he would catch six of seven World Series contests against the Tigers, hitting .353 and notching the only stolen base of the Series.

On the other hand, rookie Virgil "Spud" Davis was a more-than-adequate catcher, hitting .308 for his career. He was four years younger than the 28-year-old Wilson and would prove to be a decent defensive backstop. Don Hurst would fill the Phils' need for a first baseman much better than the weak-hitting Billy Kelly had. As you might suspect, he was a left-handed hitter and thrived in the Baker Bowl. Hurst, who would hit over .300 in four of his first five seasons with the Phils, swatted 19 homers in 1928 and won over both fans and sportswriters by midseason. It may have been an accident, but thanks to this trade the Phils had shored up

two positions. With rookies Whitney and Hurst the Phils had so-
lidified the corners of their infield for the next several seasons.

The corners may have been solid, but the pitching had the
consistency of moldy cream cheese. The next stop on the first
western swing was Cincinnati, where the Phils were welcomed
with open arms. On May 13, thanks to the Phils, the Reds moved
into first place after taking games from them on successive days.
However, on the fifteenth the tables were turned as Don Hurst hit
a three-run homer to give the Phils one of their two May victories.

The schedule maker was cruel to Philadelphia. From May 3 to
the end of the month they were on the road, with disastrous results: a trio of losses to Pittsburgh, including a two-hitter by Car-
men Hill that negated a nice effort by Benge.

By now, reported one Philadelphia paper, "Burt Shotton [was]
growing frantic over the ill success of the club." In 1927 the Phils
had led the NL in hitting as late as July 1. At the end of May 1928
they were dead last. The few moves that Shotton made were basi-
cally cosmetic. Fresco Thompson was named team captain. Russell Wrightstone was sold to the Giants, and Art Jahn, another
outfielder, was acquired from the same source, while the Phils
split a three-game set in the Polo Grounds, finally notching another
win before the month closed.

The Phils-Cardinals connection would raise its ugly head once
more in May. On the 28th, as they were arriving back in Philly to
recuperate from their lengthy travels, the Phils announced the release of lefty spitballer Clarence Mitchell. On June 4 he signed
with the Cardinals, and would go 8–9 for them, contributing in the
stretch drive. The Phils received nothing in this transaction, of
course, but Mitchell had managed to go from last place to first in a
suspiciously short time.

The Baker Bowl must have looked pretty good to the beleaguered Phils by now. As May ended, they would face the one team
in the National League that they should have had a chance to beat,
Boston. Of course, they had been unable to do so the previous
week, dropping three games in two days to the Braves. Boston had
just signed George Sisler, the great Browns first baseman of recent
years. Plagued by vision problems, Sisler was vastly reduced from

the man who had hit .420 in 1922. However, one blurry look at the Phillies rejuvenated him; in the three-game series with Philadelphia, Sisler hit .350. Sisler would tell Joe Dugan, "I still feel that I have a lot of baseball left in me even though the American League waived me out." In fact, he would finish the year with a .331 mark and would play two more seasons with the Braves, hitting .326 and .309 to close his career with a lifetime mark of .340.

June would be the best month of the 1928 season for Philadelphia. They were scheduled to play 23 games at home, a prospect guaranteed to cure their flagging spirits. However, it would be June 7 before they would win, snapping a nine-game losing streak. The losing streak was not without its interesting moments. The June 2 game was a donnybrook in which three pinch-hit homers were slugged, two by Phillies hitters Cy Williams and John Schulte, in a game that ended with the Phils on the short end of a 13–12 score. On other days Hub Pruett and Ray Benge turned in good performances but lost to the Cards and Cubs respectively. It was a typical cellar-dweller dilemma: the Phils' bats were mostly dead, so they wasted good pitching, but when they scored in double figures, their pitchers took the day off.

The second week of June marked a small turning point for Philadelphia. After losing the opening game of a three-game set to Chicago, in spite of another good effort by Benge, the Phils defeated the Cubs on a late-inning homer by Spud Davis. They came back and did it again the next day, denting the pennant hopes of the Cubs in front of many of Pennsylvania-born Cub skipper Joe McCarthy's family and friends.

If the Phils were going to make a move, they had a peculiar way of doing it. On June 12 they gave up 25 hits to the Pirates in a game they lost 15–4. That performance was an aberration by the Phils' June standards; they won the next two games with the Pirates, giving them their first series victory of the season. The best was yet to come, a three-game sweep of the Reds that toppled Cincinnati from first place. They then took two out of three from the Robins and split a doubleheader with the Giants. The time had come to leave home and go out on the road once more.

What was it about playing on the road that daunted the Phils so? Of course, travel conditions for ballplayers were a world apart from what they are today. Fresco Thompson waxed eloquent some 25 years later in describing the road experience of the late twenties to Frank Finch:

> You'd finish a ball game in Boston and ride for 36 hours to St. Louis in a tourist Pullman. The regulars and the pitchers who'd worked that day got the lower berths, the manager rated a drawing room, and the others slept in uppers.
>
> There was no air conditioning, of course, and cinders big as marbles would drift through the open windows. If you kept the windows closed you might be stifled by the heat and smoke.
>
> You'd get to St. Louis and have to fight other passengers for a taxi. You got to the ballpark the best way you could, and there was no traveling secretary who arranged for cabs or buses, saw to it that your luggage was handled, and handed you a printed itinerary accounting for your every move, as they do today.
>
> It was all daytime ball then, of course. In towns like St. Louis and Cincinnati you'd play doubleheaders in 104-degree weather. You had one set of traveling uniforms, generally of heavy flannel. . . .
>
> Before air conditioning the summer heat could turn your hotel room into a Turkish bath. I've known many a player, myself included, who would take a blanket from his room at the Hotel Chase in St. Louis and cross the street to Forest Park to spend the night.
>
> And if you were a regular, you played all the time. You never said you were tired and needed a rest. Either you were going good or bad, insofar as the manager was concerned.

Under such conditions as those, how could going on the road be anything but a trial? Of course, every team in the majors went through the same torments, but not every team was tailored to the peculiar dimensions of the Baker Bowl. The Phillies were ill suited to the wide-open spaces of the Polo Grounds, for example. And not every team was as plain lousy as the Phils; when your pitchers can't get anybody out, every minor indignity of the road seems magnified a thousandfold.

The long July road trip would spell the difference between escaping the cellar or being confined there for the remainder of the season, as James Isaminger pointed out in *The Sporting News.*

"They showed they could win at home, but they must still prove they can win on the road," he wrote. "The team is batting hard, but . . . the pitchers have been unable to hold the enemy in check." The best evidence of the truth of Isaminger's evaluation was a note in the July 12 issue of *TSN* to the effect that the Phils had been shut out fewer times at that point in the season than any other team in the league.

July would offer more of the same. In Boston the Phils would trade doubleheaders with the Braves, losing a pair of extra-inning games the first day, sweeping the Tribe the next. The third day of the series offered a good example of Phillies luck. They won the first game of yet another doubleheader, making for a three-game winning streak, but the second game was washed out. Two days later, in Cincinnati, the string would snap as Ray Benge walked Hughie Critz with the bases loaded in the ninth to give the Reds another gift victory.

A different kind of streak had begun, the longest losing streak of the season. The Phils would lose an even dozen games on the road, not winning again until July 21, when they finally defeated the Cardinals. Appropriately, the losing pitcher was Clarence Mitchell, late of the Phils. Les Sweetland and Ray Benge benefited from a savage Phils attack in the 8–3 victory.

The day before the streak ended, the Phillies made an announcement of considerable moment, although its significance was not known at the time. On Tuesday, July 24, the club would be joined by Chuck Klein, a good-natured, strapping left-handed slugger from Indianapolis. Although he had played barely a hundred minor-league games when he was purchased by the Phils from Fort Wayne, Klein would immediately tear into National League pitching with a calculated ferocity so unlike his off-field demeanor. In 1928, his rookie year with the Phils, Klein would hit .360 with eleven homers in only 253 at bats. In the years to come he would lead the NL in homers four times, runs scored three times, slugging percentage three times, and RBIs twice. He even would overcome a sojourn in Wrigley Field with the Cubs (two seasons in which his average would dip to .301 and .293 and his home-run production to twenty and twenty-one), and enjoy a trip to the 1935 World Series.

Klein would be, as Red Smith put it, "the reigning deity" of the Baker Bowl.

Unfortunately, not even Chuck Klein could resurrect the Phils now. They closed July with a 6–22 record for the month. On August 1 Philadelphia was 24–66, three and a half games behind Boston. They would be spending much of August at home, a source of some hope. The hope was misplaced to some extent. July ended with the Phils dropping a pair to St. Louis at home, followed by a sixteen-inning extravaganza in which they managed to salvage one win from the series. August began with the Pirates, who had been drubbing Philly regularly all season, coming to town. The Pirates would compile the best August record in the NL, 23–9, much of it seemingly at the expense of the Phils in doubleheader sweeps.

With the Pirates gone, however, something very nearly miraculous happened. The Cubs, who were once again in the thick of the pennant race, cruised into the Baker Bowl looking for a few easy wins to bolster their place in the standings. Instead, they ran into a buzz saw. For only the second time in the season Philadelphia put together four consecutive wins, sweeping Chicago to end the home stand on an upbeat note. "The millennium has arrived," trumpeted one *Sporting News* column. Apparently so, for even Claude Willoughby, "bullpen slave," as the *Record* labeled him, managed a victory against the Cubs.

It was a remarkable feat, one which the Phils couldn't manage a third time, but August would prove to be a more propitious month on the road too. The Phils even managed to steal one now and then. A case in point was a game with Cincinnati that was decided when Pinky Whitney dodged an inside pitch; as he fell out of the way, the ball ricocheted off his bat and landed safely for a hit, driving in the winning run. They even managed a cheapened victory in Pittsburgh when umpires halted a game in the seventh with the Phils ahead so that the road-weary Philadelphians could entrain for their next stop. Maybe it wasn't a glamorous way to win, but when you are 35–85 on September 1, you take them any way you can.

September is the month that last-place teams try to do two

things: look at prospects and short-circuit the pennant hopes of contenders. For the Phils the September of 1928 would be more useful for the latter. Klein, Whitney, Spud Davis, and Don Hurst had already won jobs with their play. Shotton wanted to concentrate on his woeful pitching staff.

John "Lefty" Milligan would win a close game with the Robins, thanks to a timely pinch single by Spud Davis. Milligan would finish the year 2–5 and end up occupying space in the Phils bullpen for the next four years, although he would only appear in thirty-three games in his four seasons as a Philly. Someone with the colorful name of Martin Van Buren Walker would make a brief appearance, starting and losing one game, then disappearing from the majors forever. Edward Lennon would pitch in five games with no decisions. Earl "Tex" Caldwell would win his first start against the Braves, then lose the next four. Ed Baecht would finally come up for a brief visit, going 1–1 in nine appearances. The pickin's were mighty slim.

Philadelphia was bound to make its contribution to the pennant race. The contribution consisted primarily of losing to every contender who came to town. The Cardinals had a particular field day with the Phils, winning five in a row in the Baker Bowl, five victories that were essential to the Redbirds' successful stretch drive. As the home season ended on September 27, Frank Ulrich, the Phils pitcher who had missed all of the season with pneumonia, was watching from the stands, a perfect symbol of yet another Phillies lost year. The season ended a couple of days later in Brooklyn as Walker got hammered by the Robins. It was a happy ending for the Robins; the victory got them up to the .500 mark for the season.

Philadelphia finished September at 8–24 for the month. Their season mark was 43–109, the worst won-lost record of any team in the 1920s, but not the worst record compiled by a Phillies team. That distinction would belong to the 1941 club, to whom we will turn briefly later.

For all their much-vaunted offensive prowess, the Phils finished with a team batting average of .267, 14 points below the league average, and a slugging percentage of .382, 15 points off the league pace. Their pitching numbers ran truer to form; the team ERA was a massive 5.52, better than a run and a half higher than the league's. Needless to say, no other team had an ERA over five.

The Phils were party to some pretty strange doings in 1928. In a year in which National League teams managed seven or more runs in a single inning on eighteen separate occasions, six of those big innings occurred in games involving the Phils. They turned the trick against Brooklyn on April 19; Cincinnati would do it to them twice; Boston, Pittsburgh, and St. Louis (who scored nine) achieved the mark once each. The Phils were also on the receiving end of one of the most spectacular exhibitions of hitting by one player all season when Cards outfielder Chick Hafey had eight hits in a July 28 twin bill; he pounded Phillies pitching for four doubles, two homers, and a pair of singles.

Spalding's Official Baseball Guide for 1929 wrote of the Phils, "It was a better team at the end of the season than it was at the beginning." That probably was true. The additions of Klein, Hurst, Davis, and Whitney gave them the nucleus of a team of sluggers that would terrorize NL pitching for another couple of years. The trade of Fred Leach for Lefty O'Doul that winter would add another big bat to the lineup. In 1929 the Phillies would improve to fifth. In 1930 they would achieve the dubious distinction of hitting .315 as a team (this was the year that the entire NL hit .303) and finishing last. When asked how that happened, Burt Shotton would reply, "My pitching staff had to work overtime to catch up."

Shotton would last through the 1933 season. He would actually manage to boost the Phils as high as fourth in 1932, the first time they had finished over .500 (78–76) since 1917. They would have their next winning season in 1949. When the Phils slipped back to seventh in 1933, Shotton was canned by Gerry Nugent, who now ran the club on the same shoestring that William F. Baker had used. Shotton was lucky. He went back to work for his friend and mentor Branch Rickey and would manage the Dodgers for Rickey in the tumultuous year of 1947, the year that Jackie Robinson broke the color line in major-league baseball.

The Baker Bowl housed the Phillies for ten more seasons, until June 30, 1938. The cheapskate ownership had allowed the elderly facility to deteriorate badly, and its meager 18,800 capacity was not up to the standards of the era. Connie Mack offered to rent Shibe Park to the Phillies. He had made the offer on several other occasions, but this time the Phils were able to extricate themselves from their lease on the Baker Bowl. The last game played in the old ballpark was, appropriately, a slugfest, with the Phils on the wrong end of a 14–1 score. The last person to leave the ballpark that day was Phils manager Jimmie Wilson, a Philadelphia native, the Opening Day catcher in 1928.

The Baker Bowl was torn down in 1950. On its site at Huntingdon and Broad streets are a parking lot and a car wash.

1928 Philadelphia Phillies Roster

Player	POS	G	AB	R	H	2B	3B	HR	RBI	SB	BA
Spud Davis	C	67	163	16	46	2	0	3	18	0	.282
Bill Dietrick	OF	52	100	13	20	6	0	0	7	1	.200
Barney Friberg	UT	52	94	11	19	3	0	1	7	0	.202
Don Hurst	1B	107	396	73	113	23	4	19	64	3	.285
Art Jahn	OF	36	94	8	21	4	0	0	11	0	.223
Bill Kelly	1B	23	71	6	12	1	1	0	5	0	.169
Chuck Klein	OF	64	253	41	91	14	4	11	34	0	.360
Freddy Leach	OF	145	588	83	179	36	11	13	96	4	.304
Walt Lerian	C	96	239	28	65	16	2	2	25	1	.272
Harvey MacDonald	OF	13	16	0	4	0	0	0	2	0	.250
Al Nixon	OF	25	64	7	15	2	0	0	7	1	.234
Heinie Sand	SS	141	426	38	90	26	1	0	38	1	.211
John Schulte	C	65	113	14	28	2	2	4	17	0	.248
Denny Sothern	OF	141	579	82	165	27	5	5	38	17	.285
Fresco Thompson	2B	152	634	99	182	34	11	3	50	19	.287
Pinky Whitney	3B	151	585	73	176	35	4	10	103	3	.301
Cy Williams	OF	99	238	31	61	9	0	12	37	0	.256
Jimmie Wilson	C	21	70	11	21	4	1	0	13	3	.300
Russell Wrightstone	OF-1B	33	91	7	19	5	1	1	11	0	.209

Figures include games played with Philadelphia only.

Pitcher	G	IP	H	ERA	ShO	SV	SO	BB	W	L
Ed Baecht	9	24	37	6.00	0	0	10	9	1	1
Ray Benge	40	202	219	4.55	1	1	68	88	8	18
Earl Caldwell	5	35	46	5.71	1	0	6	17	1	4
Alex Ferguson	34	132	162	5.67	1	2	50	48	5	10
June Greene	1	2	5	9.00	0	0	0	0	0	0
Ed Lennon	5	12	19	8.76	0	0	6	10	0	0
Bob McGraw	39	132	150	4.64	0	1	28	56	7	8
Russell Miller	33	108	137	5.42	0	1	19	34	0	12
John Milligan	13	68	69	4.37	0	0	22	32	2	5
Clarence Mitchell	3	6	13	9.00	0	0	0	2	0	0

Pitcher	G	IP	H	ERA	ShO	SV	SO	BB	W	L
Hub Pruett	13	71	78	4.54	0	0	35	49	2	4
Jimmy Ring	35	173	214	6.40	0	1	72	103	4	17
Les Sweetland	37	135	163	6.58	0	2	23	97	3	15
Marty Walker	1	0	2	00	0	0	0	3	0	1
Augie Walsh	38	122	160	6.20	0	2	38	40	4	9
Claude Willoughby	35	131	180	5.30	1	1	26	83	6	5

Figures include games played with Philadelphia only.

Chapter 5
The 1935 Boston Braves

WON: **38**   LOST: **115**   GAMES OUT OF FIRST: **61½**

DAYS IN FIRST: 3   LAST DAY IN FIRST: **April 18**

HOME RECORD: **25–50**

ROAD RECORD: **13–65**

LONGEST WINNING STREAK: **4**

LONGEST LOSING STREAK: **15**

> No matter how good you are, you're going to lose
> one third of your games. No matter how bad you
> are, you're going to win one third of your games.
> It's the other third that makes the difference.
>
> —TOMMY LASORDA

THE 1935 Boston Braves were, if nothing else, a team of distinction. For one thing, they could boast three future Hall of Famers, one of whom, Babe Ruth, was arguably the best baseball player of all time. The other two were shortstop–second baseman Rabbit Maranville, and manager Bill McKechnie.

Okay, so Ruth and Maranville weren't exactly at the top of their game. Ruth was an *old* 40, exiled from New York, a man trying desperately to show there was still a little something left in those spindly legs of his; and Maranville was an even older 43, coming off an injury so serious that it had kept him on the sidelines for the entire '34 season.

But the real reason this Brave club was distinctive was that it was a team so pathetically awful that it was destined to set a standard for losing in the National League in the 20th century—38 wins and 115 losses—a record for losing percentage that remains to this day unsurpassed as a monument to ineptitude.

♦ **Rabbit Maranville in 1935: Why is this man smiling?** (Photo courtesy of the National Baseball Library, Cooperstown, NY)

Of all the teams chronicled in this book, the 1935 Braves are perhaps the most unique because there were no warning signs on the field the year before. Nothing to tip off even the most astute fan as to what was to come. In fact, few if any would have predicted such a precipitous and incredible fall from the relative grace of the 1934 season, when, with a record of 78–73, they managed a quite respectable fourth-place finish. Remember, it took the Philadelphia Athletics two years to accomplish their steep descent, and then the reasons for their fall were obvious. Not so with the Boston Braves.

Forgetting about Ruth and Maranville, Boston had a genuine superstar in his prime—outfielder Wally Berger, who in 1934 batted .298, slammed 34 home runs, and knocked in 121 RBI. In fact, Berger was one of the few bright spots for the Braves in 1935, when, seemingly oblivious of the chaos going on around him, not to mention his team's utter incompetence, he had a career year, leading the league in RBI with 130, and home runs, with 34, while managing to hit a very respectable .295.

The last time the Braves had captured a championship was in 1914. Dubbed the Miracle Braves, the team came from eighth place on July 18 to win the pennant by 10 1/2 games and then took Philadelphia in the World Series, four games straight.

Unfortunately, at least in Boston, lightning doesn't strike twice.

♦

Usually, when a team is as bad as any of the teams we're talking about in this book are, the culprit is the same. Spell it m-o-n-e-y. The Braves had so many financial woes that their scouting program was virtually suspended, simply because there was no money to buy recommended players. In fact, it was money problems that led them to sign one of baseball's most beloved, albeit fading, stars, Ruth, and to attempt to turn Braves Field into, would you believe, a dog track.

Despite finishing no higher than fourth, the Braves franchise was a money maker in 1931, '32, and '33. Unfortunately, Judge Fuchs had the reputation of spending money as fast as he made it.

For instance, he claimed that although the Braves made a profit in 1933 of $150,000, he spent $159,000 for new players. No matter who's doing your books, that adds up to a loss.

In 1934, however, the team lost a bundle, due in no small part to the fact that over one 25-day period there were only nine, count them, nine hours of sunshine in the Boston area. Attendance was down and the interest on a $200,000 note that Judge Fuchs had taken out was mounting up. These debts were causing friction with his partners, who were starting to pull the purse strings tighter.

But Judge Fuchs was not about to throw in the towel. Think of him, if you will, as the Charlie Finley of his time. In 1935 he was 57 years old and had been president of the Braves since 1922. In 1929, after the team had dropped 103 games the previous year, Fuchs boldly named himself field manager. "The time has gone," he announced, "when a manager has to chew tobacco and talk from the side of his mouth. I don't think our club can do any worse with me as manager than it has done the last few years." Perhaps Judge Fuchs was onto something, leading us into a new era, an era when managers would speak from both sides of their mouths. (After all, the owners always had.)

In any case, with the judge at the helm the team did do better . . . marginally. They lost only 98 games. But that was hardly due to any strokes of genius on the judge's part, since he didn't actually do much of the managing. Rather, he left the dirty job to one of his coaches, Johnny Evers (who, by the way, was one of the stars, along with Rabbit Maranville, of the 1914 Miracle Braves). The next year Fuchs named Bill McKechnie manager of the Braves.

So just how bad were things for the Braves going into the 1935 season? Bad enough that Fuchs was threatening to turn Braves Field into a dog track. It seems that the Massachusetts legislature had recently voted to legalize dog racing in the state and when Fuchs heard that one of the dog syndicates was searching for a likely spot to hold their contests, he charitably offered to build a track around the field.

Ah, but what an ignominious fate for a fine old field that was first inhabited by the Braves in mid-August of 1915. Constructed on the grounds of the old Allston Golf Club, it was a spacious park, large enough so that it was possible to hit inside-the-park home runs in all three outfield directions. The stadium led a proud and honored life, at least until the park itself became a source of embarrassment eleven years after the 1935 Braves bumbled through their season. Opening Day 1946, 5000 surprised fans left the home opener with green paint on their clothing because the new paint job done on the seats hadn't been given sufficient time to dry. It cost the Braves $6000 in cleaning fees, and the team played a good number of their April home games at Fenway Park, while their seats dried. Today, the stadium has been renamed Nickerson Field, and acts as a football stadium for the Boston University Terriers.

In an effort to implement his plan to turn a few extra bucks, Fuchs had the nerve to bring up the proposition at a National League meeting conducted in December 1934. His scheme was to let the dogs have Braves Field and let the Braves, a different breed of dog altogether, play their home games at Fenway, when the Sox were out of town.

Whether Fuchs had any real notion of doing such a thing is doubtful. More likely, since he knew baseball commissioner Judge Kenesaw Mountain Landis wouldn't stand for even a hint of gambling within a horsehide's throw of the national pastime, he was instead using the dogs for leverage.

Nevertheless, in a step coolly calculated to further implement his dog-racing scenario, Fuchs actually applied to the Massachusetts Racing Commission for a license to conduct dog races at Braves Field.

Have you ever accidentally stepped on a dog's tail? Well, multiply that sound several hundred times and you probably have an idea of the high-pitched wails that emanated from Tom Yawkey, owner of the Red Sox, and Ford Frick, the National League president. And then there was the reaction of the good Judge Landis, who, pulling no punches, threatened to quit baseball if Fuchs's plan was actually executed.

The judge certainly had those good old boys by their tails. It was just the reaction he wanted, and when he got it he judiciously backed off, giving league officials time to come up with an alternative plan. The league met and it was decided that the NL would guarantee the rental on Braves Field, which was cut from $40,000 to $25,000, and would lend the Braves $7500 to meet spring-training expenses. This with the proviso that Fuchs, who was now about as popular as a rally-killing double play, would find a buyer for the club by the end of the 1935 season.

Mission accomplished, the judge embarked upon phase two of his plan toward solvency. The Babe.

It's impossible to talk about the Braves' 1935 season without focusing on Babe Ruth. The end of his career was staring him in the face and the Babe, who knew it as well as anyone, was looking ahead. He wanted to manage. More precisely, he wanted to manage the New York Yankees. One problem. The Yankees already had an able, if not brilliant, skipper in Joe McCarthy, a manager Jacob Ruppert, owner of the team, wanted to keep. And besides, even if he was ready for a managerial change, would he want the Bambino to lead the Bombers? Most decidedly not. After all, here was a man who could hardly manage himself, much less an entire team.

But there was the small matter of public relations. How do you let a legend go? After all, the Babe wasn't likely to make like an old soldier and just fade away.

It helps to have a cooperative colleague like Judge Emil Fuchs, president of the Boston Braves. Fuchs, a rather colorful character in his own right, was in a bit of a financial bind. His team, sharing the city of Boston with the Red Sox (who had been revitalized by Tom Yawkey's open-checkbook policy), was sinking deeper and deeper into debt. And Fuchs, who knew a life preserver when he saw one—or at least he thought he did probably imagined that the Babe, as over the hill as he might be, could still, especially with those extra hot dogs around his middle, float. And maybe, just maybe, he could put a few more fannies in the seats. In turn this would allow the Braves and Fuchs to grab ahold and float along with him.

In 1934, his last year with the Yankees, Ruth's diminishing skills were evident. It was the first year since 1925 (when he only played in 98 games with 359 at bats) that Ruth hadn't led the league in some category, either runs, home runs, RBIs, or bases on balls. In 365 at bats, he hit .288 and managed *only* 22 home runs, his lowest total since he played for the Red Sox in 1918, when, as a pitcher and part-time outfielder, he hit 11.

The Babe wanted desperately to manage the Yankees, but that was out of the question. What Ruppert did offer was the chance to manage the International League Newark Bears, an opportunity that the Babe took as an insult and angrily passed on. It was the big leagues or nothing.

"I would have been content to stay with the Yankees as a coach or a pinch hitter for a couple of years longer if anybody had given me the slightest encouragement that when the proper time came I would be given a chance to run the club," Ruth told sportswriter Joe Williams. "But this encouragement never came. On the contrary it was made very plain that I was never to be considered. That's why I took the Boston proposition. It turned out bad, but it was the only step I could make."

While he pondered his next move, Ruth accompanied a group of major-league players on a goodwill tour around the world. When he returned, there was Judge Fuchs waving an offer which the Babe could hardly refuse.

It was in February that the Yankees announced that they had turned over the Babe's contract to the Braves. Purely out of the goodness of their pinstriped hearts, of course, so that Ruth could fulfill his ambition of managing a major-league team.

In the meantime Fuchs had written the following letter to Ruth:

My dear George:

In order that we may have a complete understanding I am putting in the form of a letter the situation affecting our long-distance conversation of yesterday.

The Boston Braves offer you the following inducements, under the terms and conditions set forth, in order to have you sign a uniform contract plus an additional contract which will further protect you, both contracts to be filed.

1—The Boston club offers you a straight salary contract.

2—They offer you an official executive position as an officer of the corporation.

3—The Boston club offers you also the position, for 1935, of assistant manager.

4—They offer you a share of the profits during the term of this contract.

5—An option to purchase stock and become part owner.

6—The details of the amounts agreed upon will be the basis of a separate contract which shall be a personal one between you and the club, and as the case may be, with the individual officials and stockholders of the club.

In consideration of this offer, the Boston Club naturally will expect you to do everything in your power for the welfare and interest of the club and will expect that you will endeavor to play in the games whenever possible, as well as carry out the duties above specified.

You have been a great asset to baseball. . . . Your greatest value to a ball club would be your personal appearance on the field. . . . I have never seen you make a wrong play or throw a ball to the wrong base. . . . If it was determined, after your affiliation with the ball club in 1935, that it was for the mutual interest of the club for you to take up the active management on the field, there would be absolutely no handicap in having you so appointed. . . .

The grateful Babe's reply:

So long as memory serves me I shall always remember with tender recollection and appreciation the farewell testimonial accorded me at Fenway Park. . . . I am mindful of the great battle and sacrifice you have made to give Boston a good ball club and a winner. . . . In the spirit of the memory of Christy Mathewson, which we both hold sacred, and who came to Boston with you almost fourteen years ago, and in the continuation of my long friendship with you, I pledge to the people of New England that we shall keep the faith.

We now pronounce you husband and wife.

On February 27 Ruth signed a $25,000 contract as player, assistant manager, and second vice-president. He was also to share in any profits the team made that year. Good luck, Babe.

After signing, a jubilant Ruth announced to an Associated Press reporter, "I will take full charge of the Braves on the field next year. My main ambition still is to manage a big-league club, and I am going to Boston with the full understanding that it will be fulfilled."

Unfortunately for the Babe, the Braves already had a proven manager in Bill McKechnie. The Deacon, as he was known (due to his reputation as a churchgoing family man), was 48 years old and in his fourteenth season of managing in the major leagues. He'd never had a last-place team before and he never would in the eleven years more that he managed after 1935. In 1925 he'd led the Pittsburgh Pirates to a world's championship, and in 1928 he'd piloted the Cardinals to a first-place finish. In fact, he won pennants in three cities, a record that has yet to be matched.

As a player McKechnie was undistinguished, primarily a utility man with the Pirates, Braves, Yankees, Giants, and Reds. However, he had a reputation as being a scholar of the game. Frank Chance, his manager in 1913 when he was a Yankee, maintained that McKechnie "knew more baseball than all the rest of my team put together."

This sentiment was echoed by most knowledgeable baseball people, and with this in mind the 1936 *Reach Official Baseball Guide* commented thusly on McKechnie and the Braves' 1935 season: "There is little need to dwell any further on the matter except to say that in the face of troubles that would have completely distracted the average manager, Bill McKechnie gallantly stood by his guns to the finish."

The fact is, the Braves' owners were quite satisfied with McKechnie and had no intention of replacing him with Ruth or anyone else.

On the day McKechnie received a telegram from Fuchs informing him of the Babe's contract provisions, including his position as assistant manager, the Deacon also received a wire from Charles F. Adams, a majority stockholder of the team and one of the men Fuchs owed a good deal of money to, which reassured McKechnie, saying, in effect, "This move does not in any way change your position with the Braves, nor will it in the future."

Three days after signing his contract Ruth headed down to St. Petersburg, for spring training. At the station three thousand cheering fans greeted him. At the field Rabbit Maranville greeted him with tongue firmly implanted in cheek. "On this club, of course," he told the Babe, "you'll have to work your way up from the bottom."

But first, the Babe's bottom had to be outfitted. Unfortunately, the Braves didn't have a new uniform large enough to encase the Babe's bulky form. The only thing they could do was take one that catcher Shanty Hogan (six one, 240 pounds) had outgrown, and cut it down . . . but only slightly.

On the first day of practice the Babe noticed a couple of dozen new baseballs sitting on a table near his locker. "What in hell are those for?" he asked.

"They're baseballs," replied Coach Hank Gowdy. "We use them in practice."

"Oh," said the Babe. "I thought I had to autograph the damn things."

McKechnie, standing close by, laughed and said, "You're lucky to get two dozen balls to practice with on this club, let alone autograph."

"Good," said the Babe.

As far as getting into shape, McKechnie wisely let Ruth set his own schedule, much as Joe McCarthy had done. The fact is, he could do little else. From the way it was set up, Ruth wasn't working for him, but rather the other way around. The situation, such as it was, did not lend itself to a happy clubhouse. It was one set of rules for the Babe, and another set for the rest of the team.

That year a young first baseman by the name of Elbie Fletcher was invited to spring training. Fletcher was only eighteen years old, but already he'd played eight games for the Braves at the tail end of the 1934 season, going two for four.

Fletcher's entry into professional baseball was an interesting one. As he told Donald Honig in an interview contained in the latter's book, *Baseball When the Grass Was Real,* "I got my opportunity to go into professional baseball by winning a newspaper contest. A newspaper in the Boston area asked the fans to write in and recommend a high school player and say why they thought he might possibly have the qualifications to eventually become a big leaguer. Well, I organized a campaign on behalf of Elbie Fletcher. I had all my uncles and aunts and cousins and friends and everybody else write in recommending me. And as fate would have it, I won the contest. The prize was a free trip to Florida and spring training with the Braves. Talk about a dream coming true!"

Fletcher, an all-around athlete at Milton High School, who also starred in hockey, football, and basketball, was transported to his first spring training with the proviso that the team would provide him with a tutor so he could complete his schoolwork and return north in time for graduation. Fletcher did so well at spring tryout that he was assigned to a minor-league team for the 1934 season.

The next year, the fateful 1935, he was back at spring training, trying to make the club. He wasn't invited north with the team, but he did get the rare opportunity to meet the legendary Babe, up close and personal.

"In 1935," he told Honig, "I went back to spring training with the Braves. Still just a kid, eighteen years old. That was the spring Babe Ruth joined the team, right at the very end of his career. We were all awed by his presence. He still had that marvelous swing, and what a follow-through, just beautiful, like a great golfer.

"But he was forty years old. He couldn't run, he could hardly bend down for a ball, and of course, he couldn't hit the way he used to. It was sad watching those great skills fading away. One of the saddest things of all is when an athlete begins to lose it. A ball goes past you that you know you would have been on top of a few years before. And then, being a left-handed hitter, you begin to realize that most of your good shots are going to center and left-center, and you know you've lost just that fraction of a second and can't always pull the ball the way you used to. And to see it happening to Babe Ruth, to see Babe Ruth struggling on a ball field, well, then you realize we're all mortal and nothing lasts forever."

Fletcher would play most of the year at Wilkes-Barre, but he was called up near the end of the season to play in 39 games with the Braves, where he got up 148 times and batted only .236. He went on to play a dozen years in the major leagues, split almost equally between the Braves and the Pirates, compiling a respectable lifetime average of .271.

But the Babe wasn't the only one out of shape that spring. So was the diminutive Walter James Vincent "Rabbit" Maranville. Exactly one year earlier he'd had a nasty accident during a spring-training game against the Yankees. At 42 the five-foot-five-inch baseball "clown," who was nicknamed for his speed and rabbit-like leaping ability, was still spry enough to be involved on the front end of a double steal. The catcher's throw went to second and Maranville, trying to score from third, had Frank Crosetti's return throw beaten. He slid into the rookie catcher blocking the plate and snapped the tibia and fibula bones in his left leg.

When Shanty Hogan went to the plate and, cradling Maranville in his arms whispered, "You scored the run, anyway, Rab."

"Who was going to stop me?" he snapped. "Gimme a cigarette."

The bone wasn't set properly and his leg had to be rebroken. The cast wasn't removed until late August. He hobbled around with the help of a cane for the rest of the season.

For therapy, Rabbit danced three or four hours a day. "I didn't have anybody to dance with," he told sportswriter Joe Williams, "so I danced alone. People used to come into the house, look at me, and go away shaking their heads. They thought I was nuts. But all the while I was getting my leg in shape."

Now the little shortstop, who was shifted back to second base when he began to lose range, was back to give it another try. If he could make it, he would give the Braves a big lift, not so much at the plate (although he hit a creditable .251 in the dead-ball era from 1914–20, and .265 after that, he dipped to .235 for the Braves in 1932 and .218 for them in 1933), but in the field. After all, this was the man who led all shortstops in putouts with 6,413, was third in assists with 8,967, and second in total chances, with 16,020.

But as it turned out, Maranville's dancing therapy wasn't good enough. He managed to get into only 23 games and hit a paltry .149 in 67 at bats before calling it quits.

When the season ended, the Braves offered him a job managing their team at Allentown. "Where the hell is Allentown?" asked Rabbit, who was, to say the least, somewhat put out by the offer.

In the end he signed with Elmira in the New York–Penn League, as a player-manager for $3000, while the Braves agreed to kick in an extra grand. He wound up hitting .323 in 123 games. And three years later, at the age of 47, he was still at it when, while managing Albany in the Eastern League, he actually played in six games.

♦

The team arrived north a few days before the opener, so they could play a city series against the Red Sox. Unfortunately, the weather was foul. It rained for three days, and the first two games of the series had to be canceled.

On paper the Braves were, if anything, somewhat stronger than they had been the year before. Not because of Ruth, since no one really expected him to make much of a difference, but rather because, at 29, Wally Berger was in his prime. Since 1930, when he broke into the league by batting .310 and socking 38 home runs with 119 RBI, he had batted over .300 four times and had a total of 135 home runs. The fact is, Berger might have had a real shot at the Hall of Fame, if his career hadn't been cut short by a shoulder injury suffered in 1936. He played until 1940, but never on a full-time basis. Nevertheless, his numbers are rather impressive: 242 home runs, 898 RBI, and a .300 career average. Most of these stats were attained during his tenure with a team that was, at best, mediocre.

They also had a kid named Hal Lee, a slick-fielding, laconic outfielder who hit .292 with 79 RBI the year before. Lee had been discovered at the University of Mississippi by a Brooklyn Dodger scout. About him McKechnie once remarked, "He's colorless. You'd never know that he's around. If he'd advertise himself more, no doubt he'd be a lot more prominent. But he's a good fielder and a good hitter, the quiet, dependable type of player that you can always count on."

Even Lee himself admitted that "I am not much on the limelight. It has always been my nature to go about my business and try to do my best. Self-advertising and ballyhoo are not in my line. I realize that they help a fellow in a public enterprise like baseball, and I've sometimes wished that I had more taste for that sort of thing. But I haven't. So that's that."

Of course, some whispered that Lee lacked ambition and, because of that, he would never leave his mark on any club he played on. Nevertheless, if nothing else, Lee was a steady ball-player who wound up hitting .303 that fateful year. But a closer look at his stats shows that along with that average, he managed to knock in only 39 runs.

Otherwise, the regular lineup was remarkably lackluster. In fact, once you got by the Babe and Rabbit, you could color the team bland.

Third base was shared by Arthur "Pinky" Whitney and Joe Coscarart. Whitney had been with the Braves since he was traded to Boston by the Phillies in 1933. When he first broke in with Philly in 1928, he was an immediate sensation. He hit .301 as a rookie that year. In 1929 he had 200 hits and batted .327 for the Phillies. The next year he did even better, batting .342. In four of his first five years he drove in more than 100 runs. He was also an accomplished defensive player who led NL third basemen in fielding three times. In 1934 he slipped to .259, with 79 RBI. He was in the early stages of an irreversible decline. After 1930 his average dropped steadily, never rising above the .300 mark until 1937—by which time he was traded back to the Phillies and the cozy Baker Bowl—when he hit .341.

Coscarart, on the other hand, was an unproven rookie that year, when he hit .236. He was to play only one more year in the big leagues.

Randy Moore was primarily an outfielder. His best year was in 1933, when he hit .302 with the Boston team. A native Texan, he was to go into the oil business after his baseball career was finished and reportedly made millions not only for himself but for several of his Braves teammates.

At shortstop was Bill Urbanski, a sure-handed fielder but only a lifetime .260 hitter.

Sharing catching duties were Shanty Hogan, Al Spohrer, and Ray Mueller. Hogan, nicknamed "Shanty" for his physical resemblance to a small shack, was a good fielder and solid hitter. After being traded to the Giants with Jimmy Welsh for Rogers Hornsby in 1928, Hogan batted over .300 for four consecutive seasons. He was sold back to the Braves in 1933 and promptly recorded 120 consecutive errorless games behind the plate. In 1934 he batted .262, but in 1935, nearing the end of his career, he was to play in only 59 games, during which time he batted .301.

Al Spohrer was a journeyman catcher who had played sparingly for the Braves since he joined the team in 1928. His biggest claim to fame was his reputation of being a man who never walked away from a good fight. In fact, when challenged by Art Shires, a first baseman who played for Boston in 1932, Spohrer took up the gauntlet and the two, matched by a promoter, actually duked it out in the ring in front of an arena full of paying customers. Of course, spoilsport that he was, Commissioner Landis put a quick halt to any thoughts of Spohrer making this a second career.

Mueller was a rookie whose first major-league hit was to be a home run off Carl Hubbell. Nevertheless, Mueller was never more than a utility catcher until World War II when, due to the manpower shortage, he became a full-time player, catching 233 consecutive games for Cincinnati.

Baxter "Buck" Jordan played three positions for the Braves that year: first base, third base, and the outfield. He was a solid, if not spectacular, player, who hit .311 in 489 at bats in 1934, but was to dip to .279 in 1935. Nevertheless, he did get himself into the record books in a game played on August 25, 1935, when he managed to make eight hits in a doubleheader.

There were high hopes for the pitching staff of the Braves that year. They were led by Ben Cantwell, the acknowledged ace of the staff, who began his career with the Giants and was traded to Boston in 1928, where he became a relief pitcher. In 1933 he was installed in the starting rotation by McKechnie, and he rewarded his manager's decision by having his best season, winning 20 games while losing ten, and leading the league in winning percentage with .667. The next year, however, he fell upon hard times, his record dipping to 5–11. Unfortunately, the worst was yet to come. By the time the 1935 season had ended Cantwell had lost 25 games while winning only four, a winning percentage of a minuscule .138, a drop of over .500 percentage points from his record two years earlier. During this star-crossed season, when his ERA climbed to a decidedly unhealthy 4.61, Cantwell lost 13 games in a row. Poor Ben Cantwell has the dubious distinction of being the last 25-game loser in baseball.

The second biggest loser on the squad that year was Ed Brandt, who dazzled fans with a 5–19 record. But Brandt, too, had seen better days. The year before, he'd had a 16–14 record. And in both 1931 and 1933 Brandt had won 18 games for the Braves. But of course, 1935 was different. His ERA was a bloated 5.00, almost a run and a half more than he'd given up in '34, when his ERA was a far more respectable 3.53.

Almost matching Brandt in the number of losses that year was Bob Smith, whose record was 8–18. Smith began his career as a good-field, no-hit shortstop for the Braves before he switched to the mound in 1925. He had five straight losing seasons but won at least ten games each of those years. His biggest claim to fame came on May 17, 1927, when he pitched a complete-game 22-inning 4–3 loss to the Cubs, for what now stands as the fifth longest pitching effort in major-league history.

Also on the staff was Fred Frankhouse, who went 17–9 for the '34 Braves, while being named to the All-Star team. From 1933 through 1937 Frankhouse won at least ten games, finishing his career with the Braves in 1939 with a career record of 106–97. Of course, 1935 was not to be recorded as his finest hour. His record fell to 11–15 and his ERA ballooned to 4.76, a full run and a half larger than his 3.20 of a year earlier. In fact, he allowed the most runs of any pitcher in the league, 147, and the most earned runs at 122.

Essentially, the pitching staff was the same that had performed so well in 1934, but there was a difference. Now they were all a year older, and collectively, their ERA rose by about a run. The average age of the staff was 33, and all of the starters were over 30. Their relief pitchers, especially, were rather long in the tooth: Larry Benton was thirty-seven and Huck Betts was thirty-eight.

The staff ERA was 4.93, while the league average was 4.02. They gave up a total of 852 runs, while the team scored only 575 (which paled in comparison to Chicago's league-leading 847 runs scored).

Nevertheless, when the season opened, if you judged solely by the pedigree of the pitching staff, things didn't look so bad.

They only turned out that way.

Before the season opened, the National League made two announcements. First, as a token of appreciation of the old-time ballplayer, they presented lifetime passes to men who had played in baseball for ten years or longer.

The second announcement, far more momentous, was that night baseball was to be introduced into the game, first in Cincinnati. However, the rule was that you could play only a maximum of seven night games per season.

If only the Braves could have played all their games that year in the dark.

♦

When Opening Day at Braves Field arrived, the weather cooperated. Ruth was in the lineup against the New York Giants, with Carl Hubbell pitching. Hubbell was in the prime of a career in which he won 253 games. In 1933 he'd led the league with 23 wins and 12 losses, and in 1934 his record was 21–12. On this particular day he was to be a victim of the Ruth legend, as he gave up a two-run homer to the Babe, his 709th. Ruth also knocked in another run with a double and made a sensational diving catch. The final score was Braves 4, Giants 2, and there were smiles all over Beantown that evening.

The smiles were short lived.

Next, the Braves played a doubleheader against Brooklyn, which they lost by identical 4–2 scores. By this time, four days after the season opened, Ruth had pulled up lame. When he returned to the lineup on Easter Sunday, he hit a home run, but to no avail, as the Braves dropped another game to the Dodgers, 8–1.

In the field the Babe was shifted back and forth between right and left, depending upon which was the sun field, an area he wanted to stay away from. These moves neither helped Ruth's fielding ability, nor the attitude of those who were shifted to accommodate him. In fact, it seemed that the only thing Ruth could catch was a cold, which he did. It kept him out of the lineup several days, and when he came back he wasn't hitting worth a lick.

By this time the team was in what promised to be a prolonged nosedive. Their record for April was 5–7—not too bad. But by May 1 they were in seventh place, a position they were never to catch sight of again.

May was a nightmare. Their record was 4–20 for the month. They managed to score 33 runs for the month, but 12 of those runs came in a single game, a win against Pittsburgh.

The Babe Watch: On May 5 Ruth faced Dizzy Dean for the first time and didn't fare too well. He struck out, walked, and grounded out. On May 21, in Chicago, he hit his third NL home run. Two days later, against the Pirates, he failed to get a hit in four times up. The next day he was one for four. But on May 25 he temporarily awoke from his slumber and belted three home runs against the Bucs, marking only the second time in his career that he'd hit three dingers in a game.

It was an awesome performance, providing the fans a flicker of what was once the Babe. In his first time at bat, with Bill Urbanski at second, he homered into the lower tier in right off Red Lucas. In the third inning Guy Bush was pitching, and once again Urbanski was on second. Bang! the Babe pulverized a three–two pitch, sending it into the upper tier. In the fifth inning he singled off Bush, scoring Leslie Mallon, and later pitcher Bush admitted, "If he'd ever lifted that one it would have been a home run too. He really laid the wood on it."

In the seventh inning, with the bases empty, Bush threw the Babe a slow curve that he hit 50 feet over the right-field stands in Forbes Field (it was estimated to have traveled some 600 feet), the first time a ball had ever been hit over that particular spot. Pitcher Bush said, "I never saw a ball hit so hard before or since. It's probably still going." It was the 714th and last home run of the Babe's illustrious career.

Unfortunately, and for that season characteristically, despite the Babe's knocking in six runs, the Braves still managed to lose to the Pirates by a score of 11–7.

On May 22 the Braves dropped into last place and stayed there throughout the remainder of the season.

By this time Ruth knew he was going to quit the team, it was just a matter of when. He hated playing for a last-place team. His own performance was an embarrassment. He knew he'd been misled and had no more chance of managing the Braves than did the batboy. Friends, along with Bill McKechnie, urged him to go out with a bang, retiring after his phenomenal performance in the Pirate game. But Babe resisted, arguing that he had promised Fuchs that he would finish out the road trip.

The next day, playing the Reds, he went hitless in four times at bat. In this, his only complete game in the National League, he struck out three times.

His last at bat came in the Memorial Day opener in Philly. A journeyman pitcher named Jim Bivin, who went 2–9 that season, easily retired him, in more ways than one.

On June 2, while the Braves were actually winning a game against the Giants, Ruth summoned a group of Boston and New York writers and announced he was putting himself on the voluntary retired list. His voice was not without rancor as he railed at Judge Fuchs. "I was being given the runaround," he said, finally realizing what everyone else around baseball had known since his signing back in February.

Ruth was especially angry with Fuchs because the judge had refused to let him attend a party as an ambassador for baseball to be held on the *Normandie,* which was docked in New York. He attended anyway and was made even angrier because Fuchs asked him to sell 500 tickets for a retail clothier, personally autographing each ticket. The insults were piling up now. Fuchs further alienated the Babe when he wanted him to play an exhibition game in Haverhill while he was hobbling around on an injured knee.

Meanwhile, it could not be said that either the players or the manager were sorry to see Babe go. His fielding, during the 28 games in which he saw action, was atrocious. At the time of his "retirement" he was batting .181. He had only 13 hits in 72 at bats. And six of those hits were home runs.

For his part McKechnie admitted that while Ruth was on the team he could get no discipline from his other players.

The day Ruth announced his retirement, Judge Fuchs issued his own statement, which, in effect, hammered the final nails into the coffin that was to be the Braves' and his 1935 season. He admitted that he lacked the capital to get any new players. He was already a lame duck. He had until August to sell his equity in the team or surrender it to the majority stockholders.

While Fuchs was involved in behind-the-scenes machinations to try and keep the team financially solvent, poor Bill McKechnie was trying to keep the team from completely self-destructing on the field. He juggled lineups more often than a Ringling Brothers clown: by season's end, of the 31 men who were on the roster at one time or another, Wally Berger, Buck Jordan, Hal Lee, Leslie Mallon, Randy Moore, Pinky Whitney, Bill Urbanski, and Rupert Thompson were the only Braves to appear in more than 100 games. But it was all to no avail. The losing continued unabated.

The Braves couldn't win with Ruth on the team, and they couldn't win without him. In the month of June they managed to win 11 out of 30 games. As usual, the one bright spot was Wally Berger. Over an 11-game period he knocked in 14 runs. This longest run-scoring streak of the season began on June 9 in a game against New York, and ended June 19 in the second game of a doubleheader against the Cubs.

In July Boston sank lower than they had even in May. This time they went 5–23, including a fifteen-game losing streak.

August 1 rolled around and Fuchs was forced to step down as president of the club, handing the reins over to the majority stockholder, Charles F. Adams. Adams, however, was deeply involved in horse racing, and since he refused to disassociate himself from the sport, he was deemed by Commissioner Landis an unsuitable candidate to run the team. As a result Bill McKechnie was asked to serve as president pro tem until a new president could be found.

From August 18 until September 14 the Braves won only two of the thirty games they played.

In the meantime the Chicago Cubs were red hot in September, taking 21 straight games. This amazing streak allowed them to beat out the Cardinals, by finishing with a 100–54 record.

One can only imagine the collective sigh of relief that emanated through the Boston area as the season ended.

During this long—very long—season, other teams set several records playing against the Braves. For instance, in a doubleheader against the Braves, center fielder Lloyd Waner of the Pirates made nine putouts in each game (Pittsburgh won both, of course, 4–2 and 5–1). St. Louis first baseman Jimmy Collins tied a league record of only one chance in a game against Boston on August 21, which, surprise, the Braves lost 13–3. On September 5, Terry Moore of St. Louis went six for six against the Braves, tying a record shared by many other players.

Other reasons for the Braves not to be proud of this nightmare season included the fact that they were blanked 12 times; they hit into the most double plays that year, 139; and finally, they wound up 61½ games out of first and 26 games out of seventh place.

Of course, there were a few, very few, things for Braves fans to be proud of. For one thing, Wally Berger led the league in home runs with 34, including three grand slams, and in RBI with 130 (but what's even more amazing is the fact that the man on the team who had the second most homers was . . . Babe Ruth, with six—and the man only played in parts of 28 games!) Berger had more than twice as many RBIs as the next Brave, Pinky Whitney, who had 60.

As a team the Braves finished last in the league in hits (1,396 compared to pennant-winning Chicago's 1,581), doubles (233, compared to Chicago's 303), runs (575, compared to Chicago's 847), batting average (.263, compared to Chicago's .288 and a league average of .277), slugging (.362, compared to Chicago's .414), and stolen bases (20 compared to Chicago's 66). In the pitching department they were last in strikeouts with 355 (compared to 589 recorded by Chicago hurlers), shutouts, saves, and ERA, which was 4.93 compared to Chicago's at 3.26.

Understandably, the 1935 Braves were the laughingstock of baseball, the butt of all kinds of jokes.

For instance, this mock letter appeared in a national baseball magazine under the heading of LETTERS THEY NEVER RECEIVED, by W. R. Hoefer:

Wm. McKechnie, Esq.
Mgr. Boston Braves B.B. Club

Dear William:

Noting that at the National League Winter Meeting suggestions for increasing interest in the impending league pennant race were invited, I herewith accept said invitation and offer a suggestion that should make the coming pennant race more interesting, at least to the Boston Brave fans—both of them. Said suggestion is as follows: (a) Pushball, (b) Handball, (c) Volleyball, or (d) Skee-Ball. By playing one of the forementioned games of ball instead of baseball I am sure our Braves will have a much better chance for the pennant, thus automatically increasing the interest in the race for our Boston Brave fans.

Helpfully yours,

A Boston Brave Fan
(The One Who Attends
the Game on Fridays)

The Braves might have been down, but they weren't out for long. In what must be counted among the most astounding resurrections, the next year the team rebounded, moving from eighth place to sixth, winning nearly double the number of games they had the year before (their 1936 record was 71–83, nothing to write home about, but certainly a vast improvement over 1935).

One reason for this improvement was that the team named Bob Quinn to run the club. Quinn was an experienced baseball man who came to the Braves from the Dodgers, where he had been business manager. Before that he'd been president of the Red Sox. Although he'd always been associated with losing teams, he was to face his biggest challenge with the Braves. The work in front of him was pretty much summed up in a magazine article that described the job as "the reorganization of a wrecked ball club with limited capital in a city where the rival club has the edge in popularity backed by unlimited funds and directed by a princely spender."

When asked what he thought of his new team, he replied, "They look pretty well shot to me." And then he added, "But I've never had a team handed to me yet that wasn't shot."

But the first thing Quinn undertook was purely a cosmetic change, a kind of face-lift, if you will. He decided to conduct a contest to rename the Braves.

"When I took charge of this club," said Quinn, "I thought we had better make a clean sweep and have a new deal all around. The name *Braves* never did appeal to me very strongly. I felt we could have a new name that would be more appropriate. And the idea occurred to me that we could let the fans suggest a name. That might stimulate a little interest."

Fans were urged to submit nicknames and thousands poured in, among them the Sacred Cods and the Bankrupts. Finally, the judges, made up of baseball writers, chose the so very imaginative and utterly *appropriate* title of the Bees. And so, for the next six years, the Boston Braves were known as the Boston Bees, and the name of their ballpark, Braves Field, was changed to National League Park, but was far more widely known as "The Hive."

Quinn's next move, however, actually helped solved some of the problems on the field. He shipped left-hander Ed Brandt and regular right fielder Randy Moore to the Dodgers for veteran right-hander Ray Benge, second baseman Tony Cuccinello, catcher Al Lopez, and utility man Bobby Reis (he played first, second, third, the outfield, and pitched).

All of these players paid immediate dividends. Lopez, who led the major leagues in assists with 107, gave the Bees someone solid behind the plate. Benge pitched his way to a 7–9 record in 115 innings. Reis was used almost exclusively as a pitcher, turning in a 6–5 record while pitching 139 innings. And Cuccinello batted .308

and helped turn 128 double plays, tops in both leagues, while also leading all second basemen in assists with 559.

But no matter how good the Braves were to become, nothing could ever erase the ignominious season of 1935.

1935 Boston Braves Roster

Player	POS	G	AB	R	H	2B	3B	HR	RBI	SB	BA
Wally Berger	OF	150	589	91	174	39	4	34	130	3	.295
Joe Coscarart	3B	86	284	30	67	11	2	1	29	2	.236
Elbie Fletcher	1B	39	148	12	35	7	1	1	9	1	.236
Shanty Hogan	C	59	163	9	49	8	0	2	25	0	.301
Baxter Jordan	1B	130	470	62	131	24	5	5	35	3	.279
Hal Lee	OF	112	422	49	128	18	6	0	39	0	.303
William Lewis	C	6	4	1	0	0	0	0	0	0	.000
Leslie Mallon	2B	116	412	48	113	24	2	2	25	3	.274
Rabbit Maranville	2B	23	67	3	10	2	0	0	5	0	.149
Randy Moore	OF	125	407	42	112	20	4	4	42	1	.275
Ed Moriarity	2B	8	34	4	11	2	1	1	1	0	.324
Joe Mowry	OF	81	136	17	36	8	1	1	13	0	.265
Ray Mueller	C	42	97	10	22	5	0	3	11	0	.227
Babe Ruth	OF	28	72	13	13	0	0	6	12	0	.181
Alfred Spohrer	C	92	260	22	63	7	1	1	16	0	.242
Rupert Thompson	OF	112	297	34	81	7	1	4	30	2	.273
John Tyler	OF	13	47	7	16	2	1	2	11	0	.340
Bill Urbanski	SS	132	514	53	118	17	0	4	30	3	.230
Arthur Whitney	3B	126	458	41	125	23	4	4	60	2	.273

Figures include games played with Boston only.

Pitcher	G	IP	H	ERA	ShO	SV	SO	BB	W	L
Lawrence Benton	29	72	103	6.88	0	0	21	24	2	3
Walter Betts	44	160	213	5.47	1	0	40	0	2	9
Prosby Blanche	6	17	14	1.56	0	0	4	5	0	0
Ed Brandt	29	175	224	5.00	0	0	61	66	5	19
Robert Brown	15	65	79	6.37	1	0	17	36	1	8
Ben Cantwell	39	211	235	4.61	0	0	34	44	4	25
Fred Frankhouse	40	231	278	4.76	1	0	64	81	11	15
Dan MacFayden	28	152	200	5.10	1	0	46	34	5	13
Charles Rhem	10	41	61	5.31	0	0	10	11	0	5
Robert Smith	46	203	232	3.94	2	5	58	61	8	18

Figures include games played with Boston only.

Chapter 6
The 1942 Philadelphia Phillies

WON: **42**   LOST: **109**   GAMES OUT OF FIRST: **62¹/₂**

DAYS IN FIRST: **NONE**

HOME RECORD: **23–51**

ROAD RECORD: **19–58**

LONGEST WINNING STREAK: **3**

LONGEST LOSING STREAK: **13**

It was just a matter of playing anyone who
was breathing. Nobody asked too much. It was
interesting and it gave people something to do.

—RED BARBER, *broadcaster,*
on World War II baseball

When we won a few games in a row, it might have
been cause for a congressional investigation.

—DANNY MURTAGH,
second baseman with the 1941–2 Phillies

WHEN WAR was declared in 1941 in the wake of the Japa-
nese attack on Pearl Harbor, major-league baseball held its
breath. During World War I the majors had been asked to make
great sacrifices for the war effort, even shortening the season to
130 games in 1918. Travel restrictions had been imposed and many
teams held spring training in the North, with considerable discom-
fort. When President Roosevelt issued his famous "green light"
letter, urging the doyens of the game to soldier on in the name of
morale, a sigh of relief was heaved.

For the Phillies, however, it was business as usual. Under
Gerry Nugent, who took over the club after William F. Baker died

♦ **Danny Litwhiler: He *always* hustled, even in 1942.** (Photo courtesy of
the National Baseball Library, Cooperstown, NY)

in 1930, the Phillies had remained a walking austerity program for another decade. What difference could a war make?

Nugent was not a wealthy man. As sportswriter J. Roy Stockton bluntly put it, "He married the Phillies." Nugent's wife, Mae Mallen, had been Baker's secretary; Nugent joined the front office as Baker's assistant around the same time that he married her. When Baker died, he left stock in the club to his widow and Mae. Nugent had worked his way up to business manager, and after Lewis Ruch left the presidency of the Phillies three years later, Nugent became president, with Mae as his vice-president.

As anyone who watched the machinations of Cal Griffith in Minneapolis in his waning years as owner of the Twins will tell you, baseball is not a great place for an owner whose only business is baseball. It is nothing short of remarkable that Griffith lasted as long as he did in the era of free agency, no small tribute to his baseball acumen. The Phils under Nugent were a case in point long before free agency.

Gerry Nugent may have had little baseball acumen to speak of, it's hard to say. On the plus side he was not a meddlesome owner in the Steinbrenner mold. That takes an excess of capital, which leads to an excess of leisure time and ego. Nugent's every waking moment seemed to be consumed with trying to find ways to raise a few pennies. As a result his consuming passion appears to have been developing talent cheap and selling it dear. Well, not dear exactly, but for more than it cost. Danny Murtagh, the Phils second baseman in 1942 and later one of the most successful managers in Pittsburgh Pirates history, said of Nugent, "In order to maintain control of the club, he'd sell every good athlete that came along in order to meet expenses." For example, in his most unpopular move, Nugent sold Chuck Klein, the slugging outfielder who graced so many otherwise dismal Phils clubs in the first half of the thirties, to Chicago for $65,000 and three players of no great skill, the winter after he won the NL Triple Crown.

The Phillies had always been a cash-poor operation. They were the poor relations in the City of Brotherly Love, neglected for Connie Mack's (sometimes) lordly A's. And the aging rust-bucket that housed them, the Baker Bowl, didn't help matters. When the

Phils abandoned the Bandbox, however, to move in with their rich cousins in Shibe Park, things actually got worse. As Murtagh recalls, "When the Phils were playing at Baker Bowl, they had their own loyal following; but when they became tenants of the A's in Shibe Park, the people who wanted to see a ball game would always go and watch the A's play."

If you wanted to see a baseball game, you certainly wouldn't go to Shibe when the Phils were in town.

Other Phillies owners before Nugent had sold players to make their books balance. As Stockton points out, you could select a pretty good team of ex-Phils who had gone away in cash transactions. He suggested the following: Pitchers Grover Cleveland Alexander, Claude Passeau, Kirby Higbe, Curt Davis, Bucky Walters, Hal Carlson; catchers Bill Killefer, Jimmie Wilson, Spud Davis; infielders Dolf Camilli, Dick Bartell, Dave Bancroft, Johnny Rawlings; outfielders Chuck Klein, Hal Lee, Casey Stengel, Emil Meusel, and Lefty O'Doul.

"The big difference between Nugent and the Philly sales managers before him is that he either knows his young baseball broilers, or has friends who give him valuable information," wrote Stockton. "The others were always satisfied with money immediately in hand. Nugent always looks forward to a future deal, a bigger deal, with bigger money."

A classic series of Nugent-engineered deals began with Al Todd, a young catcher he purchased in 1931 from Dallas in the Texas League; He later sold Todd to the Pirates for $25,000 and two players. One of the players was Claude Passeau, a pitcher of considerable talent, who won 36 games in three years with the tail-end club. Passeau was traded to the Cubs for three players, one of them hurler Kirby Higbe, whom Nugent sold in 1941 to the Dodgers for $100,000, a considerable profit in less than a decade. Both Passeau and Higbe beat the Phils like a drum whenever they faced them.

How did he find all those young ballplayers? It apparently wasn't the scouting system. Jimmie Wilson told Stockton that when he was the Phils manager, the scouting bureau consisted "of one man—little Patsy O'Rourke." O'Rourke, Wilson noted, was supposed to cover the Pacific Coast League, the American Association, the International League, the Texas League, and anyplace else he could think of. " 'Maybe you could do it,' Wilson reminisced, 'but I don't know where O'Rourke looked. Every time I looked up in the stands, there he was.' " Probably scouting the Phils to figure out who Nugent should sell next.

A glance at the Phils roster reveals one obvious source of talent. Of the 35 players who appeared in a Phillies uniform in 1942, ten were from Pennsylvania and another two from nearby southern New Jersey. This group includes such key players as Danny Litwhiler, Ron Northey, Danny Murtagh, Tommy Hughes, and Johnny Podgajny.

Another way in which Nugent discovered young players was actually rather dubious ethically, as witness the Chuck Klein case. In 1928 Klein had actually been playing for a Cardinals farm club in the Central League, according to Stockton. At the time, Branch Rickey, the Cardinals general manager and the architect of the original farm system, was being closely watched by Commissioner Kenesaw M. Landis, an ardent supporter of the concept of independent minor leagues. It happened, says Stockton, that the Cardinals owned two teams in the Central League, an unfair business practice to say the least, so the odds were that Rickey was going to be unable to protect some of his charges in that circuit, Klein among them. Burt Shotton, a Rickey protégé, was the Phils manager at the time. He received a call from his good friend and former boss, suggesting that Klein would be a useful acquisition for the Phils, especially since the Cards couldn't keep him. The Phils purchased him posthaste.

Perhaps the most spectacular example of the Phils' edge-of-the-law scouting system was the Rube Melton deal. Melton was a big (six-five) country boy, a free spirit who once jumped the Cardinals organization to play for a semipro team. Perhaps that was why he was left off the Cardinals' list of protected farmhands coming into the 1940 minor-league draft. At the draft Nugent, broke as usual, selected Melton for the draft price of $7500, immediately dealing him to Larry MacPhail's Dodgers for $15,000. As Red Smith pointed out, this represented, "a cool hundred percent [profit], without the inconvenience of paying Melton a single day's salary, the pain of seeing him pitch a single ball, or the bother of bailing him out of a single jail." (This last remark was not an idle one; Melton was arrested for disorderly conduct by Miami police during spring training in 1942.)

The major problem the deal presented was that Commissioner Landis recognized it instantly as collusion between Nugent and MacPhail and nullified it, ruling that the Phils had to keep Melton for two years. After the 1942 season Nugent sold Melton to the Cardinals for $30,000, a 300 percent profit.

Smith noted that sportswriters and fans, as a rule, disdain such cash transactions. "It is customary for press and public to observe wittily that you can't put $30,000 out there on the mound and expect it to win any ball games. But it isn't likely to lose you more than 20 ball games, either, which was Melton's defeat quota for 1942."

Besides, as Smith adds, the money would "pay the Phils' spring-training expenses and meet the first payroll or so." In that way, he concludes, "it [would] enable the club to put a team on the field, if that can be viewed as a desirable end." And Nugent was always candid about the nature of the Phils' dilemma. Smith says that at the annual owners' meeting he bluntly told the NL proprietors, "Find me a buyer and I'll sell out. Or show me how I can operate without money." (The NL owners would have been glad to oblige. Every road trip into Philadelphia was a money loser. Stockton reported that one National League manager told him that their percentage of the gate from a series in Philly was so small that it "wasn't enough to pay for what his players ate while there.")

The same dilemma had plagued almost all previous owners of the club, the principal reason why, over a 27-year period from 1919 to 1945, the Phillies finished either last or in seventh 23 times.

♦

The 1941 season was typical.

Before the season began, Doc Prothro, in his third (and final) year as manager, secured a promise from Nugent that the Phils would stop selling off any player who showed the slightest aptitude for the game. He bubbled with pride. "The club won't make a deal now without my approval," he informed Stockton. "No more sales. We'll trade if we can help ourselves, but we're out to win."

Halfway through the season he was singing a different tune, one that bore a striking resemblance to Chopin's "Funeral March." "We couldn't go through with it," he mourned. "You know, bills. They had to be paid. We had to do something, and a hundred thousand dollars will pay a lot of bills."

Eighty games into the 1941 season the Phils had been shut out twelve times, held to one run thirteen times, two runs eleven times, three runs fourteen times. In 50 of their first 80 games that summer, the Phils had scored a total of 77 runs, an average of 1.56 runs per game. Even Walter Johnson would have lost most of his starts with that kind of offensive support, and the 1941 Phillies pitching staff didn't include any Walter Johnsons. Small wonder that Phillies hurler Hugh Mulcahy was nicknamed "Losing Pitcher."

"But we're hustling," said Prothro plaintively. "did you ever see an eighth-place club hustle like we are?"

Jimmie Wilson had a simple theory to explain the young Phils' propensity for hustle which he, too, had observed during his five seasons as Phils' manager immediately preceding Prothro. "All you have to do with the Phillies is hustle and you stand out like a lighthouse in a thin fog. . . . [Y]ou know . . . there'll be a sale soon. And if you hustle, you'll look so much better than the bums around you that the other clubs will think you're a great player. First thing you know, the Phils have a bunch of cash and you're out from behind the eight ball." Wilson knew the syndrome well; had made the trip from the Phils early in 1928 to the Cardinals, where he helped them win three pennants in four years.

All that hustle did little to advance the Phils' fortunes. Under Prothro they turned in consecutive cellar finishes with records of 45–106, 50–103, and 43–111. Their last-place finish in 1942 would give them an NL record five consecutive basement performances. They were also the first team in NL history to suffer five consecutive hundred-loss seasons.

Still, no one could say the team didn't have character. In fact the Phillies were overflowing with characters.

Once upon a time a young man presented himself at the Phils training camp, claiming to be a pitcher. He was sent to the mound during batting practice to show his stuff. Stockton reported, "After doing very poorly right handed, he turned around and did as poorly with his left arm. The Phillies, not easily irked, were indignant. As they assisted the intruder off the field, they asked him what he took them for—a big joke? 'No joke at all,' he replied gravely. 'I'm a switch pitcher and I figured you certainly needed one.' "

The real pitchers on their staff were no less eccentric. John Podgajny (pronounced "Po' Johnny," appropriately enough) was a rookie with the Phils in 1941 whom the Phils had sent to Ottawa for some seasoning. In his first start up there his manager was horrified to see the bespectacled hurler peering *over* his glasses to read the catcher's signs. When the manager urged him to get another pair of glasses, bifocals, Podgajny replied "Buy focals, nothing. I just bought these." When he was taken back to the optician's shop later, it turned out that he had bought that pair because he "liked the feel of them."

Philly backup catcher Benny Culp told Harrington Crissey, Jr., in the latter's useful oral history of World War II baseball, *Teenagers, Graybeards and 4-F's*, that only Podgajny's mastery of the Cubs kept him on the Phils major-league roster. Culp reminisced, "Podgajny . . . was tall, thin, and bespectacled. He . . . nearly drove Cub manager Jimmie Wilson crazy. . . . Wilson would take one look at Podgajny's frame and bellow, 'Put him in an iron lung.' "

Rube Melton, he of the non-draft pick draft pick, was another unique individual. In the midst of his first season with the Phils, understandably disappointed at missing a shot at the Dodgers, a real major-league ball club, Melton ran away. He later explained that he was "just discouraged about everything." Given his track record with the Cards, maybe he just liked running away.

Benny Culp recalled an incident in which Melton felt the call of nature during a lengthy inning of pitching. "He called time, trudged off the field and into the clubhouse, did his business, and calmly returned to the mound." Apparently, Melton's off-season activities were no less thought provoking. Culp told Harrington Crissey, "He once built a boat in his house, then had to tear part of the house down to get the boat out." Incidentally, although his behavior might suggest otherwise, Melton didn't get the nickname Rube because he was "country." His given name was Reuben.

The pitching staff didn't have a monopoly on eccentricity. Nick Etten, the Phils first baseman in 1941 and '42, had a quirk; he didn't like to field ground balls. Danny Murtagh told Crissey of an exchange with Etten when he was playing second alongside the rangy slugger. "There were a few balls hit between first and second that I felt Nick should have tried for, but he'd just run to the bag and let me attempt to get them. So one day I said to him, 'Nick, I think there are a few balls being hit down there that you should make an effort to reach.' He looked at me and replied, 'Son, they pay Ol' Nick to hit. You can't hit, so you catch all those balls, and I'll knock in the runs for both of us.'"

Benny Culp (whose real middle name was Baldy, honest) tells another story that seems to illustrate the Phillies' off-field behavior nicely. Culp's roommate, Lloyd Waner, the Pirates' "Little Poison" and a Hall of Famer, was nearing the end of his career, now a 36-year-old Philly. The two roomies, joined by teammate Ernie Koy, went into a St. Louis tavern owned by a former teammate of Waner's, Heinie Meine. After hoisting quite a few, they felt too inebriated to walk back to their hotel and looked for a taxi. Unfortunately, the only one in sight was parked and empty, so they took it. Happily, the St. Louis police were more understanding with ballplayers than they would have been with ordinary citizens, so the trio got off with a warning about the importance of patience.

The Phils were the first team to donate a player to the war effort. Hugh Mulcahy was drafted in the March 1941 Selective Service lottery. With typical Philly luck "Losing Pitcher" Mulcahy was denied a requested delay of six months (just enough to play a season of baseball) and inducted on March 8, right around the beginning of spring training. "I was naturally disappointed," he told Harrington Crissey, "as war had not been declared." Considering Mulcahy's major-league record—between 1937 and 1940, he averaged nineteen losses a year, against ten victories—the army may have been risking the nation's future by drafting the guy.

It certainly didn't hurt the Phils any. They still managed to lose over a hundred games without Hughie's services. At the end of the 1941 season Nugent fired Prothro and replaced him with John "Hans" Lobert, a Phillies coach who had managed the team for two games at the end of the 1938 season after Jimmie Wilson was canned. As Lobert sardonically observed in Lawrence Ritter's classic *The Glory of Their Times,* his managerial stint was "the end of a beautiful friendship."

Lobert, who was nicknamed "Hans" and "Honus" because of a superficial resemblance to Honus Wagner, had been a gifted third baseman for the Reds, Phils, and Giants during the dead-ball era. Danny Murtagh, who became a pretty good manager himself, was a big fan of Lobert's. "After spending two weeks with Lobert, I was amazed at his knowledge of baseball and his ability to teach it," he said. Lobert strongly influenced Murtagh's teaching, particularly his emphasis on base-running technique. Lobert had acquired that knowledge by experience; he stole thirty or more bases in a season seven times in his fourteen-year career, and finished with 316 thefts to his credit. Coming into the 1990 season only 66 men in baseball history had stolen over 300 bases in a career.

Lobert had been the head baseball coach at West Point for eight years before returning to the majors as a coach. The military training stood him in good stead in the first season of major-league ball after Pearl Harbor. In fact, at Lobert's instigation, Phillies players would actually get a dose of close-order drill under the watchful eye of Army instructors during spring training, and marched into an exhibition game, bats on their shoulders. They lost that game, against Casey Stengel's Braves, 6–2. Maybe they should have brought rifles.

Another element of Lobert's past would come home again during the 1942 season. It was Lobert who had been instrumental in converting Bucky Walters from a mediocre third baseman into an excellent pitcher. (Of course, if Nugent hadn't sold Walters to the Reds in 1938, we might be discussing him in this chapter.) It was a clever move, one which added many years to Walters's career, and one which Lobert would attempt to duplicate several times during the 1942 season. For example, he decided to turn strong-armed outfielder Earl Naylor into a pitcher. Naylor threw hard, but his control would have been better if he had pitched from the outfield instead of the mound. He walked 29 and struck out 19 in 60 innings. Lobert also tried catcher Mickey (real name: Thompson Orville) Livingston at first when Nick Etten's batting average and power numbers dropped. That experiment lasted only six games; Livingston hit even less than Etten.

Lobert had slightly more success in turning Bobby Bragan from a shortstop into a catcher, a fairly improbable transformation. Bragan was pretty slow afoot, and the Phils had a rookie second baseman, Albie Glossop, who pushed the speedy Murtagh out of a starting job. Murtagh, who split the year evenly between second, third, and short, became the shortstop for the time being, and Bragan was stuck behind the plate, where his considerable intelligence was an asset. Years later Bragan would tell Donald Honig that he had volunteered to go behind the plate, which is also true, although contemporary sources are mute on the subject. One thing is clear; as Bragan himself readily volunteers, it was a decision that probably added a few years to his playing career.

To hear Benny Culp tell it, Bragan wasn't much of a shortstop. Culp recalled a day on which Bragan was having more than the usual trouble at short. Si Johnson, "a dry wit," said Culp, was on the mound for the Phils. Culp came out for a conference and Johnson deadpanned, "Well, here goes a ground ball to [outfielder Danny] Litwhiler." Of course, the next batter hit a ground ball through Bragan that rolled to Litwhiler in left.

Bragan would enjoy a lengthy career in baseball, although most of it was not spent as a player. After four years with the Dodgers, interrupted by three years with the Army, he would go on to coach, to manage in the minors and majors, and eventually to become president of the National Association, the governing body of minor-league baseball.

Like Murtagh, another '42 Phil who went on to manage in the majors, Bragan had the utmost respect for Lobert. He recalled that

Hans had a unique system of signs, a different set for every player in the lineup. "My bunt sign might be someone else's hit-and-run sign," Bragan told Donald Honig. "[Lobert] had to have a hell of a memory."

♦

Spring training in Miami for the '42 season was anything but dull. For starters there was Melton's brush with the cops, which was resolved with a $300 fine. There was the usual quota of hold-outs, the most amusing of which came from pitcher Lee Grissom (brother of Marv, who was a key element in the Giants bullpen in the fifties); he had been classified 1-A by his draft board and wrote to Gerry Nugent that it probably wouldn't be worth it to report to camp. Nugent, needless to say, told him that he might not be called up for several months and should get his butt down to Miami. (Grissom was, in fact, drafted and never played for the Phils again.)

Lobert's coaches were Chuck Klein (who would even get a little pinch-hitting work during the year) and Reindeer Bill Killefer, a contemporary of Lobert who had been sold as a player by one of Nugent's predecessors. Killefer, who had played on the Phils' 1915 pennant winner, surveyed his charges and told Bill Dooly of the Philadelphia *Record,* "Maybe some of them aren't major leaguers, but I like their pep and spirit." A more accurate assessment came from a flock of ducks who rendered the Flamingo Park diamond unplayable the first day of camp by dropping a flockload of duck excrement in their wake.

When Nugent sacked Doc Prothro, he cleaned house pretty completely. As Bill Dooly observed, of 36 players who had been on the Phils roster in 1941, fifteen were gone when spring training started, not counting Hugh Mulcahy and outfielder Joe Marty, who were in the armed forces, and Chuck Klein, who was now a coach. It wouldn't be long before more were gone.

For example, Cy Blanton, who been 6–14 with the 1941 team, announced in spring training that he would double his previous season's win total. He would go 0–4 and be cut in midseason. By the end of April Lobert would send Bert Hodge, Bill Burich, and

Bill Peterman, three rookies, back to the minors. Harry Marnie, an infielder, and Bill Harman, a catcher, would be cut a few weeks later.

The war would take its toll on the majors all through the season, sometimes in unexpected ways. Early in the year National League president Ford Frick predicted that the supply of 1941 vintage baseballs would run out in midseason, forcing the majors to go with balls made under the restrictions of rubber rationing. Danny Murtagh recalled, "[S]tarting in 1942 the ball definitely became less alive. I'm not sure why. But I would say that in '42 and '43 the balls didn't travel quite as far as they did before the war." Substitute materials used in the center of the ball didn't help; a "balata" ball that was tried in 1943 was even worse.

♦

This was to be the last year of spring training in the South for the duration of the war. Travel restrictions hadn't started to take their full toll at the beginning of the season. The Phils would have had to look around for another spring-training site anyway; the Army Air Corps had commandeered their Miami base for drill grounds.

With the fear of aerial raids and submarine attacks on coastal cities rampant, night baseball nearly was another casualty. The Army ran tests of Shibe Park's visibility after a game in late May and decided that the stadium was far enough inland that the lights were not visible in restricted areas at sea. (In fact, only New York City would lose night baseball during the war.) However, blackout tests were run at the ballpark during night games on occasion. One such test, which lasted for two minutes during a game in early July, engendered a Red Smith column in which he asked where the umpires were going to go during a blackout. "Inhumane though it may seem to leave them out there in the shrapnel-spattered open, this course certainly is wiser than to toss them into a blacked-out dugout with 25 ballplayers."

One blackout test during an August game with the Dodgers lasted half an hour. Toward the end of the interruption restless smokers began to light up. Over the loudspeaker system Phils PA announcer Babe O'Rourke admonished, "You gentlemen who are lighting cigars and cigarettes, if you are Americans you won't do it." The smoking lamp was quickly extinguished, as they used to say in the military.

The Phillies did their part for the war effort in 1942. They donated the proceeds from a May 19 game with the Pirates to the Army-Navy relief fund. In spite of relentless urgings in the sports pages of the Philadelphia papers, only 3,366 showed up to watch the two worst teams in the National League in the first-ever twilight game at Shibe Park. At least the Phils won, 5–4, on Danny Litwhiler's bases-loaded triple in the eighth. The team would also be part of other charity games and would donate equipment and uniforms to the Army.

The biggest impact of the war on baseball, however, was in the area of manpower. Ballplayers were being drafted as early as 1941. The able-bodied men who remained behind were, as a song of the era went, "either too old or too young." Consequently, by midseason an unprecedented 25 percent of major-league rosters were populated by rookies. Ray Starr, who pitched for the Reds, was typical; a lifelong minor leaguer, he enjoyed his major-league rookie season at the age of 40. Lloyd Waner, who played for the Phils in 1942, had lost a lot of the speed that had made him a great player for the Pirates in the '30s, but at 36 he was past draft age. By June the minor leagues were suffering acute shortages of manpower; later that summer a team in the Western Association would activate its batboy. By the end of the war the Phils roster would include 16-year-old Putsy Caballero and seventeen-year-old Granny Hamner.

The manpower shortage went both ways. Late in the season pitcher Ike Pearson would enlist in the Marines, saying, "I want to be on a first-place team." In mid-September Hans Lobert, by then nearly 61 years old, would receive a notice requesting his presence before the local draft board. It seemed that in filling out his occupational questionnaire, Lobert had mentioned his years as West Point's baseball coach when Douglas MacArthur had been commandant of the Academy, and they wanted to learn more about his supposed military experience.

In their final spring training in Florida for the duration of the war, the Phils exhibition schedule began on an unpromising note. In an intersquad game they tied themselves, 3–3, suggesting that they were so bad, they couldn't even beat the Phils. The omen was an accurate one. They lost regularly in exhibition games with such traditional AL doormats as the Browns and the Senators. The regular season couldn't come too soon for the Phils.

Or could it? When it came, they were clearly not ready for its arrival, although Lobert said that his players "have plenty of spirit, their morale is high, and they're actually fighting to win games." Naturally, with that sterling attitude the Phils lost their season opener at home to the Braves, 2–1, in spite of a well-pitched game from Si Johnson.

That could be the story of the entire season, decent pitching and little or no hitting. As one baseball annual for 1943 noted, "The Phillies' pitching was far better than indicated in statistics. In spite of woefully weak hitting Tommy Hughes, [Rube] Melton, and Si Johnson did marvelous mound work."

The Braves would beat Philadelphia twice more in games that would set the tone for much of the remainder of the season. In the second game of the season knuckleballer Jim Tobin baffled Philly hitters while the Braves pounded out 16 hits in a 6–2 victory. In the third game of the year Tom Hughes pitched well but came out on the losing end of a 2–1 score largely because the usually swift-footed Murtagh, pinch-running for Ron "The Round Man" Northey in the ninth, stumbled on the base paths while taking a lead off third; he decided that, the damage done, he should head for home. Of course, he was tagged out. The Phils then managed a three-hit outburst, good enough to tie the game at a run apiece. If Murtagh hadn't been caught at the plate, they would have won the game then and there. Instead, they lost it in the tenth.

Lobert would sum things up elegantly in mid-June after the trading deadline passed with the Phils unable to swing a deal. "I need everything—from catchers, all the way around the infield to the outfield. Of course, the pitchers haven't been doing bad. I don't want sympathy—I want players who can win ball games."

While the Phillies lacked players who could win, they had no shortage of players who found imaginative ways to lose. For example, in a July 28 game against the Reds, the Phils achieved a rare feat, making three errors on a single batted ball. Gerald "Gee" Walker beat out a sizzler to Albie Glossop at second. Glossop hurriedly threw the ball to first—well, in that general direction. While Walker headed for second on the overthrow, first baseman Nick Etten retrieved the ball and fired it to third. Unfortunately, third baseman Merrill "Pinky" May was apparently out of the office and the ball went on its merry way, while Walker did the same. Walker scored, May was charged with an error for failing to cover his base, and Etten was charged with a wild throw.

Etten, it should be pointed out, managed a rare feat of his own during a typically inglorious 2–1 home loss to the Cubs. He spiked himself in the right heel while sliding into a base. It was one of those games, anyway. The Cubs scored their first run when Tommy Hughes gave up a dinger to Cubs pitcher Claude Passeau, and their second came as a result of a pair of fielding errors by Albie Glossop. Hughes also cost himself a run in a game against the Giants on April 22. He was on first when Stan Benjamin singled, advancing him to third until the Giants second baseman appealed, having duly noted that Hughes missed second completely. On August 28 they would lose a game to St. Louis by stranding seventeen base runners.

Another innovative performance occurred on September 2, when Frank Hoerst managed to lose a two-hitter. In the eighth he walked four batters and threw too low to the plate on a comebacker. Johnny Podgajny completed the disaster by hitting two batters with the bases still loaded. A few days later his teammates showed Hoerst their true feelings when they lost to the Braves in the second half of a doubleheader, Hoerst's last pitching performance before entering the Navy.

A few of the Phillies deserved better.

Danny Litwhiler, the Phils left fielder, went through the entire season, playing every ghastly inning of every game, without making a single error in 317 chances, then a record. He extended the streak into the following season, going a total of 187 games without a miscue. Litwhiler nearly lost the streak on a rainy day in the

Polo Grounds. The outfield was a quagmire when Johnny Mize hit a sinking line drive to left that Litwhiler gloved on the dead run. When he tried to set himself to throw the ball back in, his feet went out from under him and he dropped the ball. Litwhiler assumed the streak was over and it would be ten years before he knew why the official scorer, who had originally ruled it an error, changed his mind. Mize, who had been hitting .299 coming into the game, desperately wanted to reach the .300 mark, so much so that he ran up to the press box, in full uniform, to argue with the scorer after the game, convincing him to make the change.

Tommy Hughes would have a brief moment of a peculiar sort of glory in 1942. Hughes would go 12–18 with the Phils, with a 3.06 ERA, allowing only 224 hits in 253 innings. Only once during the season would the Phils give him a victory margin of more than one run.

Throughout the year writers would say that Hughes was as good as any righty in the league. The skinny 6–1 hurler turned in some impressive performances that year. Perhaps the most remarkable was a fifteen-inning victory over the pennant-winning Cardinals on June 28. Hughes pitched the entire 15 frames, holding the Cards to a single run. In the fifteenth he was grazed by a pitch, then had to run from first to third on a passed ball followed by a throwing error. By that time Hughes was so exhausted that Lobert had to hold him up until pinch runner Stan Benjamin could come into the game. He collapsed in the clubhouse and was revived by the team physician with a shot of brandy. He was in the bullpen the next day, ready to pitch if called upon. Lobert would tell journalists, "I wish I had eight more like him."

Hughes would go into the military after the season was over. When he came back to the majors in 1946, he was not the same pitcher. He would last two seasons with the Phils and part of another with the Reds.

Occasionally, the Phils would even win a game under bizarre conditions. For example, on July 14 they beat the Reds 2–1 on an inside-the-park homer by Rube Melton, of all people. Melton lofted a fly to left center, where Harry Craft and Max Marshall ran into each other in hot pursuit. Melton and catcher Ben Warren both scored. The Phils won another game against the Braves when Johnny Sain balked in the winning run in the bottom of the ninth.

More often, the Phils would win because their pitchers were just too stubborn to give up. Melton pitched a four-hitter against the Dodgers to win the first Philly victory of the year in the fourth game of the season, 2–1. He would throw a six-hitter to beat the Braves by the same score on May 29. Si Johnson would have to turn in the same kind of performances, going ten innings to beat Cincinnati 1–0 on June second. The next night Melton would do it again, defeating the Reds 2–1 and hitting a double to drive in the winning run in the tenth. On August 23 he would four-hit the Braves for a 2–0 shutout. Two days later he would get the last out for victor Johnny Podgajny in a game against the Cubs.

The Phils also had a pretty good record in exhibition games. They beat five minor-league teams and a team from Fort Dix on off days. They lost to Mickey Cochrane's Great Lakes Naval Station team, but that was to be expected. After all, Cochrane had a lot of major leaguers on his roster, something the Phils would have been hard put to claim.

Whatever else it was, the season wasn't dull. Hans Lobert repeatedly got into rhubarbs with the umps, trying to keep his perpetually last-place team fired up. On July 3 two fans were ejected from Shibe Park for throwing beer bottles at the Dodger dugout. That game also featured a protest from Lobert on a disputed home-run call in which two umpires disagreed. On September 15 Lobert, Chuck Klein, Mickey Livingston, and reserve first baseman Eddie Murphy charged into the stands and up to the second deck of Shibe to grab a heckler. They satisfied themselves with jawing with the leather-lunged patron and jamming him back into his seat.

Of course, there were the usual rumors that Nugent, strapped for cash, would sell Hughes and Melton, followed by the usual denials, which, for a change, turned out to be true, at least in Hughes's case. Bobby Bragan would be booed so vociferously after an error at short in late June that Red Smith would leap to his defense in a column. Bill Dooly tried to prod Branch Rickey in print into buying the team. Rickey had recently departed the Cardinals after a dispute with owner Sam Breadon.

In fact, one of the more amusing sidelights of the Phils' 1942 season took place in the pages of *The Philadelphia Record,* the paper that employed Dooly and Smith. In mid-June sports editor Bill Driscoll published the major-league standings in reverse order as a sop to the long-suffering fans of the city's two dismal baseball teams. Red Smith, who covered the A's as well as writing a column, replied with an open letter to his boss suggesting that after a few weeks of such jocular self-delusion a man would drop a net over Driscoll's head and cart him off. Smith suggested, instead, a special league for the two Philadelphia clubs, "setting them apart in a sort of detention area of their own where they can have a quiet little race all by themselves and won't have to worry about what the other teams are doing." He noted that the Phils were, at that point in the race, already seven games out of seventh place, while the A's were still taking turns in last, alternating with the White Sox. Therefore, he argued, the Phils had already established a claim on their own private party. He suggested calling it the "Phils League." Shortly thereafter the NL standings printed in the *Record* included a separate listing, "Bush League" under which the Phils could be found.

A few days later nine letters from readers were printed, berating Driscoll and Smith. They ran the gamut, from an attack on Connie Mack, who hadn't upgraded his ball club despite considerably better attendance than the Phils, to appeals to patriotism and sportsmanship.

The next day Bill Dooly, the Phils beat writer, weighed in. "I suppose all of us have now and then tried too hard for a laugh and not been funny," he wrote. "I think this is the case in our striving for humor at the expense of the Phils." However bad the team might be, he continued, they were "not so bush league in their human relations." He cited a pair of letters that were thumbtacked to the clubhouse bulletin board, thanking the team for donating uniforms and equipment to an Army Air Corps base in Sacramento where ex-Phil Joe Marty was stationed.

Finally, Driscoll authored a column parodying the famous

New York Sun "Yes, Virginia, there is a Santa Claus" editorial. He closed, "And just to prove to you, Virginia, that there is a Phillies in the Big Leagues we want you to look at the National League standings on this very page. There, 'way down at the bottom, you will find the Phillies. See? We're taking them out of the Bush League just for you, Virginia." Sure enough, at the bottom of the page, 26½ games out of first on June 22, were the Phillies.

Nobody would have blamed Hans Lobert for feeling despair, but that was not his mood. In spite of the team's impending hundredth loss, the 60-year-old manager was upbeat. "Shucks, I like it anyhow," he told beat writers in early September. "I've really enjoyed this season. I'm not down. We have a tail-end ball club but what the hell."

He waxed philosophical. "We haven't taken so many terrible beatings this year. With some breaks we'd have thirty games out of the loss column and in our wins. But a ball club's got to make its own breaks."

Strangely enough, now that their season was essentially over, now that all the jokes had been made, all the bizarre happenings had happened, the Phils would make a genuine contribution to the pennant race, one that would redeem them, if not in the eyes of their fans, at least in the eyes of the writers, players, and managers.

With only two weeks left in the season the Phillies started to play as if they were in the pennant race, and in a way they were. With the Dodgers and Cardinals dueling for first place and virtually every other team out of it, the Phils were scheduled to play both contenders eight times. They lost six of those games, but they did so in pitched battles. On the road in Brooklyn they dealt a serious blow to Dodger pennant hopes when they beat them in the first half of a doubleheader, 7–3, behind Tommy Hughes. That they lost the nightcap mattered little.

Against the first-place Cards at home the Phillies labored even more mightily. Typical of the series was a 3–2 loss in fourteen innings to St. Louis, a grueling war of nerves in which Si Johnson stopped the pennant-bound Redbirds for thirteen innings. As Bill Dooly's column headlined, PHILS FIND THEY CAN PLAY BALL.

Red Smith would write of those two series, "True, they made mistakes and committed errors. But there wasn't a moment in one of the games when they weren't in the struggle. From beginning to end they kept 'em all so close, they might have won every game." Just like Hans wanted it.

Fittingly, the season ended with the Cardinals clinching with a doubleheader sweep of the Cubs on the last day of the season while the Dodgers defeated the Phils in a meaningless game at Ebbets Field. The Phils were 62½ games behind the Cardinals. They had scored a pathetic 394 runs in 151 games, an astonishing 2.6 runs per game. Given that their team ERA was 4.12, it's a miracle that they won at all. They allowed 706 runs that season, 4.7 runs per game. It is a mark of how bad the fielding was that they allowed better than half an unearned run per contest. Well, at least they ended on an upbeat note.

For at least one Phil the blazing finale of the season would pay dividends. Danny Litwhiler nearly knocked himself unconscious scoring a run in one of the games against the Cardinals. Cardinals management was suitably impressed by the Phils outfielder and endeavored to acquire him early the following season. As a result he got a chance to play in the 1943 and 1944 World Series and won himself a World Series ring in the latter, something he wouldn't have done with the Phils. Litwhiler later coached baseball at Michigan State, where he numbered several future major leaguers among his players, including Steve Garvey and Rick Miller.

Nick Etten, in spite of a disappointing performance in 1942 (.264, eight homers, forty-one RBIs), would also luck out in Gerry Nugent's last housecleaning. He would be sold to the Yankees. He remarked, "Imagine a man in that environment hearing that he had been sold to the Yankees!" Etten would make the most of the opportunity, leading the AL in homers in 1944 and in RBIs in 1945. He would get his own World Series ring in 1943, but when the real major leaguers returned to baseball in 1946, he was on his way out. He finished his major-league career in 1947 with a fourteen-game stint with the Phils.

Rube Melton finished the 1942 season with a 9–20 record and a

3.70 ERA. That winter Nugent finally managed to send him to Brooklyn for cash. He never lived up to the promise that had led to his dramatic odyssey across the commissioner's desk. His best season in Brooklyn was 1946, when he went 6–3 with a 1.99 ERA. By the middle of the 1947 season he was gone from the majors.

Ron Northey, the beefy rookie who won the starting right fielder's job in spring training, underwent the most interesting journey in the majors. Northey's best season with the Phils, for whom he played until early in the 1947 season, came in 1944, when he had 22 homers and 104 RBIs, and led NL outfielders with 24 assists. He played decently as a part-timer with the Cards in 1948 and 1949, then was sent to the Reds and Cubs in rapid succession the following year. When he didn't play in the majors in 1951, most people assumed he was finished, but he enjoyed a surprising resurrection in 1955 with the White Sox as a pinch-hitting specialist, going 19 for 49 off the bench in 1955–6. Like Etten he finished his playing career with the Phils, only ten years later. When Danny Murtagh became manager of the Pirates, he hired Northey, a good friend as well as a former teammate, as one of his coaches. Northey's son Scott played briefly for the Royals in 1969.

Pinky May's son Milt had rather a longer career, longer than his father's too. Pinky, who hit only .238 during the 1942 season, would experience a slight comeback the following year, hitting .282. After that he went into the military and never made it back to the majors. Murtagh told Harrington Crissey, Jr., a story of Pinky's minor-league managerial days that is worth repeating. At the time Pinky was managing a Class D team in North Carolina in a game against a team whose catcher was his son, Milt. After Milt socked two home runs on his first two at bats, Pinky had his pitcher knock the kid down his third time at the plate. Murtagh recalled, "I told Pinky after the game, 'Pink, it's all right to throw at him, but if you hit him, you better not go home to Mama.' " Murtagh would manage Milt when he played for Pittsburgh, one of six teams the younger May would play for in 15 years in the majors.

After the 1942 season Gerry Nugent held another fire sale, unloading Etten, Bragan, and Melton. He probably would have sold Hughes, too, but the Army beat him to the skinny right-hander. At this point Bill Veeck entered the picture.

Veeck had already enjoyed his first success as a team owner and promotional genius with the Milwaukee AAA franchise, but he wanted a major-league team and he had a scheme that would have transformed the Phillies into the best team in major-league baseball almost immediately. Simply, he would buy the team from the perpetually beleaguered Nugent and stock it with players from the Negro League teams. He would have a team that was as good as any in baseball. It was a brilliant scheme. Veeck admitted years later that he made only one mistake. Out of respect for the man and his office, he informed Commissioner Kenesaw Mountain Landis of his intentions. Suddenly the National League owners took control of the franchise for the good of baseball, while Landis searched desperately for a buyer for the team.

He found one in William Drought Cox, who assembled a syndicate of eleven to purchase the club. The principal owner, Cox was a wealthy lumber magnate and it was assumed that he would be willing to put more money into the team than he would take out of it, a change from the Nugent regime. He made a sound first move when he hired Bucky Harris to manage the team. Harris was the first manager to take over the Phils since Harry Wright in 1884 who had actually handled a pennant winner. He had skippered the 1924–5 Senators and even had a World Series ring to show for their victory in the 1924 Fall Classic. *Baseball Magazine* would trumpet, PHILLY FANS ENVISION BRIGHTER LIFE AS COX-HARRIS REGIME TAKES HOLD.

They might have had reason to. In 1943 the Phils would escape from the basement, albeit briefly, moving up to seventh place. Of course, the honeymoon between Cox and Harris would be brief; Harris was fired after 90 games and replaced by Freddie Fitzsimmons. Still, it was progress of sorts.

Not everything the new regime tried worked. For example, they decided that the Phillies needed a new image and a new name. After a contest in which the fans would suggest the new team name, the owner selected Blue Jays. Andy Seminick, who played for the Phils from 1943 to 1951, long enough to participate in their second-ever pennant in 1950, recalled, "[It] stuck for a while, but it never really replaced Phillies. We were still considered the Phillies even though Blue Jays was on our jerseys." One group of people who were understandably put out about the name change were the students of Johns Hopkins University; their teams had been called the Blue Jays for years and they resented being identified with the Phutile Phils.

History has a way of biting back at people who try to resist its forward movement. Kenesaw Landis got a small bit of comeuppance at the end of the 1943 season when he was informed that Bill Cox, his handpicked owner for the Phils, had been betting on his own team. Cox admitted that he had placed "small, sentimental bets" on his new plaything, but only had bet on them to win. Landis, the man who had banished the Black Sox from the game, had no choice but to ban Cox from baseball. He would only serve one more year as commissioner, dying in 1944. Under Happy Chandler, his successor, baseball would have its first black player, Jackie Robinson.

Danny Litwhiler would play a small role in the successful integration of the game. At the time, he was playing for Cincinnati, a town not noted for its liberal racial attitudes. A lot of his teammates vowed they wouldn't play on the same field with a black. Litwhiler recalled in 1974, "I knew right then they were crazy. There was no way they were going to quit playing. Where were they going to get a job like they had?" Warren Giles, the president of the NL, asked Litwhiler if he would pose for a picture with Robinson when the Dodgers made their first appearance in the Queen City, hoping that such a public show of support might defuse some of the tensions. He readily agreed. Later Robinson signed a print of the photo for him and it was hung in his office at Michigan State throughout his tenure there.

If baseball was changing, so were the Phils. The Carpenter family bought out William Cox. They put money into scouting, into the farm system, into the major-league club. Gradually, the Phils climbed up the standings: last in 1944 and 1945, then fifth in 1946, then a slip back to seventh in 1947, back up to sixth in 1948. In 1949 the Phillies enjoyed their first season of winning baseball since 1917, finishing third with a record of 81–73.

The next year the team won the second pennant in its history, but lost the World Series to the Yankees in four straight games. Some habits are awfully hard to break.

1942 Philadelphia Phillies Roster

Player	POS	G	AB	R	H	2B	3B	HR	RBI	SB	BA
Stan Benjamin	OF-1B	78	210	24	47	8	3	2	8	5	.224
Bobby Bragan	SS-C	109	335	17	73	12	2	2	15	0	.218
Bill Burich	SS-3B	25	80	3	23	1	0	0	7	2	.288
Benny Culp	C	1	0	0	0	0	0	0	0	0	–
Nick Etten	1B	139	459	37	121	21	3	8	41	3	.264
Ed Freed	OF	13	33	3	10	3	1	0	1	1	.303
Albie Glossop	2B	121	454	33	102	15	1	4	40	3	.225
Bert Hodge	3B	8	11	0	2	0	0	0	0	0	.182
Chuck Klein	OF	14	14	0	1	0	0	0	0	0	.071
Ernie Koy	OF	91	258	21	63	9	3	4	26	0	.244
Danny Litwhiler	OF	151	591	59	160	25	9	9	56	2	.271
Mickey Livingston	C-1B	89	239	20	49	6	1	2	22	0	.205
Harry Marnie	Ut	24	30	3	5	0	0	0	0	1	.167
Pinky May	3B	115	345	25	82	15	0	0	18	3	.238
Ed Murphy	1B	13	28	2	7	2	0	0	4	0	.250
Danny Murtagh	Ut	144	506	48	122	16	4	0	27	13	.241
Earl Naylor	OF-P	76	168	9	33	4	1	0	14	1	.196
Ron Northey	OF	127	402	31	101	13	2	5	31	2	.251
Bill Peterman	C	1	1	0	1	0	0	0	0	0	1.000
Lloyd Waner	OF	101	287	23	75	7	3	0	10	1	.261
Bennie Warren	C	90	225	19	47	6	3	7	20	0	.209

Figures include games played with Philadelphia only.

Pitcher	G	IP	H	ERA	ShO	SV	SO	BB	W	L
Walter Beck	26	53	69	4.75	0	0	10	17	0	1
Cy Blanton	6	22	30	5.64	0	0	15	13	0	4
Hildreth Flitcraft	3	3	6	8.10	0	0	1	2	0	0
George Hennessy	5	17	11	2.65	0	0	2	10	1	1
Frank Hoerst	33	151	162	5.20	0	1	52	78	4	16
Tommy Hughes	40	253	224	3.06	0	1	77	99	12	18
Si Johnson	39	195	198	3.69	1	0	78	72	8	19
Gene Lambert	1	1	3	9.00	0	0	1	0	0	0
Andy Lapihuska	3	21	17	5.23	0	0	8	13	0	2
Paul Masterson	4	8	10	6.48	0	0	3	5	0	0
Rube Melton	42	209	180	3.70	1	4	107	114	9	20
Sam Nahem	35	75	72	4.94	0	0	38	40	1	3
Earl Naylor	20	60	68	6.12	0	0	19	29	0	5
Ike Pearson	35	85	87	4.54	0	0	21	50	1	6
Johnny Podgajny	43	187	191	3.91	0	0	40	63	6	14

Figures include games played with Philadelphia only.

Chapter 7
The 1952 Pittsburgh Pirates

WON: 42   LOST: 112   GAMES OUT OF FIRST: 54 1/2

DAYS IN FIRST: NONE

HOME RECORD: 23–54

ROAD RECORD: 19–58

LONGEST WINNING STREAK: 2

LONGEST LOSING STREAK: 10

Baseball gives you every chance to be great. Then
it puts every pressure on you to prove that you
haven't got what it takes. It never takes away the
chance, and it never eases up on the pressure.

—JOE GARAGIOLA

BOBBY DEL GRECO and Tony Bartirome grew up in
the Hill District of Pittsburgh in the late 1930s and early '40s. They
spent many lazy spring and summer afternoons learning how to
play ball in Washington Park. Tony played first base and Bobby,
faster and more agile, played the outfield. Like many kids they
dreamed of someday playing together in the major leagues.

"Maybe, someday, we'll be good enough to play for the Pirates, huh, Bobby?" Tony would say.

And Bobby would reply, "Maybe, but we got a lot of baseball
to learn."

One day, like something out of a boy's summer dream, Pie
Traynor, the Hall of Fame Pirate third baseman who was now a
scout for the team, watched Del Greco and Bartirome play and
was impressed. He became excited by their potential and eventually he was able to persuade Pirate management that these kids

---

♦ Joe Garagiola: The helmet was a Branch Rickey experiment that
worked better than the '52 Bucs. (Photo courtesy of the National
Baseball Library, Cooperstown, NY)

had promise. And so Tony and Bobby, both teenagers fresh out of high school, were signed and farmed out to the minors.

The good news is, both Del Greco and Bartirome made it to the Pirates for the start of the 1952 baseball season. The bad news is, they didn't quite fulfill their dream of playing in the major leagues.

Cruel as it may be to say, this was because the Pittsburgh Pirates of 1952 hardly counted as a major-league team. Finishing the season with a record of 42 wins and 112 losses, for a percentage of .273, 54$\frac{1}{2}$ games out of first place, and 22$\frac{1}{2}$ games behind the seventh-place Braves, they are a shoo-in for the worst team of that decade.

"If there was a new way to lose, we would discover it," said Joe Garagiola, who caught 118 games for the Pirates that year, and actually had a pretty decent season, batting .273. "We had a lot of triple-threat men—slip, fumble, and fall. They talk about Pearl Harbor being something; they should have seen the '52 Pirates. George Metkovich, our first baseman who had been around the big leagues, would holler at the umpires, 'For Pete's sake, grab a glove and help me out.' "

In many ways the team was an experiment conducted by the legendary Branch Rickey. "The Great Experiment," as Garagiola called it, "the ninth year of Mr. Rickey's five-year plan, which was known as Operation Peach Fuzz, but we were usually called the Singer Midgets and the Rickey-Dinks."

The team batting average that year was .231, 22 points below the league average, and the pitching staff had an ERA of 4.65, almost a full run higher than the league ERA of 3.73. As we mentioned in the introduction, the Pirates were last in practically every major statistical category, thus giving them more than a fighting chance of being the worst team of this century (the Cleveland Spiders being in a league all their own).

The Pirates that year were a team stocked primarily with rookies. In fact, the combined salary for the infield was, according to Ralph Kiner, $24,000, each player making the minimum of $6000. Over the course of the season 14 different players, including a catcher, Ed FitzGerald, were used at second and third bases. The clubhouse should have been outfitted with a revolving door, since, over the course of the season, 45 different players were listed on the team roster. Nevertheless, several times during the season, the team made road trips with only 18 players, seven under the major-league limit.

Perhaps the year is best summed up by Garagiola in the following passage from his book, *Baseball Is a Funny Game:* "In July our pitching and hitting slumped together, and we had a long losing streak. We got a break in August. One of our pitchers went home and we were rained out of five games. The thing that really hurt us that year was the terrible finish. We ended up losing 112 games out of 154. So that meant we won 42—not in a row, but we won them."

♦

The trouble began in 1946, when the Pirates were sold to a four-man syndicate that included crooner Bing Crosby and real-estate tycoon John W. Galbreath. During the war years the Pirates generally finished in the middle of the pack (they even managed a second-place finish in 1944). But as soon as the new ownership was in place, disaster struck. In 1946 and '47 they finished seventh. In 1948 they somehow managed to finish fourth; in '49 they returned to form, dropping back to sixth; and in 1950 they fell as far as they possibly could, into the cellar.

During this period Galbreath purchased a majority interest in the club, and as president he hired Branch Rickey with the hope that he could wave his magic wand and turn the team into a pennant contender.

Rickey, nicknamed "the Mahatma" due to his florid speech and tendency to pontificate on all kinds of subjects, especially baseball, had a well-deserved reputation as somewhat of a magician when it came to discovering and nurturing raw talent. He did this through the innovative technique of establishing a network of minor-league clubs. Through these "farm clubs" Rickey had turned the St. Louis Cardinals into a National League powerhouse in the 1930s.

After resurrecting the Cardinals, Rickey moved on to Brooklyn to do the same for the Dodgers. Here, while establishing the state-of-the-art spring-training complex at Vero Beach, Florida, he was the guiding force behind such innovations as batting cages, pitching machines, and batting helmets. Perhaps his greatest, and certainly most controversial, achievement was breaking the color line by introducing the first black, Jackie Robinson, into baseball.

By the late 1940s, however, Rickey was butting heads with Dodger owner Walter O'Malley; and so, at the end of the 1949 season, at 69 years of age, Rickey announced that he was leaving the Dodgers to join the Pittsburgh Pirates.

Upon signing, Rickey prophetically announced, "This is the greatest challenge I have faced in my more than 40 years in baseball." He also added, somewhat optimistically as it turned out, that within three years "the Pirates would be in a position to challenge for the pennant."

When Rickey joined the Pirates he was given pretty much a free hand—and he used it. On the recommendations of many of his former scouts, he quickly and indiscriminately signed dozens of free agents and bonus players. By the fall of 1951 he'd spent close to $500,000 for new "talent," most of which turned out to be disappointingly mediocre. In fact, Rickey's spending spree totaled far more than the four-year profit of somewhat over $400,000 that the team made from 1947 through 1950.

In 1951 the Pirates moved up a notch, finishing in seventh place, 32$1/2$ games out of first, but only four games behind the Reds. Ironically, this was to be the only time during Rickey's five-year reign that the team was to rise out of the cellar. Better times appeared to be around the corner. But appearances, as we all know, can be deceiving. In reality the Pirates were lucky to rise to seventh, since they barely managed to avoid last place by defeating the Cubs in the final game of the season.

That 1951 squad was a pretty hapless one in its own right. Infielder Danny Murtagh, who was to become one of the more successful managers in Pirate history, batted an appalling .199, while shortstop George Strickland didn't do much better, weighing in at .216. The only regulars who showed any talent were Ralph Kiner, who banged out 42 home runs, and Gus Bell, who, in his second year in the majors, led the league in triples with 12, had 16 home runs, and batted .278. The pitching staff consisted of Murry Dickson, Mel Queen, Bill Werle, Howie Pollet, Vern Law, and Bob Friend, all of whom were better-than-average pitchers suffering through mediocre years. One young pitcher, Cliff Chambers, actually threw a no-hitter against the Braves in May, a no-hitter that Ralph Kiner once described as "the worst no-hitter I ever saw; they were hitting line-drives everywhere."

By the time the season closed the Pirates qualified as an economic disaster area. In 1951 half as many fans paid their way into Forbes Field as had the year before. The corporate loss was set at $677,263, bringing the two-year deficit to more than $1 million. The team was hemorrhaging so much money at such an alarming rate that Galbreath was forced to dip into his own pocket to reduce the deficit.

◆

One of the problems facing Rickey as the 1952 season approached was the dearth of young talent, due in no small part to America's involvement in the Korean conflict. Still, Rickey was undaunted. He spent over $800,000 signing practically every prospect that was recommended to him. By the time this signing frenzy was over, the Pirates "owned" some four hundred players, ninety percent of them still in their teens.

"Out of quantity we get quality," "the Mahatma" opined, a theory that had worked wonders in St. Louis and Brooklyn but seemed doomed to failure in Steel Town.

As it turned out, most of Rickey's phenoms sputtered and failed miserably. For instance, consider the case of Class D farm pitcher Ron Necciai, about whom Rickey raved. "I've seen a lot of baseball in my time. There have only been two young pitchers I was certain were destined for greatness, simply because they had the meanest fastball a batter can face. One of those boys was Dizzy Dean. The other is Ron Necciai. And Necciai is harder to hit." Rickey's enthusiasm was understandable, since Necciai was a near legendary figure as a result of his having struck out 27 batters in an Appalachian League game, in 1952.

He was so hard to hit that he pitched only one season for the Pirates, won one, lost six, and had an earned run average of 7.08. The next season, due to ulcers and arm problems, he was forced to hang up his baseball spikes forever.

Oddly enough, even before the season began Rickey was angling to get rid of his only bona fide star, Ralph Kiner. In each of the six years Kiner had been in major-league baseball, he'd led the league in home runs, for a total of 257. In 1949 he hit 54 of them. In 1951 he hit 42 home runs and also led the league in runs with 124, and bases on balls with 137. His league-leading on-base percentage was .452, and his league-leading slugging percentage was .627. Not a bad set of statistics for a man denigrated by Rickey as someone who "has so many other weaknesses that if you had eight Ralph Kiners on an American Association team, it would finish last."

Naturally, with the kind of numbers Kiner had put up in 1951, he was looking for a substantial raise from his salary of $65,000. But just as naturally, Rickey was balking, which did not surprise Kiner one bit.

"Mr. Rickey is very clever about money," Kiner once said. "I remember one time Preacher Roe was holding out from the Dodgers when Rickey was over there. After a couple of conferences Rickey told Preach to stay home and think the offer over.

" 'And by the way,' Rickey told him, 'you can have my two hunting dogs if you want them.'

"So Preacher took the dogs out, and they were the finest hunting dogs he'd ever seen. He got to thinking that Mr. Rickey must be a pretty nice guy, and, well, maybe he should sign after all. So he signed the contract and sent it back.

"And you know, the day Preach put that contract in the mail, those dogs took out across the field and he hasn't seen 'em since!"

Rickey felt that this was the perfect time to dump Kiner, a time when he could get value for him, which to Rickey translated into more money to buy new players. During spring training he was asked point blank by a reporter if he would trade Kiner for three infielders. "I'd trade anybody for three infielders," he replied, without a moment's hesitation.

But no matter how much he wanted to dump Kiner, he couldn't do it without the consent of the owners. And so he began what amounted to a blatant disinformation campaign, an attempt to paint Kiner as the scapegoat for all the team's ills. He even went so far as to compose a little ditty for Galbreath's ears:

> Babe Ruth could run. Our man cannot.
> Ruth could throw. Our man cannot.
> Ruth could steal a base. Our man cannot.
> Ruth was a good fielder. Our man is not.
> Ruth could hit with power to all fields. Our man cannot.
> Ruth never requested a diminutive field to fit him. Our man does.

During spring training he also wrote Galbreath a letter citing 20 reasons why Kiner could not help the Pirates and should be cut loose. After painstakingly enumerating his reasons he beneficently added, "This relates only to his baseball value and certainly not to his personality. He is one of the nicest boys I ever met, but Ralph satisfies my requirements in only one respect—as a home-run hitter. To me that isn't enough."

But no matter what Rickey tried he was unable to convince his bosses that Kiner was worth more out of a Pittsburgh uniform than in. This was fine with manager Billy Meyer, who was a big Kiner fan.

"During all the time I managed the Pirates," Meyer commented to a *Sport* magazine writer after the close of the 1952 season, "there never was a time that Kiner didn't do everything I asked him to for the general good of the ball club. No matter what I said, it was perfectly okay with him. Having him bunt or play hit-and-run would have been ridiculous. Not only that, it would have been bad baseball too. You don't try to shoot a bird with a cannon, do you? He is our best hitter and anytime you order him to do anything else but hit away, you're throwing away your greatest power. When Ralph was in a slump we were licked. We all looked to him to lead the attack. Nine out of ten times he did. In my book he's one of the really great hitters—and a fine fellow to go along with it."

Bill Meyer had managed the Pirates since 1948. In 1910 he broke into baseball as a catcher for Knoxville in the Southeastern League, and his brief major-league career consisted of 113 games for the White Sox and A's in 1913, 1916, and 1917. After toiling eight years for Louisville in the American Association, Meyer succeeded Joe McCarthy as manager of the team. He proceeded to win a pennant his first year. He then managed sixteen years in the Yankee organization, winning several pennants along the way. He was offered the job as manager of the Yankees in 1946, but because he had recently suffered a heart attack, he declined. Instead, he returned to the minor-league Kansas City team and promptly won another pennant. In 1948, at the age of 56, he accepted the job as Pirate manager and was named *The Sporting News* Manager of the Year, as a result of his fourth-place finish.

From there it was all downhill. Nevertheless, Meyer was an extremely well respected baseball man, who had the reputation of being able to work well with young talent. This is something he would have plenty of opportunity to do with his 1952 squad.

♦

On February 18, one week prior to the official opening of spring training, the pitchers were asked to report to camp. This was a bit of unorthodox strategy proposed by Rickey, who felt that early batting practice was of little or no value to the regulars if the pitchers didn't have something of a head start. This way, Rickey reasoned, when the regulars did report, the pitchers could put something on the ball.

When the players arrived at the San Bernardino camp, there was a WELCOME PIRATES banner to greet them. Draped across the front of the hotel across the street there was also a huge banner. It read: THIS IS NATIONAL CRIME PREVENTION WEEK.

Spring training was more crowded than usual that year. More than fifty players reported, and in order to get a chance to properly assess their talent, eight more exhibition games had to be added to the schedule. According to *The Sporting News* only Gus Bell and Ralph Kiner appeared to have jobs locked up.

Meanwhile, trade rumors were flying. At the heart of them

was, of course, Kiner, who was still holding out for more money. But also, surprisingly enough, there was also talk of trading their ace starter, Murry Dickson. Dickson, because his six-pitch repertoire necessitated much experimentation, was called "the Thomas Edison of the mound." He was a rubber-armed pitcher with marvelous control and a baffling curve. But his toughest pitch was probably his slider, which, according to Gil Hodges, "comes at you like a bullet, breaks about six inches from the plate, and when you swing, all you hit is the air."

In 1946, after returning from the War, Dickson won fifteen and lost six for the Cardinals, good enough to lead the NL in won-lost percentage. In 1949 he was traded to the Pirates, where, used primarily as a relief pitcher, he won 12 and lost 14. In 1951, as a starter, he had his best year, going 20–16, which came as a surprise to many who thought of him primarily as a relief specialist.

Starting in 1947 and for the next eight years, he consistently threw over 200 innings per season. "I have an arm that never tires," he explained. "When I was a kid here in Leavenworth [after being born in 1916 in Tracy, Missouri, where he lived until he was ten, Dickson's family moved to Kansas], I played on four teams. Many times I pitched three games a day without trouble."

As a teenager he pitched for his local American Legion team. During that period he played in what was to become his most memorable game. It was Memorial Day 1933, and the team was playing the Topeka American Legion Junior in a holiday feature at the State Penitentiary at Lansing. When the game began the prison yard was filled with 1700 convicts and guards, plus a large crowd of spectators. In the second inning, in the middle of young Dickson's windup, a gunshot rang out and all hell broke loose. Eleven heavily armed prisoners led by Wilbur Underhill and Harvey Bailey, two infamous killers, had surrounded the warden, and the great Memorial Day Kansas prison break was under way.

"Sirens shrieked, women were screaming, shots were roaring all around," recalled Dickson. "Hundreds of 'good convicts' pushed us kids up against the neutral wall and stood there, their bodies offering us protection against any stray shots. I saw the eleven escaping convicts go over the wall on a ladder made in the prison twine plant. I remember the Topeka third baseman, a little chap, screaming, 'God, if I ever get out of here alive, this is one place I'll never see again.' We got out alive, all right, but the game was never finished."

One might suspect that many times during the 1952 season Murry Dickson had much the same sentiments as that Topeka third baseman.

In 1951, coming off his best season, Dickson was presented with the Dapper Dan Award for the figure who did the most to publicize Pittsburgh. Nevertheless, baseball being an unforgiving sport, Dickson was being dangled as trade bait to obtain infielders.

Evidently, however, there were no serious offers on the table and so, when spring training opened, Dickson was still a Pirate, although he may have wished he weren't. In one of the most dramatic reversals in baseball he *lost* 21 games, while winning fourteen. Still, the statistical records show that if anything Dickson actually pitched better than he had the year before, since his ERA dropped half a run from 4.02 to 3.57.

Among the highly touted rookies in camp was Bobby Del Greco. He was nineteen, fresh out of high school and draft proof (his brother was killed in World War II and he was the sole support of his widowed mother). Branch Rickey had already anointed him the outfielder of the future. "He is the best instinctive outfielder since the day of Terry Moore," Rickey excitedly if not prudently announced.

Another rookie in camp was Dick Groat, a two-time All America basketball player at Duke, who'd been the nation's leading scorer with a 23.2 average (he also signed and played part of the 1952-3 season with the Fort Wayne Pistons in the NBA, averaging 11.9 points in 26 games).

And then, of course, there was the second coming of Dizzy Dean, Ron Necciai, who, in response to a reporter's question concerning Branch Rickey's numerous philosophical "talks" to the team, replied, "Mr. Rickey is the only man I've ever listened to for more than fifteen minutes without falling asleep."

A week later the veterans began to report. Among them was

Clyde McCullough, who announced, "I'll be 34 on March 14, but I have the body of a man of 20 and the mind of a man of 50." McCullough was a strong-armed, fine defensive catcher who was reputed to be the last catcher to play without a chest protector.

Also in camp was veteran outfielder–first baseman George "Catfish" Metkovich (he was nicknamed by Casey Stengel when, while trying to pull a hook from a catfish, he injured himself). One of Metkovich's distinctions was that he was perhaps the only baseball player to also be a member of SAG. He appeared in a dozen or so movies, including Esther Williams's *Million Dollar Mermaid, The Jackie Robinson Story,* and *The Stratton Story.*

But movie making didn't stop the "Catfish" from honing his baseball skills. "If we're in a baseball picture," he said, "we always have some baseball equipment lying around. Miss [Doris] Day will play catch with us or even get into a pepper game. She's one of the nicest actors to work with."

He was once mistakenly introduced as Ralph Kiner, and in an effort to set the record straight he said, "Not for the kind of dough I'm making."

Even in spring training few Pirates were hitting. In 1951, during spring training the Pirates had had ten .300 batters, plus Gus Bell, who hit .446. In comparison this spring they had only two—Ted Beard and George Strickland—who managed to hit over .300.

When the 1951 season ended, you could count the assets of the Pittsburgh Pirates on one hand. One of those fingers would have had to represent outfielder Gus Bell.

Bell was hitting .400 at Indianapolis when he was called up to join the Pirates in 1950. He stuck around, hitting a solid .282 in 422 at bats. The next year he showed himself to be no flash in the pan, hitting .278, with 16 home runs, while leading the league in triples with twelve.

But Bell found himself at odds with Branch Rickey, which was to result in dire consequences for the '52 season. Bell's troubles with "the Mahatma" actually began in the spring of 1951, when he reported to training camp without being signed. "I didn't think there was anything wrong in that," explained Bell. "Others had done it before. But when Rickey saw me he wanted to know what I was doing there . . . he pointed out that I hadn't signed yet. He told me to go back home and then we'd talk contract. Heck, it's a long trip from California to Louisville, and I didn't have much money."

"I was so disgusted that I felt like forgetting all about baseball. I thought I had a pretty good year my first season, but I found out that Rickey doesn't believe in paying a player what he's worth."

To add fuel to the fire, just before the start of 1951 spring training Bell's mother-in-law was fatally burned in an industrial accident. In order to be with his young wife to help with the funeral arrangements, Bell had to miss one exhibition and one regular-season game. He heard about it from the boss. "You listen to Rickey, you'd have thought I committed a crime," said Bell.

In 1952 Bell again haggled over his contract. After finally coming to terms, Bell notified Pirate management that he and his family were making the trip to California by car. When he arrived, he heard complaints from Rickey about taking too much time.

Bell was brought north when training camp broke, but almost immediately he was shipped to the minor-league Hollywood squad, ostensibly at Bell's own request. Bell denied this, indicating instead that he was a victim of Rickey's vindictiveness. Still, Bell managed to play in 131 games for the Pirates in '52, though his average dipped to .250. At the end of the season Bell was shipped to Cincinnati, where he blossomed, showing both power (206 career home runs) and the ability to hit for average (.281 lifetime).

When camp broke that spring, the Pirates had promoted a whopping thirteen rookies to the parent club. Among them were Bobby Del Greco, 19, his pal, Tony Bartirome, 19, pitcher Jim Waugh, 18, infielder Lee Walls, 19, pitcher Ron Kline, 20, infielder Dick Hall, 21, pitcher Ed Wolfe, 23, and outfielder Brandy Davis, 23.

Obviously, this infusion of youth couldn't help but give the Pirates the look and feel of a minor-league team. Which, at times, is just how they played.

The pitching staff, however, was another story. The mainstays, Murry Dickson, 35, Howie Pollet, 31, and Ted Wilks, 36, were all a little long in the tooth. In fact, as *Sporting News* cruelly pointed out when all three faced the Senators in a spring-training game, this trio represented 102 years of age.

Howie Pollet began his career with the Cardinals in 1941. He had two superior years with the Cards: 1946, when he led the league in wins with 21, while losing ten; and 1949, when he was again a 20-game winner, while losing nine. He was traded along with Ted Wilks, Joe Garagiola, Dick Cole, and Bill Howerton (for Wally Westlake and Cliff Chambers) to Pittsburgh in the middle of the 1951 season, while 0–3, and ended the year with a 6–13 record.

According to Jackie Robinson, Pollet, whose career record was 131–116, "was one of the toughest pitchers I ever faced. He threw a fastball and most of his other pitches with the same motion."

Unfortunately, he was to fool few opponents in 1952, going 7–16, with a 4.12 ERA.

Ted Wilks, obtained with Pollet, had joined the Cards in 1944, when he was already 28 years old. In large part due to his excellent control he surprised everyone by compiling a 17–4 record, for a league-leading .810 winning percentage. For the years 1946 to 1950 Wilks went 30–9. In 1946 (8–0) and 1947 (4–0), used primarily in relief, he was undefeated. In 1949 his 59 appearances, ten relief wins, and nine saves were league highs. In his split season with the Cards and Pirates in 1951, he once again led the NL in games pitched with 65 and saves, with 13. In 1952 he was one of the few Pirate pitchers to have a fairly decent season, appearing in 44 games and going 5–5.

Also on the staff was Bob Friend. The previous year, as a rookie, Friend had gone 6–10 with a 4.27 ERA. Bobby probably didn't think things could get any worse, but they did. Friend was fated to lose 17 games in 1952 while only winning seven, yet better times were on the horizon. In 1955 he became the first player to lead a major league in ERA (2.83) while pitching for a last-place club. In 1958 he tied for the league lead (with Warren Spahn) with 22 wins against 14 losses, and in four other seasons he managed to win 17 games or more. Still, in his 15 seasons with the Pirates he pitched on five last-place teams and is the only pitcher to have lost more than two hundred (230) games, while winning fewer than two hundred (197).

The other members of the staff, which included, at one time or another, folks like William Bell, Don Carlsen, Harry Fisher, Calvin Hogue, Ron Kline, Paul LaPalme, Harry Main, Joe Muir, George Munger, Mel Queen, and Jim Waugh, were either rookies or cast-offs.

Before the close of spring training Pirate fans did have something to cheer about. It was announced that Ralph Kiner was finally able to settle his salary dispute with the club, signing for $75,000, a $10,000 raise over his 1951 stipend. Thus, the cast of characters for the 1952 season was securely in place.

♦

The Pirates' opening game was against the Cardinals. The Bucs were behind from the beginning all the way to the end. They did manage a rally, three singles in a row, but it was killed when Clyde McCullough and his 50-year-old mind in a 20-year-old body was picked off first base. Later, shortstop Clem Koshorek tripped over Cardinal catcher Del Rice's foot at the plate and was tagged out.

From that inauspicious beginning things actually got worse for the Pirates. They won only two out of their first seven games, those two being won by rookie pitcher Joe Muir and sophomore Bob Friend. In the first week Dickson and Pollet lost two starts each. In his first 14 innings Dickson gave up ten runs and 15 hits. Pollet gave up 12 earned runs and 15 hits in 11⅔ innings.

In one game against the Reds, manager Bill Meyer used 20 players, ten of them rookies. In fact, in those first seven games Meyer, trying desperately to come up with a winning combination, started seven different lineups.

The day before they lost their third straight game to the Reds, Pirate management announced they would probably train in Havana the next spring. One Red cracked, "Wait until those Cubans get a load of this Pirate act. It might start another revolution!"

During an early ten-game losing streak Meyer used 31 pitchers in eight of the games. They rewarded his spreading out of the work load by giving up 72 runs and 97 hits during this period.

Rickey's pet project, Bobby Del Greco, started the season on fire. He had three-hit games in two of his first four starts. But it was hardly enough to take Pirate fans' minds off the awful truth: that, as a team, they were little better than a Triple-A club.

As Joe Garagiola put it, "With all our inexperienced players we got off to a slow start. We lost ten out of the first fourteen and then had a slump."

Using a host of rookies presented some unique problems for Bill Meyer and his staff. The majority of his club was so raw that he was forced to use three simple offensive signals.

"When a coach puts his hands on his cap, that means hit," Meyer explained. "When he rubs his belt, you bunt, and when he rubs the letters on his uniform, that means to take the pitch."

"But excuse me," one rookie interrupted, "you didn't say which coach would give the signals."

Apropos of this aspect of the Pirate game, Joe Garagiola wrote, "I have often said that the 1952 Pirates . . . were the only ball club that I knew that had foolproof signs. Nobody ever got our signs. Many of the clubs thought they had them, but we would miss our own signs so much they could never prove it."

♦

It didn't take long for Pittsburgh fans to give up on their team. As Samuel Goldwyn might have remarked, "They stayed away in droves." On April 25, for instance, a mere 1,945 fans showed up at Forbes Field.

By mid-May the Pirates were mired in last place and virtually the whole team was in a batting slump, with the club average an embarrassing .206. Ralph Kiner was hitting .217; George Metkovich, .215; Joe Garagiola, .200; and Clyde McCullough, .124.

In addition to his troubles at the plate McCullough was also having his problems with management, problems that prompted McCullough to question his value to the organization.

The Phillies' Richie Ashburn was on second base with one out in the sixth inning when Don Carlsen knocked down a drive by

Granny Hamner and threw to first for the putout. Ashburn raced around third and headed home. First baseman Tony Bartirome threw to the plate, but McCullough made a late tag and Ashburn slid in safely. Branch Rickey, who evidently didn't like what he saw, picked up the phone in his private box and called the dugout. The next thing McCullough knew he was on the bench and Joe Garagiola was behind the plate.

McCullough steamed. After the game he confronted Meyer in the locker room. "I've been in this game a long time," he said, "and never have been insulted in this way. I can't catch here after what happened. I've never been shown up like this before. I think I would be better off if you sold or traded me."

Unfortunately for McCullough, the incident blew over and he remained with the club for the rest of the season.

No matter what lineup poor Billy Meyer tried, his team still managed to lose. In one stretch the Bucs scored only one run in 30 innings. During this period Kiner went one for 19, then two for 25. When he walked with the bases loaded in the first inning of a game against Chicago, forcing in a run, it was his first RBI in ten straight games.

When his regulars, such as they were, didn't hit, Meyer was forced to go to his bench, which didn't offer much relief. In the first 24 games Meyer called on a total of 50 pinch hitters. Only five of them came through with hits. Worse yet, 19 of them struck out.

By the time the Pirates had lost 30 out of the first 36 games they played, the fans and sportswriters were understandably restless. Many clamored for a trade. Rickey heard the din, but what could he do? "No Pirate has performed well enough to attract attention," he complained, and who could argue with him?

Opposing pitchers seemed to present unsolvable mysteries for the Pirates. Only two Bucs were hitting over .300, second baseman Johnny Merson, and Pete Castiglione. The average for the rest of the team was .222.

Some of the veterans tried to smooth the way for the rookies through their experience, but as Joe Garagiola explained, it wasn't easy.

George Metkovich was one of the players that had an answer for every pitch. We were playing the Braves in Boston on a cold night (another one of our many private games that year). [Max] Surkont was the Boston pitcher. Late in the game we were hurting for a base hit. Bill Meyer . . . looked down the bench and said, "Cat, grab a bat and hit. You know this Surkont pretty good."

"Yeah, I played against him last year out on the Coast," Metkovich said.

So he went up to hit. First pitch was a fastball for a called strike. Cat backed out, rubbed some dirt on his hands. Next pitch was a fastball that the Catfish took for strike two. Back out of the batter's box, looked around, and back in. Next pitch a fastball and called strike three. Metkovich came back to the bench, politely put his bat in the bat rack, and sat down. "He threw me that radio ball," said Metkovich.

"Radio ball?" asked Dick Groat, then a rookie.

Metkovich looked up and said, "You can hear it, but you can't see it."

The veterans also offered advice. Like the time the Pirates were playing in Cincinnati. "Bubba Church was pitching for the Redlegs with a two-run lead going into the sixth," recalled Garagiola. "Gus Bell . . . hit a home run on the first pitch. Ralph Kiner hit a home run on a two-ball, no-strike pitch to tie the game, and I came up and hit the first pitch for a home run to break the tie.

"Bobby Del Greco . . . was the next hitter. On the first pitch down he goes. Up he comes. Next pitch and down he goes. On the two–two pitch he flied out to the left fielder. When Del Greco came back to the bench he sat down next to Clyde McCullough. . . . Bobby said, 'Man, he's wild! I thought he was supposed to have pretty good control.'

"McCullough, the philosopher, looked at Bobby and in his best southern drawl said, 'Son, when the three previous hitters have hit the ball out of the park, go up there and go down before you see the whites of their eyes.' "

♦

Rickey and the rest of the Pirates also had to deal with some of the critical barbs coming from the other teams, as well from sportswriters. For instance, the following passage appeared in *The Sporting News* of July 9, concerning a game played on June 29:

> The Pirates were on their third-longest losing streak of the year when the rain came to their rescue. The Bucs held a 3–2 lead over the Cards at the end of five innings in the first half of a doubleheader when a thunderstorm burst over Pittsburgh and called off festivities. The Bucs had lost seven straight prior to the storm and previously had dropped ten in a row, six in a row, and eight in a row.

"We'll have some of these teams crying before long," Rickey threatened, which, as things turned out, may have been the case, but obviously not for the reasons he had in mind.

Amazingly, the Bucs didn't win their first game against a lefty until May 29. Unfortunately, not many people in Pittsburgh knew about it, since only 1,070 fans showed up to witness the prodigious feat.

Perhaps the man suffering most from the club's ineptitude was Murry Dickson. In May he lost three straight but gave up only nine earned runs and 21 hits. According to newspaper accounts his fastball seemed to be even better than it was the year before when he'd won 20. Yet he kept on losing. By the time September rolled around, Dickson had suffered through his twentieth setback, making him the first Pittsburgh pitcher in this century to lose 20. He was also the first pitcher in the NL to lose 20 games after winning 20 the year before since Joe Oeschger did it for the Braves in 1922.

In fact, Dickson's twentieth loss was a rather memorable one, coming as it did in a 13-inning duel against the Giants, when Don Mueller, leading off the inning, rapped his tenth homer into the nearby right-field seats. It also happened to be Dickson's twentieth complete game of the season, his eighth one-run setback, and the eighth straight game he lost due to a home-run ball.

By the time the end of July rolled around, Meyer must have been pulling his hair out. George Strickland and Tony Bartirome were still hitting below .200. To Ralph Kiner, Gus Bell, Dick Groat, and Bobby Del Greco .250 was still as elusive as the Holy Grail.

And then, just when Billy Meyer thought things probably couldn't get any worse, they did. Injuries, including a broken elbow suffered by first baseman–outfielder Pete Castiglione when he was hit by a pitched ball, brought the Pirate roster down to twenty. The next day Ted Wilks pulled a thigh muscle and the count was nineteen, only seven of them pitchers.

Ah, but there was a ray of hope . . . of sorts. Luck, which had been conspicuously absent from the Pirate lineup since opening day, threatened to join the team.

In mid-July, Dick Groat was in the throes of a terrible slump, going zero for nineteen. After a game against Boston, Les Biederman, baseball writer for the *Pittsburgh Press* and *The Sporting News,* approached an obviously dejected Groat in the locker room and said, "Here, put this ten-cent piece in your uniform pocket for good luck. You might go four for four today."

Groat shoved the coin in his pocket and that afternoon against the Braves he went five for five. And in the next two games the rookie had three singles and hit three hard line drives for outs.

The next day Biederman told Ralph Kiner the story and gave him a quarter to put in his uniform pocket for luck.

"I gave Dick Groat a dime yesterday and he got five singles," Biederman explained. "Maybe this quarter will help you hit a home run."

His first time at bat Kiner fouled out. Next time he walked. In his third appearance he stroked a home run against the scoreboard, breaking a zero-for-twenty hitless string.

This sort of baseball black magic was old hat to Biederman, who, in 1943 when he was in New Guinea with the Air Force, sent Rip Sewell, Bob Elliot, and Vince DiMaggio each an Australian shilling for good luck. That season Sewell won 21 games, Elliot led the Pirates in hitting with .315, driving in 101 runs, and DiMaggio led the Bucs in home runs (fifteen) and was selected for the All-Star team.

Meanwhile, Groat, whether due to Biederman's good-luck coin or not, was beginning to find his batting eye. He finished that Braves series with eight hits in thirteen trips to the plate, jumping his average from .216 to .250. And, as one of the few bright spots on the Pirate team, he ended the year batting an impressive .284.

The Pirates were now not only losing games but also losing money at an alarming rate. This was understandable, as fans refused to pay major-league money to see minor-league players. Management figured they had to do something to get folks back into the park, so they came up with the brilliant idea of giving hometown boy Bobby Del Greco a Night. Though it may have been an esthetic and economic success, as far as Del Greco was concerned the "honor" was a dubious one. A mere 24 hours after celebrating the "Night" named in his honor, he was unceremoniously optioned to Toronto. He was batting .208 at the time.

The Pirates reached a milestone of sorts on September 7, when they lost their hundredth game. The countdown had begun. Only 12 more losses to go.

One interesting side note is that Pittsburgh was the end of the road for one player who was to move on to some renown in another area, John Berardino, while it was the beginning of the road for another, Frank Thomas, about whom we shall hear more of in the next chapter.

Berardino, who had appeared in a few of the *Our Gang* comedies as a child actor, began his career with St. Louis in 1939. (As a publicity stunt Bill Veeck once insured his face.) He was a utility man who was called a "one-man infield," an allusion to his versatility. He played for the Cardinals until 1948, when he was traded to the Indians. In 1950 he was traded to the Pirates; then, in '51, he was back with the Cards. In '52 he began the season with the Indians, and then ended it with the Pirates, where he played only nineteen games. He fit in fine, batting .143 in 56 at bats (his career average was .249). The next year he was out of baseball and things became so bad, he had to hock his 1948 Cleveland Indian World Series ring. Dropping the second *r* in his name, he finally decided to return to acting and became rather well known for playing the part of Dr. Steve Hardy on the soap opera *General Hospital*.

Frank Thomas began his career with the Pirates in 1951. He played in only 39 games and batted .264. When the 1952 season opened, Thomas was not on the team. He was brought up during the season, but he appeared in only six games and batted a minuscule .095 (one hit in 21 at bats). Better days were in store for him (and some worse ones too). In 1953, with Kiner gone, Thomas, who was a big man at six-foot-three and 200 pounds, was tabbed as his successor. That year he almost filled Kiner's shoes, slugging 30 home runs and knocking in 102 RBI.

That season was especially tough on someone like Ralph Kiner, who, although he was having a relatively miserable year at the plate, batting only .244 (35 points below his career average), had not lost his power. He wound up leading the league in home runs with 37 (tied with Hank Sauer of the Cubs), making it a record seven consecutive times that he'd led the league in that category, and bases on balls with 110. This was typical for Kiner in his years with the Pirates, because opposing pitchers could always pitch around him, which makes his lifetime home-run total of 369 even more astounding.

In an interview that appeared in Donald Honig's *Baseball Between the Lines,* Kiner mused about playing with a loser.

"Throughout most of my years with the Pirates we were a second-division club, and there's no question about it, the hardest thing in the world is to play on a losing team. The mistakes and the failures are all the more glaring and frustrating. It's an altogether different game when you're winning; it's easier to play and, obviously, more enjoyable. I always had a strong competitive drive and I hated to lose. I took an awful lot of pride out on that field with me. . . ."

For Dick Groat, who went on to have a marvelous career with the Pirates (especially in 1960, when he hit a league-leading .325 and helped pace the Bucs to the World Championship over the Yankees), it was an interesting introduction into major-league baseball.

"The funny thing about it all now," Groat recalled, "is the players didn't realize how bad a team we were. The club was loaded with young guys like me and we all thought we were hotshots. We were sort of like a high-school team that had won a state high-school tournament and gone to Yankee Stadium to beat the Yankees. We had the enthusiasm, foolish enthusiasm.

"Even in the cellar we thought we were pretty good. On days we were clobbered, say ten to one or thirteen to two, we would just sit around the clubhouse or the bus taking us to the airport brooding like high-school cheerleaders. The next day we played like it was a World Series. I firmly believe we were overwhelmed more by our own enthusiasm and overestimate of our own ability than by any ball club. They didn't beat us, we beat ourselves."

And they did it 112 times.

♦

The next year the Pirates improved, slightly. They won 50 games and lost 104. Still, Branch Rickey prevailed. On June 4 the Pirates traded Kiner, Joe Garagiola, Howie Pollet, and George Metkovich to the Cubs for six second-string players: pitcher Bob Schultz, catcher Tobie Atwell, outfielder Gene Hermanski, first baseman Preston Ward, outfielder Bob Addis, and $150,000 in cash.

Kiner spent the rest of the 1953 season with the Cubs, playing in the outfield alongside Hank Sauer, with whom he'd shared the home-run lead in 1952. He was suffering from back problems, but nevertheless Kiner managed to hit 35 home runs in 1953 (seven of them were hit while he was still a Pirate), and then hit 22 homers in 1954. Before the 1955 season opened, Kiner was traded to the Cleveland Indians. Plagued by back problems he could not overcome, this turned out to be his final season. In only 321 at bats Kiner rapped 18 home runs, giving him a career total of 369, leaving him with an average of one home run hit in every 14.1 at bats. In 1975 Kiner, who now broadcasts the New York Met games, was elected to the Hall of Fame.

Joe Garagiola has made a career out of making fun of himself over what he purports to be his somewhat less than mediocre baseball skills. For the most part these jokes obscure the fact that Garagiola was actually a pretty good ballplayer. For instance, while all else around him was going to hell, Garagiola did hit .273 for the Pirates in 1952. And the next year he hit .272 for the Cubs.

The next year, playing for the Cubs and then for the Giants, while appearing in only 68 games, he batted .280, giving him a career average of .257 for his nine years in the major leagues. In 1955 he began his broadcasting career with the Cardinals.

After trading Kiner, Garagiola, and Metkovich, Rickey wasn't finished cleaning house. He then turned around and traded his best pitcher, Murry Dickson, to the Phillies for $72,500 and two players.

The 1952 season was the last straw for Billy Meyer. Before the start of the 1953 season he phoned Rickey and said he could not continue managing the team due to serious personal problems, which most certainly included his precarious health. Later, Meyer worked as a scout for the Pirates. He died in 1957, at the age of 65.

You would also be hard pressed to find any familiar names in the 1953 lineup from the year before. Rickey hired Fred Haney to take Meyer's place, and he and his new manager were the brooms that swept the roster clean, so much so that by the end of the season the only player of note left from the '52 squad was Bob Friend.

Ironically, the one budding star Rickey discovered in 1952, Dick Groat, was lost to the team for the next two years, as he fulfilled his military service. When he returned, in 1955, the Pirates were still in familiar territory: last. In fact, it wasn't until 1958 that the team finally began showing signs of life, rising from the lock they'd held on seventh place for the last two years to come in second, eight games behind Milwaukee. From that time on the Pirates, led by Danny Murtagh, were a team to be reckoned with.

We're not sure if it had anything to do with the horrible season the Pirates had in 1952 but, not unlike the Boston Braves, who thought a name change might make people forget about the miserable season they'd had, Pirate management decided to remove the name Pittsburgh from the face of the travel uniforms. It was not to return to its rightful place on the chests of Buc players until the 1990 season. Maybe the Chamber of Commerce preferred it that way.

1952 Pittsburgh Pirates Roster

Player	POS	G	AB	R	H	2B	3B	HR	RBI	SB	BA
Tony Bartirome	1B	124	355	32	78	10	3	0	16	3	.220
Ted Beard	OF	15	44	5	8	2	1	0	3	2	.182
Gus Bell	OF	131	468	53	117	21	5	16	59	1	.250
Pete Castiglione	3B	67	214	27	57	9	1	4	18	3	.266
Brandy Davis	OF	55	95	14	17	1	1	0	1	9	.179
Bobby Del Greco	OF	99	341	34	74	14	2	1	20	6	.217
Ervin Dusak	OF	20	27	1	6	0	0	1	3	0	.222
Ed FitzGerald	C	51	73	4	17	1	0	1	7	0	.233
Joe Garagiola	C	118	344	35	94	15	4	8	54	0	.273
Dick Groat	SS	95	384	38	109	6	1	1	29	2	.284
Dick Hall	OF	26	80	6	11	1	0	0	2	0	.138
Bill Howerton	3B	13	25	3	8	1	1	0	4	0	.320
Ralph Kiner	OF	149	516	90	126	17	2	37	87	3	.244
Clem Koshorek	SS	98	322	27	84	17	0	0	15	4	.261
James Mangan	C	11	13	1	2	0	0	0	2	0	.154
Clyde McCullough	C	66	172	10	40	5	1	1	15	0	.233
John Merson	2B	111	398	41	98	20	2	5	38	1	.246
George Metkovich	1B	125	373	41	101	18	3	7	41	5	.271
Jack Phillips	1B	1	1	0	0	0	0	0	0	0	.000
Manny Senerchia	3B	29	100	5	22	5	0	3	11	0	.220
Dick Smith	3B	29	66	8	7	1	0	0	5	0	.106
George Strickland	2B	76	232	17	41	6	2	5	22	4	.177
Frank Thomas	OF	6	21	1	2	0	0	0	0	0	.095
Lee Walls	OF	32	80	6	15	0	1	2	5	0	.188

Figures include games played with Pittsburgh only.

Pitcher	G	IP	H	ERA	ShO	SV	SO	BB	W	L
William Bell	4	16	16	4.60	0	0	4	13	0	1
Don Carlsen	5	10	20	10.80	0	0	2	5	0	1
Murry Dickson	43	278	278	3.57	2	2	112	76	14	21
James Dunn	3	5	4	3.58	0	0	2	3	0	0
Harry Fisher	8	18	17	6.87	0	0	5	13	1	2
Bob Friend	35	185	186	4.18	1	0	75	84	7	17

Pitcher	G	IP	H	ERA	ShO	SV	SO	BB	W	L
Calvin Hogue	19	84	79	4.84	0	0	34	68	1	8
Ron Kline	27	70	74	5.40	0	0	27	66	0	7
Paul LaPalme	31	60	56	3.92	0	0	25	37	1	2
Forrest Harry Main	48	153	149	4.46	0	2	79	52	2	12
Joe Muir	12	36	42	6.31	0	0	17	18	2	3
George Munger	5	26	30	7.27	0	0	8	10	0	3
Ron Necciai	12	55	63	7.08	0	0	31	32	1	6
Howard Pollet	31	214	217	4.12	1	0	90	71	7	16
Mel Queen	2	3	8	29.70	0	0	3	4	0	2
Jim Suchecki	5	10	14	5.40	0	0	6	4	0	0
Jim Waugh	17	52	61	6.36	0	0	18	32	1	6
Ted Wilks	44	72	65	3.63	0	4	24	31	5	5

Figures include games played with Pittsburgh only.

Chapter 8
The 1962 New York Mets

WON: **40**   LOST: **120**   GAMES OUT OF FIRST: **60½**

DAYS IN FIRST: **NONE**

HOME RECORD: **22–58**

ROAD RECORD: **18–62**

LONGEST WINNING STREAK: **3**

LONGEST LOSING STREAK: **17**

> You know, they's teams been playing together
> forty years and they's still finishin' down in last
> place or something. Just because you have a team,
> that don't mean it got to finish on top.

—MARV THRONEBERRY

IT WAS April 9, 1962, and there was a definite aura of anticipation and excitement in the air. At least that's the way it felt for the New York Mets, who had just landed in St. Louis, where the next day they would be making their debut as one of the two new entries in the National League.

A group of 28 Mets, plus assorted coaches, newspaper reporters, and supporters, emerged from the bus after it pulled to a stop in front of the Hotel Chase. Most of the passengers dispersed in different directions, perhaps to get a bite to eat, or to check out the action in the hotel lobby. But a group of road-weary Met players, 16 in all, spiffily attired in their spanking new blue team blazers, moved directly to the front desk, where they received their keys and then made their way to the elevator that would take them to their rooms. Among this group was Opening Day pitcher Roger Craig and his battery mate, Hobie Landrith.

The elevator arrived and all sixteen players pushed their way

---

♦ **Marv Throneberry: The legend himself.** (Photo courtesy of the National Baseball Library, Cooperstown, NY)

on. The doors closed. The elevator began to move. Only, it didn't move quite far enough. Two and a half floors, to be exact. And then it stopped. The sixteen players looked at each other. They looked at the door. They looked back at each other. They waited. They listened to a recorder in the elevator that announced that "dinner in the Tenderloin Room is now being served. Charcoal broiled steaks the succulent specialty of the house." They listened to this announcement once. They listened to it twice. In all they listened to it 67 times.

"I knew it," moaned Roger Craig. "The first time in my life I'm going to open a season, I get stuck in an elevator. I'll probably be here for 24 hours."

"It wasn't so bad for the other guys," the five-foot-ten-inch Hobie Landrith recalled afterward. "I'm not built high enough. I couldn't get any air down where I was."

Eventually, their screams were heard by someone in the hotel. An elevator repairman was immediately dispatched to the scene and twenty minutes later the Mets, all sixteen of them, were freed from elevator bondage.

As it turned out, there was no immediate rush. The next day it rained, so Opening Day was pushed back. And when you consider how the Mets did that first year of their existence, would being stuck in an elevator for the entire season have been so bad?

♦

How bad were the 1962 Mets? Bad enough that they set a modern major league (162-game schedule) record for losses in a season—120—and the fewest wins—40. Bad enough that their team batting average of .240 was 21 points below the league average and 38 points below the average of the pennant-winning Giants. Bad enough that their team ERA was a bloated 5.04, more than a run above the league average of 3.94. And bad enough that their .967 fielding average put them last in the league.

There's more. That year the Mets gave up a total of 948 runs, 322 more than the fourth-place Pirates. They had losing streaks of nine, eleven, thirteen, and seventeen games; and they wound up

60 1/2 games out of first place; eighteen games behind the ninth-place Cubs.

But these are only figures. The true measure of how bad the New York Mets were in 1962 comes in *how* they played the game and *who* they were. For this was a team so inept yet so lovable that it is to be remembered and immortalized for all time. If you like to think of baseball purely as a form of entertainment, as some romantic souls insist upon doing, then the 1962 Mets have to be considered as one of the most entertaining losing teams of all time. They didn't win, well, they hardly ever won, but they sure as heck kept their fans, and there were plenty of them, mightily entertained.

Once upon a time there was no such team as the New York Mets. It was a time when baseball was played primarily between the foul lines. It was a time when fans came to the ballpark to see their team win; and if they didn't win, they stopped coming to the park.

But a new era in baseball was to dawn shortly after the 1960 World Series, when the National League announced that they would be awarding two new franchises. One of them would be in Houston, the other in New York. This was fine with New Yorkers, who had been clamoring for an NL team ever since the Dodgers and Giants drove a double stake through the hearts of the fans when they abandoned the city in the mid–1950s.

Thus was the league expanded to ten teams and thus did Mrs. Charles Shipman Payson, the former Joan Whitney, a woman worth several hundred million dollars in her own right, find herself the principal owner of a baseball team. To actually oversee the team affairs she appointed M. Donald Grant. In turn Grant wanted Branch Rickey to run the club. However, the venerable Mr. Rickey wanted, as usual, a free hand along with several million dollars to develop talent (we've already seen what this free hand gripping mucho bucks did for the Pirate teams of the late 40s and early 50s). Grant, with the heart and nature of a Wall Street banker, balked.

Instead, in mid-March 1961, seventy-one-year old George Weiss, formerly general manager of the Yankees (he had "voluntarily" resigned a month earlier in deference to a newly instated retirement age of sixty-five), was appointed president and Grant moved up to chairman of the board.

Almost immediately, he began to assemble a renowned scouting staff that included Rogers Hornsby, Babe Herman, Johnny Murphy, and Gil McDougald.

That fall Weiss dipped into the Yankee gene pool and convinced Casey Stengel that retirement was for old fogies. Stengel had spent twelve years managing the Yankees and during that time he set several records, including the most years as a championship manager in the American League (ten); the most consecutive first-place finishes (five); the most World Series games managed (63); and the most World Championship wins (37). In all he won seven World Championships, 1949–53, 1956, and 1958.

On October 2, two days prior to the Yankees meeting the Reds in the first game of the 1961 World Series, and 50 weeks after having been dismissed as the Yankee manager, the 72-year-old Stengel put his John Hancock on the dotted line, signing on as the first-ever manager of the latest New York franchise.

This occasion called for a little speech, and the "Old Perfessor" gladly obliged. "It's a great honor for me to be joining the Knickerbockers," he said, alluding to both the basketball team and the historic Knickerbockers, the New York club that had played in the first formal game of baseball in America on the Elysian Fields in New Jersey in 1845. He also referred to the Polo Grounds, where the new club would play their home games, as "the Polar Grounds."

The fun had just begun.

♦

In the meantime Mrs. Payson, et al. were trying to come up with an appropriate name for the new team. Choices included the Continentals, Skyliners, Jets, Meadowlarks (for Flushing Meadow, where their new stadium was to be completed sometime in 1963), Burros, Skyscrapers, Rebels, Avengers, and the Mets. Mrs. Payson was rather partial to Mets, so the New York Mets it was.

The original Mets were an entry in the American Association, a major league extant from 1883 through 1887. The last Met team,

1887 variety, finished seventh out of eight teams. The club was owned by one Erastus Wiman and played most of its home games on Staten Island and a few at Weehawken, N.J., not far from the heights where Alexander Hamilton and Aaron Burr engaged in their famous duel.

On October 10 the expansion draft was held. Each of the eight NL clubs put up fifteen players. Seven of these had to be players from their 25-man active roster as of August 31, and the remaining eight were to come from the farm system. New York and Houston (the other expansion team), were permitted to select sixteen players from the first pool at a price of $75,000 each. At the conclusion each club could then select two more from a second pool for $50,000 each. The final round would be from the "premium" players list. Each premium pick would cost $125,000, and each club would be permitted four picks.

Houston's first pick was Eddie Bressoud of the Giants. As for the Mets, their first selection was the Giants' catcher, Hobie Landrith. The logic that went into this choice was faultless. "Ya gotta start with a catcher," Casey reasoned, " 'cause if you don't you'll have all passed balls." As it turned out, Landrith was one of the first Mets traded. After only 23 games behind the plate, in what would turn out to be a move of historic significance, Landrith was sent to the Orioles for a first baseman named Marvin Eugene Throneberry (initials, M.E.T.). In fact, the Mets wound up using six catchers that season and still managed to suffer 26 passed balls.

When the draft was completed, the new Mets roster was as follows:

$125,000 premium picks: pitchers Jay Hook and Bob L. Miller; infielder Don Zimmer; outfielder Lee Walls.

$75,000 picks: pitchers Craig Anderson, Roger Craig, Ray Daviault, and Al Jackson; catchers Chris Cannizzaro, Clarence "Choo Choo" Coleman, and Hobie Landrith; infielders Ed Bouchee, Elio Chacon, Sammy Drake, Gil Hodges, and Felix Mantilla; and outfielders Gus Bell, Joe Christopher, John DeMerit, and Bobby Gene Smith.

$50,000 picks: pitcher Sherman "Roadblock" Jones; and outfielder Jim Hickman.

The final cost to stock the team was $1,800,000.

The first player signed by the Mets, however, did not come from the expansion pool. Rather, this distinction went to Ted Lepcio, a free agent from the Red Sox. To Lepcio also went the distinction of being the last player cut by the Mets before they returned north after spring training.

In addition to these players the Mets undertook negotiations to bring other "name" players to the team. These included Johnny Antonelli, who made his name pitching for the New York Giants and now toiled with the Braves; and Billy Loes, an ex-Dodger pitcher. Antonelli, purchased from the Braves, just plain refused to report. The Braves, spoilsports that they were, refused to return the money that the Mets had shelled out for him. As for Loes, he appeared to indicate by his appearance in the Macy's Thanksgiving Day parade that he would, indeed, be happy to join the new entry into the league. But when it came time to report for spring training, he changed his mind and chose retirement. Too bad—as a pitcher who once lost a groundball in the sun, he would have fit in splendidly.

The Mets did add two players of note when they purchased outfielders Richie Ashburn from the Cubs and Frank Thomas from the Braves—the same Thomas who, you may recall, made a brief appearance with another one of our worsts, the 1952 Pirates. He was a power hitter who came up in the Pittsburgh organization with the promise of being the successor to Ralph Kiner. In fact, in his first full major league season (1953), he slugged 30 home runs, and in 1958 he finished second to Ernie Banks with 35 homers and 109 RBI (this included three home runs in a game). By the time he reached the Mets, he'd already smacked over two hundred home runs. A strapping six-foot-three-inch, 200-pound man, he got pleasure out of betting all comers that he could catch their hardest throw barehanded. It appears he never had to reach into his pocket to pay off such a bet.

Thomas had one particular quirk that must have amused those

around him, not to mention raised a few eyebrows. Evidently, he held the secret desire to be a flight attendant, since he had the rather odd penchant for serving meals on team flights. It was estimated that by the time his baseball career was over, Thomas must have served several thousand airline meals.

Thomas was to hit 34 home runs for the Mets in 1962, while hitting for a .266 average, but was never to reach those heights again. He played with the team until 1964, when he was traded to Philadelphia. He ended his career in 1966 with the Cubs, after having hit 286 career home runs.

Center fielder Richie Ashburn, a singles hitter who batted leadoff for 15 years, came up to the Phillies in 1948. He hit over .300 nine times and won two batting titles, finishing second three times. He was a member of the 1950 Philadelphia Whiz Kids, who won the NL pennant on the last day of the season over the Dodgers. (When he was once asked the reason why the club never won another pennant, he replied, "We were all white.") He had just turned 35 when he came to the Mets from the Cubs, where he'd had his lowest batting average (.257) since coming to the major leagues.

♦

Spring training arrived. Facing his troops for the first time, Stengel proceeded to lead his new charges on a walk around the bases. When the short jaunt was completed, Stengel turned to the assembled crew and announced, "Them are the bases. We just went around them." Someone in the crowd had the temerity to snicker. Casey simply growled and said, "Well, show me a better way to score runs."

Later, a writer asked Casey how he thought he'd do, "managing this new team?"

"I don't know," Casey replied, his logic, as always, irrefutable. "It ain't been managed yet."

Putting his players through their paces, Stengel could see that it would be a long season. He called one of them "a lower intestine." Another was "my road-apple left-hander." Of another he said, "Look at him. He can't hit, he can't run, and he can't throw. That's why they gave him to us."

In public Stengel never let an opportunity go by without uttering a few optimistic words about his team. In private, however, he admitted that "this team is a fraud."

All the while Stengel kept the press corps mightily amused. For instance, he had trouble with names. The catcher, Chris Cannizzaro, somehow, after emerging from the caverns of Casey's mind, became Canzoneri. About him Stengel once said, "Canzoneri is the only defensive catcher who can't catch."

One of Casey's favorites that spring was a fellow by the name of Rod Kanehl, soon to be known affectionately as "Hot Rod." Kanehl had played eight years in the minors as an infielder-outfielder. He had once impressed Stengel in a Yankee training camp by jumping over a fence to try and snag a fly ball. Kanehl's contract was purchased from Nashville, where he'd batted .304 in 1961. Over the course of the 1962 season "Hot Rod" was to play seven different positions. He was fearless and once allowed himself to be hit by a pitched ball with the bases loaded. He had the rather unusual hobby of regularly exploring the New York subway system, which led some to refer to him as "The Mole." Stengel preferred to call him "My Little Scavenger."

Other potential Met players seemed to come out of the woodwork, looking for a chance to make the team. For instance, there was a young Queens, New York, man named John Pappas who simply showed up in camp one day and asked for a tryout. He informed the team and the press that he'd read about the team's shortage of pitchers and was sure he could lend a hand. Sure, he had no professional experience, but he said he worked himself into shape by throwing a baseball against the wall under the Queensboro Bridge for two months. Because of the publicity Pappas generated, he was given a tryout. Unfortunately, the reports were unanimous: Pappas probably could not even have made a mediocre high-school squad.

There were two pitchers named Bob Miller, one a lefty, the other righty. R. G. Miller, the lefty of the duo, was last in the major leagues in 1956 when he pitched for Detroit, appearing in 11 games for an 0–2 record. He was literally spirited off the lot of an automobile agency, where he was employed selling cars. His record that year was 2–2, with a 7.20 ERA.

Righty Bob Miller had begun his career in 1957 with the Cardinals. With the Mets in '62, he was to go 1–12.

The Miller boys were roomed together on the road, primarily as a favor to hotel switchboard operators. But telephone operators weren't the only ones who couldn't keep the Millers straight (or anyone else, for that matter). One day Casey called the bullpen and asked for a relief pitcher named Nelson. One problem: the Mets didn't have a pitcher named Nelson. So Joe Pignatano, who'd answered the phone, explained what he did. "I just took a baseball and put it on the rubber and said to the guys in the bullpen, 'He wants Nelson.' Bob Miller got up immediately and grabbed the ball. 'He always calls me Nelson,' Miller said." Which Bob Miller this was, is a question that will remain one of those unanswered mysteries of life.

In one of their early spring-training games they faced the Yankees. Somehow, probably because the Yanks took the contest far less seriously than did the Mets, the upstart team took the game, 4–3.

You would have thought the Mets had won the Series. There was rejoicing up and down the East Coast. The Mets hosted a victory cocktail party at a local hotel. From New York, Stengel took a call from restaurateur and Broadway character Toots Shor, who told Casey that "it's like New Year's Eve in this joint." The win even merited a front-page story in the New York *Daily News*.

When Casey was asked to comment on the game, he waxed eloquent, as usual. "Oh, it was just lovely. It's terrific and it should be very good for the players. This will make the Mets believe that if you can beat a great team like the Yankees you should be able to defeat numerous clubs in our league."

Five days later the two teams met in a rematch. This time a sense of order was restored to the world. The Yankees had all their regulars go the full nine innings and consequently won the game, 3–2. Even Stengel had to admit, "We wouldn't've done so good if their team was trying."

Meanwhile, players came and went. Evans Killeen, a promising pitcher, cut his thumb while shaving and never returned to the team. More than one observer probably wondered what in the world Killeen was doing shaving his thumb. (These kinds of injuries seem to happen to players on teams like the Mets. For the record, later in the season, a Met pitcher by the name of Grover Powell actually injured his arm while combing his hair.)

A player without any discernible experience named Dawes Hamilt, told one reporter he didn't believe he'd get a fair shot at making the team because he was Jewish. Obviously, he never heard of a fellow with a fairly lively arm named Sandy Koufax who would, as it happened, toss a no-hitter against the Mets later in the season.

By the time spring training ground to an end, Casey was referring to his team as "the Amazin's," a sobriquet which stuck, in a slightly altered form, as the Amazing Mets. "Come out and see my Amazin' Mets," he dared.

Overall, the Mets went 12–15 in spring training, which may have lulled some into a false sense of complacency, a sense that they did, indeed, belong in the major leagues. But not old Casey. "I ain't fooled," he said. "They play different when the other side is trying too."

♦

The opening of the 1962 baseball season was close at hand, and in New York the excitement was starting to build. Finally, after the perfidy suffered at the hands of the Dodgers and Giants, New York would have another National League club to kick around.

The Mets were to play their home games at the Polo Grounds, which had been unused since 1957 when the Giants slunk out of town. The place had been refurbished for a reported $350,000, but still Coogan's Bluff, as it was affectionately known, had been around a little more than half a century and was showing definite signs of wear and tear. It was an oddly shaped field, with the dimensions of 279 feet in left field, 475 feet in dead center field, and 257 in right field. After playing for the Dodgers for all those years, Gil Hodges's feelings about the place were conflicted. "The Polo Grounds always was the enemy park," he said. "I felt strange in it." So did many of the other Met players.

Expecting a groundswell of support, the Mets' first ticket office was set up at the Martinique Hotel, not far from the Metropolitan Opera House. The sign in front of the office read, METS TICKET OFFICE. An opera patron came by and asked the clerk for "two for *Traviata.*" Without missing a beat the clerk replied, "First- or third-base side?"

♦

Stengel once said that there were "three things you can do in a baseball game. You can win, you can lose, or it can rain." Since the third option was what happened to the Mets on their originally scheduled opening day in St. Louis, the Mets were forced to wait another 24 hours before they could see whether or not they were for real. Casey's lament concerning Mother Nature's uncharitable blow was right in character. "Somebody is putting the Whammy on us before we even start."

The next day, however, dawned dry and the Mets, champing at the bit, made ready to take on the Cards, who, led by Stan Musial, had, the year before, finished in the middle of the pack, fifth place.

Casey announced the starting lineup in his patented idiosyncratic fashion. "In left field," he opined to the assembled news media, "we got Frank Thomas, who hit 25 home runs last year in Chicago, two in Milwaukee gets him 27, hit balls over buildings, he's got experience and power, very good, we can use him. In center field we got Richie Ashburn, who's one of the quiz kids in Philadelphia, gets on base 200 times a year, which is excellent, delighted to have him on our side, and in right field we got five or six fellas is doing very excellent. . . ." Here, Casey ran into a little bit of trouble remembering just who his right fielder was, so he improvised a bit till it came to him. ". . . and the best played for Hornsby in Cincinnati . . . he's a splendid man, and he knows how to do it. He's been around and he swings the bat there in right field and he knows what to do. He's got a big family and he wants to provide for them, and he's a fine outstanding player, the fella in right field. You can be sure he'll be ready when the bell rings . . . and that's his name, Bell!"

Whew!

The opening lineup, in somewhat more succinct form, looked like this:

Richie Ashburn, CF
Felix Mantilla, SS
Charlie Neal, 2B
Frank Thomas, LF
Gus Bell, RF
Gil Hodges, 1B
Don Zimmer, 3B
Hobie Landrith, C
Roger Craig, P

♦

And so, on the night of April 11, 1962, the New York Mets took the field for the first time ever. Don Zimmer, at third base, took the first ground ball of the year and proceeded to throw it wildly over the first baseman's head. Minutes later the ball dropped out of Roger Craig's hand during his motion to the plate and he was called for a balk, which sent a run across the plate.

After only three innings the Mets were behind 5–2. It was the closest they got. They lost the game 11–4, despite the first-ever Met home run delivered by ex-Dodger great Gil Hodges, and an additional one hit by yet another ex-Dodger, Charlie Neal.

The harshness of reality was beginning to set in.

Some time later Casey got into a cab in St. Louis with several young writers following the club and the curious cabdriver asked, "Are you fellows players?" "No," replied Stengel, "and neither are my players."

Roger Craig took the loss, one of a record 24 he was to sustain

over the course of the season (this was a 162-game schedule record that remained intact until it was tied by another Met, Jack
Fisher, in 1965). Later in the season Craig would look back and
say, "You can't win the game. You go out there knowing that. So
you try harder. Try too hard, it usually turns out. You're out there
concentrating so hard that the first thing you do is make a mistake.
Anyway, I'll tell you one thing. I want a raise next year. I'm going
to pitch over 220 innings for this team before the season is over [he
pitched 233], and I want to get paid for it."

About the escalating number in the loss column beside his
name, he said, "The losing doesn't bother me. It's the not winning
that hurts." And hurt it did. Five of his losses were by scores of
1–0. He finished the season 10–24, with an ERA of 4.51. Craig was
to pitch for the Mets in 1963 and did even worse, tying a league
record with eighteen straight losses and finishing with a 5–22 record, although he did lower his ERA to 3.78. He ended his playing
career in 1966 with the Phillies. Craig went on to manage the San
Diego Padres in 1978–79 and later became a successful pitching
coach with Detroit and Houston, teaching the split-fingered
fastball to both Jack Morris and Mike Scott, which resulted in both
pitchers becoming 20-game winners. He became manager of the
Giants in 1985, leading them to the NL pennant in 1989.

♦

When the team arrived in New York, they were honored with
a parade up Broadway. Stengel, a genuine folk hero, was presented with a key to the city. "I got a lot of keys to a lot of cities,"
he said, "but this one I'm gonna use to open a new team."

The home season opened, fittingly, on Friday, the thirteenth
day of April. Snow flurries and temperatures in the forties greeted
the 12,447 fans in attendance. Earlier that day, in what might have
been considered an ominous sign among dozens of ominous signs,
Stengel had slammed the door of his new office and when he tried
to get back in there was no key that fit the lock. Workmen had to
be called in to disassemble the door frame.

Brian Sullivan, of the Metropolitan Opera, and the St. Camil-
lus Band rendered their version of the National Anthem. It would

have been especially nice if they'd done so at the same time instead of a few beats apart. And when the starting lineup was announced over the PA system, it turned out to be the wrong one.

Sherman "Roadblock" Jones was the pitcher. Jones began his career with San Francisco in 1960, when he appeared in sixteen games and went 1–1, with a 3.09 ERA. The next year he was with the Reds, appearing in twenty-four games, again with a 1–1 record, and 4.42 ERA. In fact, Jones was scheduled to start the second game of the season, but on the flight from Florida, he burned himself with a matchbook. He was to go 0–4 with the Mets before he was sent to the minors. Eventually, he was forced to retire from baseball due to recurring arm problems.

Unfortunately, Gil Hodges, one of the few genuine links the Mets had with a team of past glory, was out of the lineup due to a pulled leg muscle and a bad knee. Hodges was an eight-time All-Star first baseman with first the Brooklyn, then the Los Angeles, Dodgers. He had over 100 RBIs for seven consecutive seasons (1949–55), and he hit 20 or more home runs in 11 straight seasons (1949–59). For a good while, prior to the time it was eclipsed by Willie McCovey, Hodges held the NL mark for lifetime grand slams with 14 (McCovey had 18). In one game against the Braves on August 31, 1950, Hodges hit four home runs. But now, at 38, Hodges's career was winding down. In the previous two seasons he'd hit .198 and .242. And in 1962 he was destined to play in only 54 games for the Mets (the next year, his final season, he played in only 11 games). In 1963 Hodges was sent to the Washington Senators in exchange for outfielder Jimmy Piersall. He took over as manager of the Senators that season and remained in that position until 1967. He was traded back to the Mets as manager in exchange for pitcher Bill Denehy and cash. In 1968, under Hodges's leadership, the club finished ninth, but the next year Hodges took the Mets to the pennant. They swept the Braves in the LCS, then beat Baltimore in the World Series in five games. Hodges went on to manage the Mets to two third-place finishes before he died of a heart attack after a spring-training golf game on April 2, 1972, at the age of 47.

The Mets lost their home opener to the Pirates, 4–3. An easy fly ball dropped between Ashburn and Bell, after they both called for it. "My head knew I had it," Ashburn explained later, "but my legs forgot to get it."

After the game it was discovered, one can only imagine how, that the shorts Stengel was wearing were emblazoned with the emblem of the New York Yankees.

The Mets proceeded to lose nine straight, including two to the other expansion team, the Houston Colt .45's. During this period poor Don Zimmer, who had come to the Mets from the Cubs, after having a fine career as the Dodger second baseman and shortstop (he was supplanted by Maury Wills) had his problems at the plate. He was 3–12, then he fell into an 0-for-34 swoon. He finally ended his skid with a double on May 4. Two days later he was traded to the Reds for infielder Cliff Cook. "They traded him while he was hot," cracked one reporter.

During the first few weeks of the season Mrs. Payson, the owner, was out of the country (coincidence or prescience?). Before she left, she asked that she be sent a daily telegram informing her of how the team was doing. After several arrived chronicling the team's losses, she wired back, "PLEASE TELL US ONLY WHEN METS WIN."

"That was about the last word I heard from America," she recalled when she returned.

The Mets finally won their first game on April 23. Jay Hook, an engineering student from Northwestern, was the winning pitcher. About him Stengel once said, "I got the smartest pitcher in the world until he goes to the mound."

After a few weeks it was apparent to Casey that his catching corps, which consisted of first Hobie Landrith, then Choo Choo Coleman and Chris Cannizzaro, left something to be desired. And so, the front office went to work. The fruit of their labor was a catcher named Harry Chiti, who was obtained from the Cleveland Indians farm system for "a player to be named later." After appearing in 15 games for the Mets, Chiti was hitting .195. Casey had seen enough. He shipped him back to the Cleveland farm system, thus making Chiti "the player to be named later." This has to be one of the few times a player was actually traded for himself.

By May 5 the Mets' record stood at three wins and sixteen losses. The pitching staff was allowing close to seven runs a game. Seven players were hitting .300 or better, but the team batting average was only .236. At this point, however, the Mets went on a tear, winning nine of their next twelve.

In mid-May they won five of six, two of them with late-inning rallies. In a thirteen-inning night game that didn't end until almost one A.M., the Mets won 6–5 when Hobie Landrith walked with the bases loaded. The next day they won another extra-inning game by the same score and actually moved out of last place.

But disaster was no more than a booted ball away. Following a doubleheader victory in Milwaukee on May 20, the Mets went on a tear in a different direction, losing seventeen in a row. In one game against the Giants at Candlestick the Mets had a 5–4 lead going into the eighth, when Willie Mays hit a home run off Jay Hook in the bottom of the inning to tie the game. In the tenth Felix Mantilla homered to put the Mets ahead again. Unfortunately, Mays was still in the game and in the bottom of the inning he hit another homer with a man on to win the game for the Giants.

During this streak they also lost a doubleheader to the Giants. In the seventh inning of the first game, with Mays on first, Roger Craig hit Orlando Cepeda with a pitch. Cepeda was not pleased. Glaring at Craig, he slowly made his way to first. Unintimidated, Craig, who was known for his artful move to first, immediately proceeded to turn and pick off the angry Cepeda. Only one thing wrong. Ed Bouchee, the first baseman, forgot to hold on to the ball. So Cepeda was safe. On the next pitch a fight broke out between Mays and Met shortstop Elio Chacon. Taking this opportunity to mete out some frontier justice on Craig, Cepeda charged the mound. After the fight was quelled, Craig, cool as could be, simply picked Cepeda off first again. Out? Not quite. Once again Bouchee neglected one of the cardinal rules of the game: You gotta hold on to the ball. Safe.

Things like this happened with startling regularity to the Mets and rather than turn off the crowds, these trials and tribulations seemed rather to endear them to folks. First one, then several, then many of these fans showed up at the park with banners proclaiming their various allegiances. LET'S GO METS; WE'RE FOR ASHBURN FOR PRESIDENT; WE LOVE ELIO; STENGEL'S LANCERS; HOT ROD; WHAT, WE WORRY? I'M A METS FAN; WE DON'T WANT TO SET THE WORLD ON FIRE—WE JUST WANT TO FINISH NINTH; TO ERR IS HUMAN, TO FORGIVE IS A METS FAN; and, simply, the word, PRAY!

By the time the season ended, the Mets had drawn an incredible 922,530 fans, the second largest attendance in history by a last-place club (exceeded only by Detroit's 1,026,846 in 1952).

◆

The inept antics of his players would have led a lesser man to check himself into a rest home. But not Casey. He seemed to thrive on it. Yet the ineptitude of his players did prompt Stengel to moan in absolute frustration, "Can't anybody play this here game?" (This phrase was later transposed to read, "Can't anybody here play this game?")

The tales were myriad. Take the problems Richie Ashburn was having in the outfield. In going for short fly balls he was constantly being run over by shortstop Elio Chacon. Finally, Ashburn took Chacon aside and tried to explain to him that as a matter of tradition, the center fielder had the option of calling for all fly balls that he thought he could get to.

But the next time there was such a short fly, and Ashburn called for it, Chacon ran him over again. Ashburn, beside himself, finally figured out that maybe Chacon, due to a language problem, simply didn't understand what he meant when he waved his arms and yelled, "Mine! I got it!" So Richie approached teammate Joe Christopher, who happened to be bilingual, and asked him for help. Christopher simply suggested that Ashburn use the Spanish phrase, "¡Yo la tengo!" He also promised that he would speak to Chacon and explain the situation one more time.

Before the beginning of the next game Ashburn approached Chacon and tentatively asked, "¿Yo la tengo?" Chacon smiled and nodded his head vigorously. "¡Sí, sí! ¡Yo la tengo!"

That night, in the early inning of a game, a short fly was lifted to center. Ashburn raced for the ball. Chacon raced back for the ball. *"¡Yo la tengo!"* Ashburn yelled, waving his arm.

Chacon stopped abruptly and gestured for Ashburn to take it, whereupon the center fielder reached up to make what should have been an easy catch. It wasn't easy, because this time he was knocked on his butt by Frank Thomas, the left fielder.

It was incidents like these that must certainly have prompted an obviously confused Ashburn to say, "I don't know what's going on, but I know I've never seen it before."

One of the most lovable yet inscrutable Mets on the team was a catcher named Clarence "Choo Choo" Coleman. Coleman came up through the Philly organization and was known primarily for his defensive skills. He was, for some reason, a particular favorite target of Stengel's wit. At one point in spring training Casey said, "Do you know who my player of the year is? My player of the year is Choo Choo Coleman, and I have him for only two days. He runs very good."

He also supposedly fielded "very good." As Stengel once said, "He can handle a low-ball pitcher because he crawls on his belly like a snake." In fact, he moved around behind the plate so much that when Phillies pitcher Chuck Churn, who'd played with Choo Choo, was once asked who the toughest man in the league to pitch to was, he replied, "Coleman."

Coleman was something of an enigma. Gene Mauch, who was with the Phillies, recalled Coleman well. "I remember one time when we were playing the Dodgers and Charlie Neal, their second baseman, said Choo Choo wouldn't recognize him despite the fact that they had been roommates in the minors. During batting practice Charlie asked, 'Do you know who I am?' and Choo Choo said, 'Sure, you're number four.' "

One day, in an interview with Met TV broadcaster Ralph Kiner (who, you'll recall, had plenty of experience with losers from his days with the '52 Pirates), Coleman was asked how he got his nickname.

His reply was as economical as possible. "Dunno."

Stretching for some possible area of connection with the catcher, Kiner asked innocently, "Well, what's your wife's name and what's she like?"

"Her name is Mrs. Coleman," replied Choo Choo, "and she likes me."

But without doubt the fans' favorite, and the player who came to most symbolize those 1962 Mets, was Marvin Eugene Throneberry, best known to all as "Marvelous Marv."

Throneberry came to the Mets in that trade from the Orioles for Landrith. He was a first baseman with power. In the summers of 1956 and '57 he hit 42 and 40 home runs for a team in the Yankees' minor-league system. Okay, it was in the rarefied air of Denver. But they still counted.

Marvin Throneberry metamorphosed into "Marvelous Marv" on one particular Sunday afternoon in mid-June. It began at the top of the first inning, when Throneberry (who was often referred to as Thornberry by Casey) found himself smack in the middle of the baseline during a rundown of the Cubs' Don Landrum after pitcher Al Jackson had picked him off. He was, of course, charged with interference. That alone wouldn't have meant much, especially on a club that had as many miscues as the Mets. But in the bottom of that inning Marv hit what appeared to be a two-run triple. Unfortunately, he was called out for missing first base. Stengel, his face turning red, leapt out of the dugout to argue the call, but he was intercepted by first-base coach Cookie Lavagetto. "It won't do any good, Casey. He missed second base too." To give the day the verisimilitude of a perfect ending, in the bottom of the ninth, with the Mets down 8–7, with two outs and two men on, who should show up at the plate? You guessed it. Marv. And what did Marv do? Why he struck out, of course.

Thus are legends born.

And thus is how they survive:

Coach Solly Hemus had just been kicked out of the game and Cookie Lavagetto was moved to coach at third. Another Met player, 40-year-old outfielder Gene Woodling, was drafted to coach first. At one point in the game Stengel called for Woodling to pinch-hit. This left the first-base line uncoached. Richie Ashburn volunteered Marv for the job.

"What do I know about coaching?" Marv asked.

"Nothing," replied Ashburn, who was one of Marv's chief supporters and good-natured tormentors, "so do it just like you're playing and stand out there."

The crowd went wild when Marv trotted out to the first-base line.

In the ninth inning Ashburn, Joe Christopher, and Jim Hickman all got base hits, bringing the score to 4–2, Pirates. There were two outs, two on, and a pinch hitter was due up. A roar went up from the crowd. A thunderclap of appreciation. WE WANT MARV! WE WANT MARV! There was no stopping it. It knocked upon the mountains and recoiled upon the flats. Casey motioned to the newest first-base coach to come in and grab a bat. When he got into the dugout Marv said, "If I strike out, I'll blame it on Ashburn. He got my timing off by making me wave runners around."

Some stories do have a happy ending. This one does. All Marv proceeded to do in his one time at bat was to hit a three-run homer to end the game.

The crowd went wild. They stood. They cheered. They refused to leave the stadium until their hero made one last appearance. And so he did. Smoking a tremendous black cigar, Marvelous Marv made his curtain call . . . wearing only his torn underwear.

New York might not have had a winning NL team, but they did have Marv. He became an instant hero. Fans chanted, "Cranberry, strawberry, we love Throneberry." One night five fans printed the letters M-A-R-V on their T-shirts and danced on the dugout roof. They reversed their position to spell out V-R-A-M. When they were promptly ejected for their efforts, they simply turned their shirts inside out and paid their way back in.

Marv was, if nothing else, a man of many miscues. He made 17 errors at first base, including an underhand toss that went over the pitcher's head on what should have been an easy play at first. Another time he ran down a runner caught in a rundown between first and second while the runner on third trotted home easily.

After games reporters flocked to Throneberry. Richie

Ashburn, who had the locker next to Marv's and never missed a chance to stick the needle into his teammate, once cracked, "Tell them how you're going to throw a party for your fans . . . in a phone booth."

As for Marv, he appeared to be a little bewildered by it all. Still, he was the proud possessor of a self-deprecating sense of humor. For instance, concerning a doubleheader, he once announced to the assembled sportswriting corps, "Hey, I've got good news for you. I'm only playing in one of the games today."

When the other first baseman, Ed Bouchee, once made an error and then struck out with two runners on base, Throneberry approached him and, feigning anger (or at least he appeared to be feigning it), said, "What are you trying to do, steal my fans?"

And upon leaving New York after the season was over, Throneberry, the man the fans loved to hate, cracked, "You think the fish will come out of the water to boo me this winter?"

Few honors came to Throneberry that year, but there was one that turned out to cause him a heap of problems. There was, in right field, a sign paid for by the Howard Clothing Company that dared Met hitters to strike it with a ball. If they did, they received a certain number of points. Those points were to be added up at the end of the season and the player with the most points was to receive a $6000 luxury cabin cruiser. During the season Stengel suspected that Frank Thomas was trying a little too hard to pull the ball. One day he took Thomas aside and told him so. "If you want to own a boat, join the Navy," he said.

Despite the fact that Thomas had 34 home runs, most of them pulled to left, he wasn't the winner. In fact, it was a left-handed batter that copped the prize. And wouldn't you know it, it was Marvelous Marv.

"In my whole life," he said, upon taking receipt of the boat at the end of the campaign, "I never believed they'd be as rough a year as there was last season. And here I am, I'm still not out of it. I got a boat in a warehouse someplace and the man tells me I got to pay taxes on it and all we got around here [here being Collierville, Tennessee] is, like I say, filled up bathtubs and maybe a crick or two. . . ."

Life can be so ugly sometimes.

When it came time to sign for the next season, Marv was adamant about his worth to the team. The following exchange between Throneberry and Johnny Murphy, the ex-Yankee pitcher who negotiated salaries for the Mets, was reported by sportswriter Leonard Shecter.

Marv: "People came to the park to holler at me, just like Mantle and Maris. I drew people to games."

Murphy: "You drove some away too."

Marv: "I took a lot of abuse."

Murphy: "You brought most of it on yourself."

Marv: "I played in the most games of my career, 116."

Murphy: "But you didn't play well in any of them."

Case closed.

♦

Hard as Casey might try, he couldn't seem to find a winning pitching combination. And he had plenty to choose from. There was Ken MacKenzie, a Yale graduate. Casey once put him into a game in a tight spot with the sage advice, "Make believe you're pitching against the Harvards."

MacKenzie once announced that "I have taken a survey and I find that I am the lowest-paid alumnus in the entire class of 1956."

MacKenzie also had some serious thoughts on the season. "When we started out this spring, I really thought we'd be all right, maybe even play .500 ball. I don't know what happened. *Something* happened, of course. You hear about clubs that win pennants. What happens is one guy picks up if another lets down. We've worked in reverse. We found a different way to lose every day.

"I don't think we were quite as bad as we looked. There was something this year that made every player a little worse than his potential. Our pitching, well, our pitching had a pattern. Error, base hit; error, base hit. When you're pitching good ball and there's an error behind you, you bend your back and make the pitches. This is exactly what we didn't do. We probably set a record for unearned runs. That's no alibi for the pitchers, not when he's giving up the runs after the error."

And then there was another college man, Craig Anderson. Anderson had a gentle, educated manner that seemed to drive Stengel crazy. When Casey learned that Anderson had a very generous annuity plan, he cracked, "He's got an-noo-i-tees, but he won't knock a batter on his butt."

The high point of Anderson's ill-fated season came on May 12, when the Mets managed to sweep a doubleheader. Pitching in relief, Anderson won both games, bringing his record to 3–1. Unfortunately, he never won another game all season, losing sixteen straight, then another two in 1963, and one more in 1964. Thus, he hung up his spikes with a nineteen-game losing streak.

By the time the season ended, the Mets had gone through seventeen pitchers—Craig Anderson, Galen Cisco, Roger Craig, Ray Daviault, Larry Foss, Darius (Dave) Hillman, Jay Hook, Willard Hunter, Al Jackson, Sherman Jones, Clem Labine, Ken MacKenzie, Robert G. Miller, Robert L. Miller, Wilmer Mizell, Herb Moford, and Bob Moorhead—and only one of them, Roger Craig, won in double figures. Al Jackson lost twenty, while winning eight. Jay Hook lost nineteen, while winning eight. Craig Anderson lost seventeen, while winning three. Only one pitcher had a winning record, MacKenzie, and that barely, going 5–4.

All in all, the team, and you'd have to say it was a team effort rather than simply the fault of the pitching staff, yielded ten or more runs 23 times that season.

When the final tally was in, the Mets had used, at one time or another during the season, an astounding 45 different players. And when you came right down to it, only a handful, including Frank Thomas and Richie Ashburn, could actually *play* this here game.

At the end of June, Ashburn had his 2500th hit. He finished the year with 2,574 and his batting average ended up over .300 (.306) for the ninth time in his career. In September the feisty Ashburn crashed into a wall in Pittsburgh while chasing a double hit by Bill Mazeroski. The collision knocked him silly and he couldn't remember any of the game the next day. A week later he slammed into the bullpen in Houston and hurt his right shoulder.

At the end of the season Ashburn was voted the Mets MVP. One would suspect that the vote was hardly a close one.

In trying to sum up that amazing season Ashburn said, "Any losing team I've ever been on had several things going on. One, the players gave up. Or they hated the manager. Or they had no team spirit. Or the fans turned into wolves. But there was none of this with the Mets. Nobody stopped trying. The manager was absolutely great, nobody grumbled about being with the club, and the fans we had, well, there haven't been fans like this in baseball history. So we lose 120 games and there isn't a gripe on the club. It was remarkable. You know, I can remember guys being mad even on a big winner."

♦

Ashburn's point about no one giving up was well taken. A week after they'd been officially eliminated from the pennant race in a loss against the Dodgers in LA on August seventh, the Mets hit two pinch-hit home runs in a game. The first was hit by Choo Choo Coleman, batting for pitcher Craig Anderson; the second by Jim Hickman batting for Coleman.

♦

The last game of the season came—finally—on September thirtieth. It was an afternoon game in Chicago. In the top of the eighth, losing 5–1, Sammy Drake opened the inning with a single off Bob Buhl. Then Ashburn singled. Nobody out, runners on first and second, Joe Pignatano up. He hit a looper into right. Drake, thinking the ball was going to drop, took off for third. Ashburn, thinking the ball was going to drop, took off for second. Second baseman Kenny Hubbs, thinking the ball wasn't going to drop, tore off into right and snagged the little sucker. When he turned around he saw that two Mets weren't where they were supposed to be. So, he did what he was supposed to do. He threw the ball to Ernie Banks at first base. And then Ernie Banks did what he was supposed to do. He threw the ball back to second. The result: a triple play.

How fitting.

♦

Now all that was left were the postmortems. And they came aplenty. After all, no team had been quite this bad since, well, since the Pirates of 1952.

The first came from Bill Veeck, who delivered his eulogy not at the end of the season, but in the middle. He spoke, as you'll see, not with rancor, but rather in awe of a team that was, if nothing else, unique in the annals of baseball's losers.

"They are without a doubt the worst team in the history of baseball. I speak with authority. I had the St. Louis Browns. I also speak with longing. I'd love to spend the rest of the summer around the team. If you couldn't have any fun with the Mets, you couldn't have any fun anyplace."

The next assessment came from the owner, Joan Payson.

"Just before last season opened, this wonderful writer from the *Daily News,* Dick Young, told me not to expect anything good at all. I said, oh, couldn't we beat out the Cubs and Phillies? They weren't particularly good clubs, you know. He said absolutely not. So I said to him, 'Well, can't we please expect to finish ahead of the other new team, Houston?' He said, 'No, I told you to expect nothing.' So I said, 'All right then, I'll settle for tenth place.' I certainly was not disappointed."

And the last words on that never-to-be-forgotten season must come from Casey Stengel himself. "Strangers," said Casey, "are hard to manage. It was like spring training all year. But I expected to win more games. I was very much shocked." And then he added, "The public that has survived one full season of this team got to be congratulated."

Postscript

In 1963, after the Mets lost their opener, Stengel said, "We're still frauds. We're cheating the public." The cheating continued, as they went on to lose seven more games before finally winning one. In 1964 the team lost sixteen of their first nineteen and Stengel, referring to the fact that the Mets would finish in tenth place for the third straight year, predicted, "We're gonna finish thirtieth."

Stengel remained as manager of the team until the middle of 1965, when, one week before his seventy-fifth birthday, a broken hip forced him into retirement. He died on September 29, 1975.

1962 Mets Roster

Player	POS	G	AB	R	H	2B	3B	HR	RBI	SB	BA
Richie Ashburn	OF	135	389	60	119	7	3	7	28	12	.306
Gus Bell	OF	30	101	8	15	2	0	1	6	0	.149
Ed Bouchee	1B	50	87	7	14	2	0	3	10	0	.161
Chris Cannizzaro	C	59	133	9	32	2	1	0	9	1	.241
Elio Chacon	SS	118	368	49	87	10	3	2	27	12	.236
Harry Chiti	C	15	41	2	8	1	0	0	0	0	.195
Joe Christopher	OF	119	271	36	66	10	2	6	32	11	.244
Choo Choo Coleman	C	55	152	24	38	7	2	6	17	2	.250
Cliff Cook	3B	40	112	12	26	6	1	2	9	1	.232
John DeMerit	OF	14	16	3	3	0	0	0	1	0	.188
Sammy Drake	2B	25	52	2	10	0	0	0	7	0	.192
Joe Ginsberg	C	2	5	0	0	0	0	0	0	0	.000
Rick Herrscher	1B	35	50	5	11	3	0	1	6	0	.220
Jim Hickman	OF	140	392	54	96	18	2	13	46	4	.245
Gil Hodges	1B	54	127	15	32	1	0	9	17	0	.252
Rod Kanehl	2B	133	351	52	87	10	2	4	27	8	.248
Ed Kranepool	1B	3	6	0	1	1	0	0	0	0	.167
Hobie Landrith	C	23	45	6	13	3	0	1	7	0	.289
Felix Mantilla	3B	141	466	54	128	17	4	11	59	3	.275
Jim Marshall	1B	17	32	6	11	1	0	3	4	0	.344
Charlie Neal	2B	136	508	59	132	14	9	11	58	2	.260
Joe Pignatano	C	27	56	2	13	2	0	0	2	0	.232
Bobby Gene Smith	OF	8	22	1	3	0	1	0	2	0	.136
Sammy Taylor	C	68	158	12	35	4	2	3	20	0	.222
Frank Thomas	OF	156	571	69	152	23	3	34	94	2	.266
Marv Throneberry	1B	116	357	29	87	11	3	16	49	1	.244
Gene Woodling	OF	81	190	18	52	8	1	5	24	0	.274
Don Zimmer	3B	14	52	3	4	1	0	0	1	0	.077

Figures include games played with New York only.

Pitcher	G	IP	H	ERA	ShO	SV	SO	BB	W	L
Craig Anderson	50	131	150	5.35	0	4	62	63	3	17
Galen Cisco	4	19	15	3.32	0	0	13	11	1	1

Pitcher	G	IP	H	ERA	ShO	SV	SO	BB	W	L
Roger Craig	42	233	261	4.51	0	3	118	70	10	24
Ray Daviault	36	81	92	6.22	0	0	51	48	1	5
Larry Foss	5	12	17	4.63	0	0	3	7	0	1
Darius (Dave) Hillman	13	16	21	6.19	0	1	8	8	0	0
Jay Hook	37	214	230	4.84	0	0	113	71	8	19
Willard Hunter	27	63	67	5.57	0	0	40	34	1	6
Al Jackson	36	231	244	4.40	4	0	118	78	8	20
Sherman Jones	8	23	31	7.71	0	0	11	8	0	4
Clem Labine	3	4	5	11.25	0	0	2	1	0	0
Ken MacKenzie	42	80	87	4.95	0	1	51	34	5	4
Bob G. Miller	17	20	24	7.20	0	1	8	8	2	2
Bob L. Miller	33	144	146	4.89	0	1	91	62	1	12
Vinegar Bend Mizell	17	38	48	7.34	0	0	15	25	0	2
Herb Moford	7	15	21	7.20	0	0	5	1	0	1
Bob Moorhead	38	105	118	4.53	0	0	63	42	0	2

Figures include games played with New York only.

Chapter 9
The 1979 Toronto Blue Jays

WON: **53**   LOST: **109**   GAMES OUT OF FIRST: **50½**

DAYS IN FIRST: **NONE**

HOME RECORD: **32–49**

ROAD RECORD: **21–60**

LONGEST WINNING STREAK: **4**

LONGEST LOSING STREAK: **7**

> It's not very often we get to see the Lone Ranger
> and Toronto the same night.
>
> —BOBBY BRAGAN,
>> *Texas Ranger administrator, after a game against*
>> *the Blue Jays featuring an appearance by Clayton*
>> *Moore, television's original Lone Ranger.*

SOME DAYS it just doesn't pay to get out of bed. For the Toronto Blue Jays of 1979 there were, lamentably, far too many of those days. This was one of them.

It was September 7. The Blue Jays were in Cleveland for the first game of a three-game series. By this time the Jays were comfortably nestled in last place, an all-too-familiar position—the club had filled that lowly site for the past two years, ever since they'd been admitted into the American League.

The team was now in the midst of yet another losing streak, again familiar territory. The club had just arrived from Baltimore, where they'd slunk out of town after losing three straight to the division leader. Their record now stood at 43–97. They were closing in fast on the 100 mark.

But today things were looking up. After six innings the Jays

♦ Mark Lemongello has already thrown the ball past Jays skipper Roy Hartsfield and is on his way to baseball oblivion. (Photo courtesy of the National Baseball Library, Cooperstown, NY)

were leading the team just ahead of them in the standings by a score of 8–0. In the seventh inning the Indians had begun making their move, closing the gap to five runs. But in the eighth the Jays, with the help of a triple play, the third in their three-year history, put on the brakes. They were almost home free. Just one more inning. Three more outs.

But, alas, it was not to be. Returning to form, the Jays committed five errors in the ninth inning, leading to six Cleveland runs. And so, by a score of 9–8, they wound up losing a game they appeared to have had sewn up.

This loss, no more frustrating than scores of other losses under their belt, left the Jays a mere 50 games behind the Orioles.

Ah, so many ways to lose. Let us count the ways.

♦

In 1979 the Toronto Blue Jays could count at least 109 ways to lose and only 53 ways to win. They wound up $50\frac{1}{2}$ games behind the Eastern Division–winning Orioles; $28\frac{1}{2}$ games behind sixth-place Cleveland. Their team batting average was .251 (the league average that year was .270), higher only than the Western Division's last-place Oakland team's average of .239 (as it happens, Toronto just nosed out Oakland for the honor of worst team of the seventies by the slimmest of margins—one game). They hit the fewest home runs (95), had the highest ERA (4.82), and gave up the most home runs (165, though in this category they had to share the dubious honor with both Seattle and Kansas City). They set a modern-day AL record for most losses on the road in a 162-game schedule with 60.

♦

In 1976 it was clear that the city of Toronto would be the newest site for major-league baseball. At first it appeared as if the San Francisco Giants, who were on the block, might be sold to interests who would relocate to the Canadian city. But instead the club was peddled to a group of owners who wanted to keep the team in San Francisco. Consequently, the American League seized the opportunity to award Toronto an expansion franchise.

Stocked primarily by players chosen through an expansion draft, the Blue Jays were a team of has-beens and untried rookies or, as relief pitcher Tom Buskey put it, "young players on their way in and old players on their way out." Early on the front office made the decision to shun the expensive free-agent draft and rather concentrate on developing a minor-league system. In the meantime, however, they would have to make do with cast-offs from other clubs.

In their first season the Blue Jays lost 107 games, an unsurprising figure, since the 1962 Mets lost 120. The next year they did improve, but only slightly, losing 102. But despite losing five fewer games they still brought up the rear in hitting, fielding, and pitching. There seemed to be no place left to go but up. Or was there?

In fact, 1979 turned out to be the worst year ever for the Blue Jays. While every other team in the Eastern Division compiled a winning record, the Jays lost often and early. In fact, during the stretch between April 15 and June 5, they won only nine games out of the forty-eight they played. During this period the team never won two in a row and every win was followed by at least two losses. As a result there was little suspense in Toronto that year as to where the team would end up in the final standings.

Spring training opened on a familiar note for the Blue Jays. For the third year in a row power-hitting outfielder Otto Velez failed to report on the assigned date. This time his excuse was income-tax problems. Then there was pitcher Tom Buskey, who spent a week of spring watching soap operas in his hotel room, compliments of a long-overdue case of chicken pox. Once this problem was cleared up, the ill-fated Buskey suffered a muscle pull, which left him even farther behind in the battle to get into playing condition.

On the other hand, veteran sluggers Rico Carty and John Mayberry were in pretty good shape. At thirty-nine Carty was at the end of an illustrious career. Born in the Dominican Republic, Carty, who called himself "the Big Boy," broke into baseball in 1960 when he naively signed not one but ten pro contracts. After this slight technical error was finally cleared up, he found himself the property of the Milwaukee Braves. Originally, he was a catcher, but the Braves turned him into an outfielder (and a pretty poor one, since speed was never one of his noticeable assets). However, there was never any doubt that his true value to any team was to be at the plate. As a rookie in 1964 he hit .330, barely losing the batting crown to Roberto Clemente, who hit .339. He was also just nosed out of the Rookie of the Year award by Dick Allen. In 1968 he was out the entire year, due to a case of tuberculosis. The next year he returned to the team, and despite seven shoulder dislocations he suffered during the season, he still batted .342. In 1970 he hit .366, good enough to take the batting crown and, incidentally, the highest major-league average since Ted Williams hit .388 in 1957. That year he was elected as a write-in candidate to start for the NL All-Star team. In 1978, splitting the season between Oakland and Toronto, he had a career-high 31 home runs, while batting .282. The Jays were hoping he could repeat this performance in 1979.

Though there was little doubt about his baseball pedigree, some Blue Jay players, especially utility infielder Tim Johnson, thought Carty took himself a bit too seriously. Next to his own locker Johnson had installed what he referred to as his "Hall of Shame," which, according to Alison Gordon, a sportswriter for the Toronto *Star*, was "composed of photographs out of newspapers with rude captions. Carty made the wall one day, with a vengeance.

"It had been Poster Day at Exhibition Stadium, and Carty was that season's pinup. The pose was a standard baseball one. Carty knelt on one knee, resting his hand on his bat, flashing that famous smile. Johnson put it up on the wall with the legend, 'Here's Rico, running out a ground ball.' "

John Mayberry, also a bona fide "big boy" at six-three, 215 pounds, broke into the major leagues with Houston in 1968. For the next four years he totaled only 298 at bats and in those appearances managed only 57 hits. But in 1972 he was traded to the Kansas City Royals, where he became the regular first baseman. He rewarded the Royals' faith in him by hitting .298 and showing plenty of power along the way, stroking 25 home runs, with 100 RBI. Over the course of the next ten years or so, Mayberry hit over twenty home runs eight times (he hit 30 twice) and had 100 RBI three times. Twice, he hit three home runs in a game.

In her book *Foul Ball! Five Years in the American League,* Alison Gordon describes what was probably a typical good-natured exchange between the two veteran sluggers that spring.

Standing at the batting cage they began needling each other.

"You sure didn't get any better looking over the winter, John," Carty said.

"I don't know what you're talking about, Rico," Mayberry replied. "At least I didn't get any balder!" Mayberry then snatched Carty's cap from his head, baring his receding hairline.

"Bald! That's not bald," Carty protested. "That's a sign of intelligence. You look at all the lawyers and presidents. They all have high foreheads."

♦

Surprising even themselves, the Jays managed to have a respectable spring, going 12–12. One casualty, however, was catcher Ernie Whitt, who broke into the major leagues with Boston in 1976. Whitt played only eight games for the Sox and was then chosen by Toronto in the expansion draft. In '77 Whitt, a good defensive catcher who was especially adept at handling pitchers, played in only 23 games for the Jays. The next year he played in only two games. But in 1979 he appeared to be ready to stick with the club for the entire season. There was only one thing (or person) standing in his way, as Alison Gordon points out in her book.

"Whitt's career got stalled by one very simple factor: Roy Hartsfield didn't like him, and since Hartsfield was the major-league manager, it meant that the catcher had no chance of making it out of Syracuse while Hartsfield was in charge. In 1979 the two had a confrontation in spring training. Hartsfield told him he would never be more than a minor league player because he couldn't hit, couldn't handle pitchers, and couldn't throw out runners at second. Then he handed Whitt yet another ticket to Syracuse."

As a result of being demoted to the minors once again, Whitt almost quit baseball. However, after being assured by the front office that Hartsfield was not the manager of the future, he decided to remain in the farm system, while he waited his turn when, as promised, Bobby Mattick would become the new manager. When Mattick did, indeed, take over the next season, Whitt was rewarded for his patience. He wound up playing with the Jays throughout the next decade. Consequently, of all the players selected in any expansion draft, with the exception of Jim Fregosi, Whitt played more games with the team that selected him.

Perhaps the best move the Jays made that spring was to trade their 1978 Rookie of the Year and co–Rookie Pitcher of the Year Victor Cruz to Cleveland for infielders Alfredo Griffin and Phil Lansford. In 1978 Cruz was 7–3, with nine saves and a 1.71 ERA, but due to weight problems he was never to fulfill his potential. Griffin, on the other hand, turned out to be a steal. Before the 1979 season Griffin, who made a brief appearance with Cleveland in 1976, had played a total of 31 major league games. With the Jays in 1979, he was installed as the starting shortstop, and after a slow start at the plate (after the first three weeks of the season he was hitting .082, but he ended up the season at .287), he came on strong to share Rookie-of-the-Year honors with the Twins' John Castino.

Besides Rico Carty, John Mayberry, and Griffin, the team the Jays brought north with them included outfielder Bob Bailor (who was the Jays' first pick in the 1976 expansion draft and rewarded the team's faith by hitting .310, a record for a first-year player on an expansion team); outfielder Al Woods, who debuted with the Jays in 1977, when he hit .284 in 440 at bats, but was unfortunately somewhat of a liability in the field; second baseman Dave McKay, the only native-born Canadian on the squad; outfielder Rick Bosetti, about whom we will hear more later; and third baseman Roy Howell.

Ernie Whitt's loss was Rick Cerone's gain. The catcher, who came to the Jays in 1978 after playing parts of two seasons with Cleveland, played 88 games that year and hit .223. Most of his popularity and acclaim stem from the years he played for the Yankees, from 1980 through 1984.

The Jays' pitching coach that year provided a link with another worst team of the century, the New York Mets. Robert L.

Miller was the same Bob "Righty" Miller who pitched for the Mets in 1962, compiling a 1–12 record. Miller remained an active player for another twelve years, his lifetime record 69–81, with an ERA of 3.37.

His pitching staff was, if nothing else, young and eager. There was Dave Lemanczyk, who was plucked from Detroit in the expansion draft and proceeded to win thirteen games (tying a record for wins with an expansion team), losing sixteen, for the Jays in their maiden season. That year he led the team in wild pitches, hits, and runs allowed. The next year, however, his record fell to 4–14.

Tommy Underwood began his career with the Phillies. In his rookie season he went 14–13. He never quite fulfilled his promise, and when he came to Toronto in 1978, he'd already spent part of his career in the bullpen as a reliever. Now, he was a starter again and he was to end the season with a 6–14 record. Still, he did lead the club in strikeouts with 139. In an interesting sidelight, that season Underwood was one of three major-league pitchers who suffered two 1–0 losses, the second of which was to his own brother, Pat, who was making his major-league debut for Detroit. This was the first time a pitcher made his debut with his brother on the mound for the opposition. With their mother in the stands Tom Underwood pitched a shutout until Jerry Morales hit a home run in the top of the eighth inning. His brother, Pat, gave up only three hits before leaving in the ninth.

Jim Clancy began his career with the Blue Jays in 1977, after being selected from Texas in the 1976 expansion. He went 4–9 that year, improving to 10–12 the next. At 23 he appeared to be hitting his stride. Unfortunately, 1979 would prove to be a setback year for Clancy, though he would recover to become one of the most consistent pitchers in the league.

Phil Huffman played only 34 games in the minors before he was rushed into the majors. He was to lose eighteen games (leading the AL that season) while winning only six. In what was to be his only season in the majors (he had a very brief cup of coffee with the Orioles in 1985), his highlight had to be a one-hitter he tossed against Oakland.

At nineteen, Balor Moore was the first draft pick of the Montreal Expos in 1969. A power pitcher, he was often referred to as a left-handed Nolan Ryan. In 1972 he went 9–9 for the Expos, averaging nearly ten strikeouts per game. He underwent elbow surgery in 1975 and didn't win another major-league game until 1978, at which point he'd resurfaced at Toronto. He went 6–9 that year but had to get by without his overpowering fastball.

Dave Freisleben, who'd come up with the Padres in 1974, joined the Blue Jays during the season and finished with a 2–3 record. It was to be his last season in the major leagues.

Tom Buskey was a reliever who'd begun his career with the Yankees in 1973. He was traded that year to Cleveland and promptly set a Cleveland record (since broken) for saves, with seventeen. In 1978, pitching for the Jays, Buskey appeared in only eight games, for an 0–1 record.

One acquisition made that spring that Blue Jay fans would remember for a long time came in a preseason trade with the Houston Astros. In November 1978 the Blue Jays announced that they had traded their promising catcher, Alan Ashby, to the Astros for pitcher Mark Lemongello, along with outfielder Joe Cannon and shortstop Pedro Hernandez. But the key man in the deal was Lemongello, who, in his second full season with the Astros, had compiled a 9–14 record with a 3.94 ERA.

"It's always difficult to give up a player of Ashby's caliber," said Pat Gillick, the Blue Jays' vice-president of baseball operations, "but we have acquired three excellent young prospects, one of whom, Lemongello, is an established major-league pitcher."

Lemongello may, indeed, have been "an established major-league pitcher," but he was also, as described by sportswriter Alison Gordon, "a migraine headache . . . a crazed pitcher best remembered for beating himself up after games. . . ."

Okay, so Mark was a little . . . eccentric. After all, this was the same Mark Lemongello who reportedly bit himself on the shoulder out of sheer frustration after being knocked out of the box one day in Houston.

From a cursory examination of Lemongello's checkered past, short as it was, since he was only twenty-three, one is inclined to wonder why the Jays made the trade in the first place. Sure, the young pitcher showed some promise, but those who knew him might argue that his elevator didn't always go up to the top floor. For instance, whenever Mark lost a game for the Astros, his teammates would beat a hasty retreat into the clubhouse to watch as the crazed pitcher ravaged everything in sight: hair dryers, mirrors, lockers (mostly his own), and even his own person. "He was unreal," one Astro was quoted as saying. "One time he bit his shoulder until it bled. He's also pounded on his pitching hand with his fist, crying, 'Goddamn SOB!' Once he kicked a cigarette machine and the flying glass cut him all up. . . . I mean, it wasn't funny, but it was impossible to keep a straight face."

One player who came up through the minor leagues with Lemongello recalled Mark returning to the clubhouse after a poor performance and throwing himself headlong onto the buffet table. "He just lay there covered with mustard and butter for a half hour."

Another time, again in the minors, during a game in Memphis, Lemongello stomped off the mound in a snit, walked through the stands, got into his car, and drove away. "I quit and went home to New Jersey," he explained. Astro general manager John Mullen followed him north, and it was only his promise that Mark would get a shot with the Astros if he worked hard that convinced the high-strung Lemongello to give it another chance.

For his part Lemongello felt that the end of his career as an Astro came as the result of a game against the Cubs. The score was tied 1–1, in the ninth inning. Fellow Astro Joe Sambito recalled that "Mark had pitched a beautiful game. He had runners on first and second, one out, a full count on Gene Clines. The pitch *was* a strike, no doubt about it. The videotape showed it. But Dutch Rennert called it a ball, and Mark just lost it."

Stomping off the mound Lemongello screamed at the ump, "What was that?" Rennert ignored him. Lemongello screamed again, "What the *fuck* was that?"

Rennert tossed him. Losing complete control, Lemongello raced from the mound, charging at the ump, screaming, giving him the finger. Several Astros had to wrestle him away from Rennert.

"Then," Lemongello said, "I cleaned out the dugout. Bats, towels, helmets—I threw out anything I could grab. I think the Astros gave up on me after that."

But the kid did have talent. After all, in 1977, when he ended up with 9–14 with a 3.47 ERA, he almost threw a no-hitter against the Reds, losing it in the ninth inning when Johnny Bench nicked the foul pole for a home run. "That game, that game. . . ." Lemongello later recalled rather wistfully. "If I could've gotten that no-hitter, I would have had a *name*. I would have established myself."

Lemongello (a cousin to both Peter Lemongello, the erstwhile singer whose career, such as it was, could best be described as being a blueprint for a promotion man's dream—all hype and very little substance—and his brother, Mike, who earned some minor renown as a professional bowler) was not exactly thrilled with the trade. Two weeks after the deal was announced, the Jays were still unable to contact their new pitcher. In fact, a Houston paper carried a story that quoted him as saying he'd rather be driving a Coke truck than playing ball in a foreign country.

"I slugged a lot of cases of Coke working in a supermarket when I was going to college, and I've also been in Phoenix in August when the temperature is about 120 degrees," Blue Jays president Peter Bavasi countered. "I can assure him playing ball in Toronto is preferable to either one."

Three more weeks passed, and still there was no word from the elusive Lemongello. One local newspaper ran the headline JAYS NEED RADAR TO LOCATE LEMONGELLO. The Jays, who were by this time perhaps having second thoughts about the swap, weren't able to home in on Mark, but they did reach his agent, who assured them that his client was, in fact, alive and well. A lot of good that was doing the Blue Jays.

Three more weeks passed and finally Lemongello surfaced, but only after he'd received a letter from Peter Bavasi that ostensibly helped dispel some of the fears he had pitching for a team based in a foreign country. In any case, the Jays obviously believed that if they could get Lemongello's head screwed on right, he might be a valuable asset to the organization.

Leading the Blue Jays was manager Roy Hartsfield. Hartsfield had a short-lived major-league career playing for the Boston Braves from 1950 through '52. Hampered by injuries, he still managed to have a career average of .273. In 1977 Hartsfield was named manager of the fledgling Blue Jays, and promptly led them to two, soon to be three, consecutive last-place finishes. According to Rick Bosetti the problem wasn't necessarily with Hartsfield. "I liked Roy as a person," said Bosetti, "but he didn't really have the respect of the team because they knew he wasn't running things."

♦

The Blue Jays opened the season on April 5 in Kansas City against the 1978 Western Division Champion Royals. To the surprise of few they were completely overmatched, dropping three straight, by scores of 11–2, 7–4, and 8–3.

But things began to look up when they moved on to Chicago, where they took two straight from the White Sox, 10–2 and 9–7. Then, it was back to K.C., where, much to everyone's surprise, they beat the Royals two straight, 4–1 and 8–6, before losing the last game of the series 12–10.

From that point on, however, the *real* Blue Jays took the field. A definite pattern was established. They lost their next four straight (in this streak the Jays' pitching staff gave up 45 runs), won one, lost two, won one, lost four.

There were a few bright spots along the way. On April 24 Dave Lemanczyk pitched a gem of a game, a one-hit shutout against the Rangers.

In the end, however, their record for April was a disappointing 7–15.

May was no better. In fact, it was worse. They won only five games and lost 23. After they'd lost their sixth game in a row, third baseman Roy Howell was practically moved to tears. "This is probably the lowest point since I've been here," he moaned.

Bob Bailor summed up the problems rather neatly. "When we get a well-pitched game, we don't hit, and when we score some runs, we give up even more."

The pitching staff was having severe problems. In 27 games

toward the end of April and beginning of May, the staff gave up 117 walks. In one game Tom Underwood walked two men with the bases loaded in the ninth inning to turn a 4–3 lead into a 5–4 loss to Milwaukee. Underwood, particularly, was having his problems. He would lose nine straight before finally winning a game at the end of June. This win ended a personal fifteen-game losing streak that dated back to August 8, 1978.

"It was frustrating," recalled Bosetti. "No matter what you did, it was never good enough. We didn't have a stopper. We tried everyone, but nothing seemed to work."

During this period Toronto general manager Pat Gillick was offered a job with the Atlanta Braves. No rat deserting a sinking ship was he. "We have a big job to finish with the Jays," he said, in turning down the offer. He was not exaggerating. The Jays promptly lost the next five games and then, injury being added to insult, Jim Clancy, their best pitcher, had to undergo surgery on a dislocated tendon in his right ankle and was lost for eight weeks. As it turned out, Clancy only managed to pitch 64 innings that season, for a record of 2–7.

Is it possible Mr. Gillick might have been, at least for a moment, regretting his loyalty?

In early June the front office decided to make some changes. Second baseman Dave McKay, the only native Canadian on the team, was hitting only .218, so he was expendable. To take his place the Jays promoted Danny Ainge. Ainge, a three-sport star in his Eugene, Oregon, high school, had been drafted by the Jays in the fifteenth round (the 389th pick overall) of the 1977 June draft. His low position in the draft reflected the belief that he would play college basketball, not professional baseball. In fact, in the spring of that year the San Diego Padres approached him and said they'd draft him high if he'd sign with them. He refused. The Blue Jays never even asked.

"We took a flyer," said Pat Gillick. "If you're fainthearted, you better not run an expansion club. You've got to gamble, be it in trades or drafts."

The Jays sent Ainge three contracts and several letters urging him to report to their minor-league club in Utica, New York. He tossed the contracts and the letters into the trash. "It was the last thing on my mind," he said. "I never answered them."

Eventually, the Jays made Ainge an offer he couldn't refuse. If he'd sign while in college, he wouldn't have to report to the Jays until school was out in April, and then he could return to Brigham Young University for the beginning of classes in September, even if it was before the baseball season was over. He was also offered a bonus, reportedly of $50,000 for three years, and it was strongly hinted that Ainge could go straight to Triple-A ball.

On Sunday afternoon, May 20, the twenty-year-old Ainge, in Rochester playing for the Syracuse Chiefs, got the call. "Be in Toronto for a Victoria Day holiday game tomorrow."

Arriving at Exhibition Stadium the next morning, he found that batting practice had been canceled because of an early-morning rain. The artificial turf remained covered until shortly before game time, at which point the Jays and the Indians took infield practice.

In his first time at bat Ainge, starting at second, grounded out. The second time up Ainge found himself in the middle of action. Rick Bosetti was on third with two outs. "Bo had the green light to steal home and the kid had the green light to bunt for a hit," said Roy Hartsfield.

"I saw him coming and it was the first time this ever happened to me," Ainge admitted later. "I thought of getting out of the way. Then I tried to push the pitch past the pitcher. I didn't see what happened after that, but I got a good bounce and got a hit."

His next time up he singled, and in his final trip to the plate he singled again—off Victor Cruz, the former Blue Jay right-hander who'd been dealt to Cleveland for Alfredo Griffin.

There was excitement in Toronto the next day. Could the Jays have unearthed a star? Two stars, counting Alfredo Griffin. The Blue Jay public-relations machine began to crank up. Now, they proudly announced, Danny Ainge and Alfredo Griffin had teamed up to form the youngest double-play combination in the major leagues. Between them that day they accounted for six of Toronto's thirteen hits in their 8–1 win over the Indians. They also chalked up two double plays. A jubilant Blue Jay front office believed they'd found the middle of their infield for at least the next decade. This was not to be the case.

Ainge struggled the rest of the year. He wound up batting .237. The next year he appeared in only 38 games for the Jays, batting .243, and in 1981, appearing in 86 games, he batted an anemic .187. Ainge realized that his future in sports was on the hardwood. He therefore announced that he would concentrate on pro basketball in August of 1981, and in November of that year the Boston Celtics agreed to compensate the Blue Jays for Ainge's release from a baseball contract. He didn't have much better luck playing hoops at first. The joke around the league in 1984, according to Bill James, was that "Ainge had proven so far that he couldn't play shortstop, second base, third base, or the outfield, hit left handed, hit right handed, hit a jump shot, or guard Andrew Toney." But Ainge had the last laugh, improving markedly and becoming a member of the Celtics' World Championship team.

♦

On June 19 the Blue Jays, who were now in the midst of a modest three-game win streak, breezed into New York for a four-game series against the Yankees. Normally, since this game was in the middle of the week, it would have been a ho-hum affair. But this was the Yankees, and owner George Steinbrenner had just shaken things up a bit by hiring back Billy Martin to coach the team. Already Billy was working his magic, putting some 36,000 fannies in the seats against a bumbling team like the Blue Jays.

As Alison Gordon reports in her book, "At the beginning of the week Steinbrenner, perhaps realizing that advance ticket sales were pathetic for the series, perhaps wanting to guarantee Martin a few quick wins, had announced that Bad Billy would replace Bob Lemon, the man who had replaced him the season before. The move was cynically motivated, but the fans lined up around the block to be there."

Tommy John, 10–2 at the time, was moved up in the rotation. Against him the Blue Jays threw rookie Phil Huffman, who had a 3–7 record and would turn twenty-one the next day.

"Banners hung from every tier of the stadium to welcome Martin back," Gordon writes, "and when he came jogging out of the dugout with the lineup card before the game the din was frightening, especially to Huffman, out in the bullpen warming up."

"When they all started yelling for Billy, I got the chills," Huffman recalled some time later. "I got the butterflies real bad. I was so pumped up, I couldn't even hear the names of the batters when they were announced." In fact, Huffman was so pumped up that in the third inning he hurled a pitch over the catcher's head and into the screen.

Huffman lasted six innings, holding the Yankees to three runs, while virtually every time the Jays hit the ball it seemed to find an open spot on the field. The final score was Jays 5, Yankees 4.

"The heroes of that night," writes Gordon, "were men who will never be called to Cooperstown. Not one of them lasted in the majors past the end of the next season. Huffman lost eighteen games that year and was sent to the minors, never to return. . . . J. J. Cannon, who made the catch of the game to rob Graig Nettles of a home run, now coaches in the low Blue Jay minors. . . ."

♦

In the meantime Mark Lemongello was having his problems as a Blue Jay starter. His woes culminated when, in the midst of losing his sixth decision in seven starts, Lemongello was visited on the mound by manager Hartsfield after the right-hander had given up a grand-slam home run to Cleveland's Andre Thornton. When Hartsfield announced that Mark was due for an early shower, the erratic pitcher snapped. He tossed the ball past the manager's outstretched hand and stalked off the mound. When his next turn to pitch came up against Detroit, Hartsfield returned the favor by bumping him from the starting rotation, instead handing the ball over to left-hander Jerry Garvin. From then on Lemongello's days as a Blue Jay were numbered. On July 23, his twenty-fourth birthday, Lemongello pitched one and a third innings in relief against the Twins. This marked his first appearance in a game since July 1. Two nights later he threw a wild pitch in the bottom of the ninth, allowing the winning run to score as the Jays lost 7–6.

"I've gone from a regular starter on one of the best pitching staffs in baseball to not pitching on one of the worst," Lemongello complained. "I just want to be moved, preferably back to the National League."

He got his wish . . . almost. He was moved, but it wasn't to the NL. With his record at 1–9 (he'd given up 97 hits, including fourteen home runs, in 83 innings and his ERA was 6.29), the Jays designated the right-hander for assignment to the Syracuse Chiefs in their minor-league system. Lemongello had better luck there. On August 22 Syracuse established a club record of 12 consecutive victories, as Lemongello notched his second win. "It's been so long since I've been on a team that wanted to win," he lamented. "It's just a frustrating atmosphere up there [Toronto]."

Poor Mark was due for a lot more frustration in his life. For one thing, he never did make it back up to the major leagues. In 1980 he was invited to spring training by the Jays, but didn't make the squad. In 1982 he got into a spot of trouble when, with Manny Seoane (also a former pitcher with a short-lived career for the Phillies and the Cubs), he was arrested on kidnapping and robbery charges. The twosome were accused of abducting at gunpoint Mark's cousins, Mike and Peter Lemongello. Both cousins were dropped off in a wooded area north of St. Petersburg. The incident stemmed from business dealings between the cousins concerning a house that was being built for Houston Astro relief pitcher Joe Sambito. This brush with the law pretty much finished any chance that Mark might have had to make it back into baseball. And so, at the age of 27, he was through as a player.

♦

But if Mark Lemongello was finished, the career of another rookie Blue Jay was just beginning. In mid-June the Jays called up Dave Stieb to pitch his first major-league game in Baltimore.

Stieb was drafted out of college in 1978 and spent the season in the Florida State Class A League, where he alternated between pitching and playing the outfield. He began the 1979 season playing for the same team. After winning five games he was jumped to Triple-A, where he played for the Syracuse Chiefs. Here he pitched well enough, winning five more games, to catch the eye of the parent club.

At 22 he made his major-league debut against the Orioles in Memorial Stadium, where they had won eighteen of their last twenty games.

Stieb turned in a laudable performance, striking out five. But he was ultimately done in by sixth-inning back-to-back homers by Doug DeCinces and Lee May.

"After the game," writes Gordon, "he sat slumped at his locker, sad and vulnerable, refusing to content himself with having impressed both teams with his pitching. 'I don't mind the runs I gave up early,' he finally admitted, 'but no one had ever hit a home run off me before.' At that moment he was still only a kid, albeit an extraordinarily talented one. Not many pitchers get to the major leagues without giving up a home run. Stieb went on to become one of the best pitchers in the league, but that night, that loss, his shyness and chagrin were touching."

♦

Stieb finished the season with a very creditable 8–8 record and an ERA of 4.33.

Meanwhile, Dave Lemanczyk was pitching quite well, but experiencing more than his share of bad luck. In one stretch in late May and early June the Jays had seven wins in 35 games and Lemanczyk accounted for four of them. By the time August rolled around, he was 8–8. But then he succumbed to a nerve inflammation in his lower back that affected the feeling in his right leg. The rest of the season was pretty much a wash, as he wound up at 8–10, with a 3.71 ERA.

The injury list grew larger by one "big boy" when designated hitter Rico Carty suffered a freak injury when he stabbed himself at the base of his middle finger with a toothpick, which attacked him as he reached into his carry-on bag. "That's my power hand," Carty complained after the accident. "I can take the pain. That doesn't bother me. But I can't hit for distance." Though a piece of the toothpick remained in his swollen hand for some time after the accident, he refused surgery. Whether due to the accident or simply to advancing age and declining skills, Carty wound up having a disappointing season. His home-run total dropped from 31 to 12, and his RBI from 99 to 55.

♦

In early August, in order to juice up attendance, the Jays added yet another of their many promotional gimmicks, proclaiming Italian Heritage Night at Exhibition Stadium. Evidently, Italians weren't very big in Toronto, because only 15,130 fans showed up. Furthermore, things looked pretty dim for the Blue Jays until Toronto's own contribution to Italian Heritage, Rick Bosetti, came up with the bases loaded and delivered a single, knocking in two runs. It turned out to be the Jays' first win after five straight losses. At this point in the season the Jays' record stood at 33–76.

Bosetti, hero of Italian Heritage Night, was something of a character. He was a member in good standing of the Turds, whose other members included leader Tim Johnson (a utility infielder, described by Alison Gordon as "a bit of an outlaw . . . older than the rest, just putting in his last major-league season . . . a hard-nosed jock who raced motorcycles in New Mexico during the off-season"), Dave Lemanczyk, Dave Freisleben, Balor Moore, and Rick Cerone. These were the rebels who stayed out late, carousing and drinking. Occasionally, they even showed up at game time with serious hangovers. They gave Roy Hartsfield headaches all year. But he did manage to have the last laugh when, on the last day of the season, he made sure that each of them got into the next day's game, after he knew they'd been on an all-night binge.

"The Turd Club kept things loose," said Bosetti. "For instance, Timmy Johnson had this obscene little award, called the Fuck-up of the Night Award. He had this fourteen-inch manual crank dildo that he taped to the locker of that night's winner."

Bosetti had the reputation of being something of a flake. For one thing, he was described by one teammate as "a nature lover. He has real basic tastes. Like he doesn't like to wear clothes. We keep waiting for the day when he forgets to wear anything when he goes out on the field, because every other time we see him he's got only his socks on."

Bosetti's explanation was simple. "Hey, I grew up with eight other kids—nude bodies are nothing unusual for me. I've never been ashamed to go around naked."

At the time there was a story making the rounds about Bosetti trying to take a few friends to a very trendy restaurant without benefit of reservations. Supposedly, Bosetti informed the maître d' that he was with the last-place Blue Jays and so he would agree to enter through the back door. "He didn't appreciate the humor," Bosetti said. "He told us to get lost." A few weeks later Bosetti was back inside the restaurant. He headed straight for the bathroom, emerging only moments later with all his clothes under his arm, whereupon he proceeded to march through the dining room and out the front door. "That's Bo's way of thumbing his nose at people," said a Blue Jay. "Only, he never uses his nose."

Unfortunately, according to Bosetti this story is utter nonsense. "It never happened," he said. "If it had, don't you think I would have been arrested?" Nevertheless, it has been added to the Bosetti legend.

Bosetti also had the quaint habit of painting eyes on his bats, and making dramatic diving catches in the outfield, even when he didn't have to. Bosetti admitted as much. "I've reached the point where if I do hot-dog it, it's not because I want to show up anybody, I just want to put a charge into the team."

Another legend that sprang up around Bosetti was that he had a rather unusual life's goal: that is, to urinate in every natural-grass outfield in baseball. "I've gotten all the American League parks," he supposedly claimed. "That's why I want interleague play. To water that beautiful grass in Wrigley Field would be a dream come true." Bosetti insisted that he only did his "watering" when there were no fans in the park, but one teammate insisted otherwise. "He also does it during games, like at pitching changes. He doesn't want anyone to know; he wants it to be his secret, to know that he can do it before 20,000 and not be noticed. . . . But we see him turning to the wall and putting his glove in front of his waist. Now we're waiting for him to do it between pitches."

Again, this made for a good story, but was it true? Not according to Bosetti. "The urination thing was an exaggeration. It started in the minor leagues. It was pregame stuff. We were playing in Oklahoma City, I wasn't feeling too good and they didn't have the proper facilities, so I did it. One day some reporter asked Rick Cerone about it and he said, 'Oh, yeah, he's done this in every ballpark.' I started playing along with it. I even said, 'Yeah, but never on Astroturf.' People actually believed it. I even had Fred Lynn come up to me one time and ask me not to do it in his outfield."

But crazy things did happen to Bosetti and the Jays that year. Like the time they finished a game and there was no bus to take them back to the hotel. "Here we were, 37 games out of first place, just trying to get out of town, and there's no bus."

Another time Bosetti had a rather unique experience at the plate. "We were in Oakland, there were about 350 people in the stands—and 50 of those were on passes from me, since I grew up in the area—and I walked on three balls. Ron Luciano was the umpire and I guess he hadn't cleared his counter. Matt Keough was pitching, and after ball three Luciano told me to take my base. The catcher said, 'Ron, it's only ball three. Look at the scoreboard.' He looks up and the scoreboard reads three and one. He looks back down at his counter and says, 'This says ball four, take your base.' "

Ironically, Bosetti had his best year in 1979. He batted .260, led the league in total chances—"Obviously, with that team, I had a lot of chances"—and played in all 162 games. "I almost didn't," he explained. "My wife was pregnant and gave birth on a day we were supposed to play Boston. But the game was rained out, so I got to play the next day without missing a game."

In mid-August the pitching staff began to rebel against Roy Hartsfield. It began with ace reliever Tom Buskey, whose record at the time was 5–5 with five saves and a 2.28 ERA. Oddly enough, his outburst came after the Jays had busted a 12-game losing streak on the road with three straight wins.

"We need a new manager," Buskey complained to a reporter. "Roy Hartsfield just doesn't know how to handle a pitching staff. Nobody knows what he's supposed to be doing."

When told of Buskey's comments, Jays President Peter Bavasi wryly responded, "Just another superstar popping off."

But Buskey was not alone in his criticism of Hartsfield. "The way they silver-spoon the kids around here bothers guys like us," said 25-year-old third baseman Roy Howell (could he possibly have been referring to Danny Ainge?).

Tom Underwood, who'd just become the first fifteen-game loser in the American League, added his two cents. "The rest of us are tired of being baby-sat, we're men." And Rick Bosetti bitterly complained that when he was ejected from a game in Chicago for throwing his bat, Hartsfield chewed him out in front of the umpire.

"There was a lot of I-Me going on. If you have a good day, go two for three, but you still lose, well, it's hard not to feel, shoot, at least I did my job."

Today, Tom Buskey has his own feelings about what was happening on the Jays and why they were such big losers. "You got the feeling from the front office—not directly, but you still got it—that they didn't worry about winning. They just wanted to make sure you showed the logo. They seemed to say, 'Since we are an expansion team, no one expects us to win.' This attitude bothers you a little.

"And there was another thing. Most ballplayers want to know what their job is. We didn't, and that was the problem as far as the pitchers were concerned. Management had no faith in what we were doing. You got the quick hook. One mistake and you were gone. The pitchers got frustrated. For instance, we had this thing in the bullpen—the Totem Pole Theory of Relief Pitching. There was no such thing as a specialist. There was no short man, long man, mop-up man. No matter what the situation was, if you were at the top of the totem pole, if you were the only one who hadn't pitched the day before, then you came in. And you only came in when it was your turn."

As if the controversy stirred by the pitchers wasn't enough, on the same day this story broke, a newspaper carried the story of an eighteen-year-old ticket-taker at Exhibition Stadium who had been dismissed because she'd been seen getting into a player's car at the stadium (evidently, this was counter to a security-company policy of nonfraternization with the players).

When asked to comment Peter Bavasi added fuel to an already sizzling fire when he said, "I certainly wouldn't want my daughter"—who happened to be eight years old at the time—"dating a Blue Jay."

This didn't go over too well with the players. "How do you think our wives feel about that remark?" said Roy Howell.

Bavasi wasn't exactly a favorite of the players anyway. "Bavasi had what he called the artichoke theory," explained Bosetti. "He'd get us all in a room and he'd make this speech. 'Gentlemen, don't take this too hard, but this team is like an artichoke. You peel an artichoke, throw away the leaves, and keep the heart. Some of you are hearts and you'll be here all summer; some of you are leaves, just passing through.' That kind of talk didn't inspire a whole lot of confidence or professionalism."

Somehow, all this controversy seemed to work in the Jays' favor. At least for a while. They went on to have only their second winning week of the season. Tom Buskey threw 2⅓ hitless innings to save a 6–4 win over the Angels. He received an ovation from the fans . . . but no handshake from Hartsfield. Buskey then went on to pitch seventeen scoreless innings before finally giving up the winning run to Seattle in a 3–2 loss.

In mid-September, when every other also-ran was just playing out the string, the Blue Jays appeared to be hitting their stride. They had only their third winning week of the season, beating the league-leading Orioles twice.

♦

While all this was going on, the Toronto fans continued to pour into the ballpark. "They were so hungry for baseball entertainment," explained Bosetti, "that they even gave a cheering ovation for the opposing player who hit a home run. But the problem was, they really didn't understand the game, and so they weren't able to get into carrying the momentum of the game, like cheering for a rally in the seventh or eighth inning."

In fact, the Canadian fans were very different from American fans. According to Bosetti, "We used to say that it was so quiet in the stadium that you could hear a nun fart in the tenth row. I could actually hear people talking in the dugout from the outfield."

♦

Losing as much as teams like the Blue Jays did can certainly do something to a ballplayer's psyche. Does it turn him into a misanthrope? Does it cause tension in the clubhouse? Do players tear at each other? Blame each other? Shun each other? At least in the case of the Blue Jays, it seems not. In fact, it was just the opposite.

"In all my years in the game," explained Tom Buskey, "major and minor leagues, I only played with one team that was .500 or better, so I know something about losing. Normally, when you're losing, the fans don't show up. And those that do often turn on you. So, in the end, you've only got yourselves. So what losing does is bring you closer together as a team. It's the guys who play beside you who understand what you're going through. As a team we were expected to lose, but we knew we wanted to win as bad as anyone else."

♦

The Blue Jays went out of the season pretty much the way they came in . . . abysmally. They lost their last five straight, the first two to Boston, the last three to New York. After the final game, which was a 9–2 blowout, with their record standing at 53–109, the ax fell on Roy Hartsfield. Evidently, three hundred-plus-loss seasons were more than enough for the Blue Jay front office. "We are grateful to Roy Hartsfield for having established the foundation for the future," said team vice-president Pat Gillick. "His was a most difficult task. We hope Roy will remain with the Blue Jays and assist us with the many challenges ahead."

A short time later Bobby Mattick was hired to lead the team, and although they wound up in the cellar the next year, they did improve their record to 67–95, only 36 games behind the division-winning Yankees. The next season they also brought up the rear, but from then on they began to rise steadily until 1985 when, with

Bobby Cox at the helm, they actually won the Eastern Division crown (Dave Stieb and Jim Clancy were still on the team and played a large part in Toronto's rise to the top).

The Blue Jay player who came off best in 1979 was co–Rookie of the Year Alfredo Griffin. Hitting .347 in the month of September, when he was named AL League Player of the Month, Griffin ended the season batting .287, leading the team in triples with ten, and stealing a team-record 21 bases. Another pleasant surprise was Otto Velez, who socked fifteen home runs, which matched the combined number hit by his outfield cohorts Rick Bosetti, Al Woods, Bob Bailor, and J. J. Cannon.

John Mayberry wound up actually boosting his batting average to .274 (from .250 the year before) and set a team record with 74 RBIs, and this despite missing the last week of the season due to an injury.

After his disastrous 0–9 start Tommy Underwood managed to go 9–7 for the rest of the season, lowering his ERA from 5.00 to a respectable 3.69.

As for Rick Bosetti, he was out of the game by 1982, a victim, he says, of the change in management. "Bobby Mattick was the one who scouted Lloyd Moseby, who was supposed to be the next great superstar. So he had a vested interest in seeing that he played." Today Bosetti is the owner of a computer company called Team Solutions.

But none of these individual feats could quite erase what was the worst performance of a team in the 1970s.

1979 Toronto Blue Jays Roster

Player	POS	G	AB	R	H	2B	3B	HR	RBI	SB	BA
Danny Ainge	2B	87	308	26	73	7	1	2	19	1	.237
Bob Bailor	OF	130	414	50	95	11	5	1	38	14	.229
Rick Bosetti	OF	162	619	59	161	35	2	8	65	13	.260
Rogers Brown	OF	4	10	1	0	0	0	0	0	0	.000
Joe Cannon	OF	61	142	14	30	1	1	1	5	12	.211
Rico Carty	DH	132	461	48	118	26	0	12	55	3	.256
Rick Cerone	C	136	469	47	112	27	4	7	61	1	.239
Bob Davis	C	32	89	6	11	2	0	1	8	0	.124
Luis Gomez	SS	59	163	11	39	7	0	0	11	1	.239
Alfredo Griffin	SS	153	624	81	179	22	10	2	31	21	.287
Pedro Hernandez	U	3	0	1	0	0	0	0	0	0	.000
Roy Howell	3B	138	511	60	126	28	4	15	72	1	.247
Tim Johnson	2B	40	60	6	10	2	1	0	0	0	.100
Craig Kusick	1B	24	54	3	11	1	0	2	7	0	.204
John Mayberry	1B	137	464	61	127	22	1	21	74	1	.274
David McKay	2B	47	156	19	34	9	0	0	12	1	.218
Bob Robertson	1B	15	29	1	3	0	0	1	1	0	.103
Tony Solaita	1B	36	102	14	27	8	1	2	13	0	.265
Otto Velez	OF	99	274	45	79	21	0	15	48	0	.288
Thad Wilborn	OF	22	12	3	0	0	0	0	0	0	.000
Al Woods	OF	132	436	57	121	24	4	5	36	6	.278

Figures include games played with Toronto only.

Pitcher	G	IP	H	ERA	ShO	SV	SO	BB	W	L
Tom Buskey	44	79	74	3.42	0	7	44	25	6	10
Jim Clancy	12	64	65	5.48	0	0	33	31	2	7
Claude Edge	9	52	60	5.19	0	0	19	24	3	4
Dave Freisleben	42	91	101	4.95	0	3	35	53	2	3
Jared Garvin	8	23	15	2.74	0	0	14	10	0	1
Stephen Grilli	1	2	1	0.00	0	0	1	0	0	0
Phil Huffman	31	173	220	5.77	1	0	56	68	6	18
Jesse Jefferson	34	116	150	5.51	0	1	43	45	2	10
Dave Lemanczyk	22	143	137	3.71	3	0	63	45	8	10

Pitcher	G	IP	H	ERA	ShO	SV	SO	BB	W	L
Mark Lemongello	18	83	97	6.29	0	0	40	34	1	9
Stephen Luebber	1	0	2	0.00	0	0	0	1	0	0
Dyar Miller	10	15	27	10.80	0	0	7	5	0	0
Balor Moore	34	139	135	4.86	0	0	51	79	5	7
Tom Murphy	10	18	23	5.50	0	0	6	8	1	2
Dave Stieb	18	129	139	4.33	1	0	52	48	8	8
Jackson Todd	12	32	40	5.91	0	0	14	7	0	1
Tom Underwood	33	227	213	3.69	1	0	127	95	9	16
Michael Willis	17	27	35	8.33	0	0	8	16	0	3

Figures include games played with Toronto only.

Chapter 10
The 1988 Baltimore Orioles

WON: **54**   LOST: **107**   GAMES OUT OF FIRST: **34$^1/2$**

DAYS IN FIRST: **NONE**

HOME RECORD: **34–46**

ROAD RECORD: **20–61**

LONGEST WINNING STREAK: **3**

LONGEST LOSING STREAK: **21**

All the things I've learned about baseball over the years made what happened impossible. Teams don't have stretches like that. Especially at the beginning of the year, the very first twenty-one games.

—JON MILLER,
Baltimore Orioles and ESPN broadcaster

THERE IS no other team in this book quite like the 1988 Baltimore Orioles. They were not a longtime dog like the Phils, Braves, and Senators, an expansion team like the Mets and Jays, or a bad team rebuilding around youth like the Pirates. Given the Orioles' record of success, one might want to compare them to the 1910 Athletics, but the Orioles were not an undercapitalized team struggling against the big bankrolls of other owners. Edward Bennett Williams, who owned the team at the outset of their worst season, was a wealthy man who wanted a winning team badly.

The Orioles were one of the great success stories of baseball in the era of divisional play. Including the 1988 and 1989 seasons they have the best record in baseball since the four divisions were created, going 1,853–1,470 over 21 years. Indeed, their success goes

♦ **Cal Ripken, Jr.: He's smiling because he's on his way to Cooperstown to join Maranville.** (Photo courtesy of the National Baseball Library, Cooperstown, NY)

back even farther; over the past thirty seasons the Orioles have the highest winning percentage in the majors, .555. From 1968 through 1985 they never had a losing season, a string of eighteen consecutive winning years, second in history only to the Yankees' 39-year skein (1926–1964). As recently as 1983 they had been the World Champions, and there was no Connie Mack to tear the team down in the false hope of rebuilding on the cheap.

The Orioles organization was considered a model in baseball, like a big, happy family from the owner to the guy who swept out the stadium that housed their lowest minor-league team. The Orioles actually used a manual called *The Oriole Way* to teach minor-league players, coaches, and managers the organization's methods and techniques. Oriole baseball was sound fundamentals, drilled endlessly, "good pitching and three-run homers," as longtime O's manager Earl Weaver would have put it. And it really did work for a long time.

However, the slippage had been steady since the 1983 title. After going 98–64 that year the O's had compiled the following records: 85–77 in 1984, 83–78 in 1985, 73–89 in 1986, 67–95 in 1987. Clearly some changes were in order.

The symbols of the old guard had to be swept away, yet the Orioles family had to be left intact. At the end of the 1986 season Earl Weaver, back from retirement for a futile last season, retired again. He was replaced by third-base coach Cal Ripken, Senior. Ripken, father of star shortstop Cal Junior and highly touted second-base prospect Billy, seemed to be the kind of tough skipper the Orioles needed.

Ripken Senior was one of the authors of *The Oriole Way.* He had spent thirty years in the organization as a coach and minor-league manager. Ray Miller, former Baltimore pitching coach, had called him "*the* true Oriole." He had nearly had the job twice before, in 1982 when Weaver retired the first time, and again in 1985, when Joe Altobelli, Weaver's successor, had been fired and replaced by Earl. Each time he had been passed over and had reacted with total loyalty to the organization. Williams, who admitted that bringing back Earl was a mistake, told *Sports Illus-*

trated that Ripken "handled himself with such class and loyalty in difficult situations that you had to be impressed."

He was entering another difficult situation in taking the manager's job. The team he inherited from Earl was aging. General Manager Hank Peters and his director of minor-league operations, Tony Giordano, had presided over the demise of a great farm system. Cost cutting hurt the scouts, and many of the top baseball people began leaving the organization. The Ripken brothers were two of the last regulars to be bred by the Orioles in their own nest. Mike Boddicker was the last homegrown pitcher. Under Peters no player selected by the Birds in the first round of the amateur draft had made it to the majors. (Of course, he wasn't helped by all the picks the team had given up to sign free agents like Lee Lacy.)

There had been murmurings among some baseball people that the free-agency era of baseball had passed the Orioles by, that the front office had never adjusted to the realities of the long-term multimillion-dollar contract. In the '80s the Orioles had certainly made some errors in judgment, signing part-timers like Lacy and over-the-hill superstars like Fred Lynn to big pacts. Confronted with the reality of a team that had slipped all the way to seventh in 1986, Peters had applied Band-Aids, signing second baseman Rick Burleson, 35, third baseman Ray Knight, 34, and trading Storm Davis, a much-needed member of the rapidly thinning rotation, for Terry Kennedy, a 30-year-old catcher, for the 1987 season. The idea was to plug three holes in the lineup and bring in some guys with World Series experience to spark the clubhouse.

None of the deals addressed the real needs of the team. In 1986 the Orioles had set a new major-league record for the fewest triples hit by a team (thirteen) and had been twenty-fifth in the majors in stolen bases. They scored three runs or fewer in nearly half their games. Clearly, team speed was lacking, something that neither Burleson, Knight, nor Kennedy would add.

Defensively, the O's were a disaster, with a team fielding percentage of .978, their worst since 1959. Pitcher Mike Flanagan spoke truer than he realized when he told *Sports Illustrated*'s Hank Hersch, "This franchise was built on defense. As pitchers we always complained about not having enough runs, but that meant we took the defense for granted. But the last couple of years have made us realize just how important it was."

This was the team that Cal Ripken, Sr., had inherited, a team that lost 42 of its last 56 games in 1986 to land in last, 22½ games behind the first-place Red Sox.

As they used to say in war movies, "He never had a chance."

First, the pitching collapsed. Only two starters, Boddicker and Eric Bell, started as many as sixteen games. Nine other pitchers split the starting duties, including such old Orioles hands as Scott McGregor and Mike Flanagan. McGregor and Flanagan both spent parts of the season in the minors. The rest were rookies like John Habyan, Tony Arnold, and Jose Mesa, all of whom have long since departed. Two others, Mark Williamson and Jeff Ballard, would still be around in 1990. The rookies went 27–40 with a 5.20 ERA.

The only player with more than ten steals in 1987 was Alan Wiggins. Wiggins had been suspended several times by his previous team, the Padres, for drug use and was hardly the sort of model citizen around whom Orioles teams traditionally were built. More than that, he was a lousy fielder and unhappy in the organization. He would be gone in the off-season.

The 1987 season was an odd one for Baltimore and in some ways made the debacle of 1988 possible, maybe even inevitable. As Jon Miller, the team's play-by-play man, explains, "the Orioles really fell apart." Oddly enough, the team had enjoyed a scintillating May, hitting 50 home runs over a 22-game stretch in which they went 17–5. "They ran roughshod over some teams for a while," Miller said. "People went in with this feeling that the Orioles had a chance to do something. Then just as quickly, they went 5–30, which put them at 35–53 at the halfway point, which was about right for them."

In July the Orioles brought up Billy Ripken, a fiery kid who was fiercely loyal to his father and the organization. Playing for his dad at the major-league level, Ripken lit up the failing O's briefly. They strung together an eleven-game winning streak and looked like the Birds of old for a moment. His youthful enthusiasm brought back some of the looseness in the clubhouse that had been one of the hallmarks of the winning Baltimore teams of the

'70s. As Flanagan said, "Things are a lot more normal all of a sudden."

It was an optical illusion, a costly one. Over the last two months of the season the Birds went 20–39 and limped home in sixth place, ahead of the even more woeful Cleveland Indians. Their darkest hour probably came on September 14, when they gave up a major-league record ten homers to Toronto, while losing 18–3. Orioles pitchers surrendered a total of 226 dingers that year, also a new record. But to some optimistic eyes the two hot streaks had disguised the fact that this was a team in need of a complete face-lift.

Ed Williams must have suspected something. Over the winter he fired Hank Peters and Tony Giordano and replaced them with Rollie Hemond and Doug Melvin. Hemond had been Bill Veeck's general manager when the wily Veeck had taken over the White Sox in the mid-70s; Veeck fans retain an indelible image of the two of them sitting at a card table outside the winter meetings their first year at the helm of the Chisox with a sign that advertised their willingness to trade. More seriously, Hemond had helped Veeck design his "rent-a-player" system of using one-year free agents to boost his club, and had made some clever little deals that helped Veeck rebuild the previously dreadful Sox into something more respectable. The new farm director, Melvin, was young, only thirty-five at the time, a former righty pitcher who had even spent time as the Yankees' batting-practice pitcher. He was considered a shrewd judge of talent, like both Hemond and another new member of the management team, Hall of Famer Frank Robinson.

Robinson, former Oriole, was named special assistant to Williams. The appointment answered several needs. First, it gave the increasingly active Williams an experienced baseball man to oversee operations. Second, it reclaimed one of the brightest lights of the O's' championship history. Third, it put a highly visible black face in the management of the club at a time when Williams was disturbed by what he perceived to be racial insensitivity in his organization.

Still, says Jon Miller, after the 1987 season there was a feeling of optimism. After all, the team had hit 211 home runs. Maybe a legitimate leadoff hitter, someone who can run, a couple of pitchers. . . . After all, this team had Eddie Murray, Cal Ripken, Larry Sheets (who had hit .316 with 31 homers in '87), Fred Lynn, Terry Kennedy. The pitching staff was being retooled completely, with younger arms being brought in regularly. If only some of those kids could pitch. . . .

Rollie Hemond explained to the Baltimore *Sun,* "Part of the plan was to find help for 1988. We weren't in a position to trade for the future. . . . We added some players who are in the good age bracket, the mid-twenties. They give us help now, but it also allows our farm system to work in players without rushing them."

Philosophically, it was sound thinking. Of course, nobody expected much from the Orioles going into the 1988 season. Most sportswriters picked them to finish last in the AL East. "The Orioles need time," opined *Sports Illustrated,* "Or better yet, another Ripken or two in the lineup."

At least on paper it was a lineup that should have won more than 54 games. Lynn was nothing like the ballplayer he had been in his heyday in Boston, but he had hit 23 homers in 1987. Sheets looked like an outfield star in the making, and Ken Gerhart showed promise. Granted, by trading Ray Knight for pitcher Mark Thurmond, the O's were left without a third baseman, but young Rick Schu had possibilities; after all, hadn't the Phils moved Mike Schmidt to first to give the kid a shot? And Billy Ripken, hadn't he hit .308 in 58 games (before being sidelined by injuries) and shown a lot of fire? At least he gave his big brother a second baseman to turn the DP with. Cal Junior had played with 19 different second baseman before Billy came up.

At the heart of the team were Cal Ripken, Jr., and Eddie Murray, a pair of perpetual MVP candidates. Never mind that Murray, never garrulous but always gracious before, had turned taciturn and unhappy in Baltimore, a target for fan disenchantment who was now getting friction from management as well. Forget that Ripken's numbers were dropping as his consecutive-game streak mounted. These guys were the kind of clutch hitters who could carry a team for weeks on end.

The pitching was almost all question marks, not a good sign. Mike Boddicker had gone 10–12, with a 4.18 ERA, in 1987, and his repertoire of junk pitches no longer seemed to tantalize AL hitters as it had when he was a rookie in 1983. Maybe the wear and tear of throwing 1,088 innings over five years was beginning to hamper him. Dave Schmidt had helped out in '87, going 10–5 with a 3.77 ERA. Mike Morgan won twelve games in 1987 with the woebegone Mariners; certainly he would do more with the proud Orioles behind him. Mark Thurmond had been to a World Series with the Padres in 1984 and knew what it was to be a winner (although he was 35–31 lifetime, entering the 1988 campaign). Bullpen ace Don Aase had gone from 66 appearances in 1986 to seven the following year, plagued by a bad back. The off-season acquisition of Doug Sisk from the Mets should have given him some help. Could Scott McGregor have a year left? Maybe some of the kids would come around.

Spring training was less than promising. In fact, it was lousy. The team went 9–19, their worst exhibition record since 1980, when they had played to a 7–14 record in Florida. That team had gone 100–62 under Earl Weaver and finished second to the Yankees. Of course, nobody expected the 1988 Orioles to do the same, but anything was possible.

In fact, Bill James had put his finger on the team's problem in his 1988 edition of the *Baseball Abstract*. At the time, he wrote that the recent changes in the team's starting lineup "rather than fighting off the natural aging process and the natural accumulation of incentive problems which occur within any lineup, made the team immediately older, less well conditioned, less well motivated, and more injury prone."

The O's dropped their last five spring training games. Opening Day, in spite of drawing their largest regular-season crowd ever, 52,395, was a disaster for Baltimore. The Brewers pummeled the Birds, 12–0, tying a major-league record for the worst shutout in an opener. Rumors were starting to fly that manager Ripken would be canned soon. (On the other hand *Sports Illustrated* had probably been premature in deriding the O's for starting five lefties against the left-handed Ted Higuera; he had actually been more effective against right-handed batters in 1987. Not that it helped.)

Lots of good teams lose on Opening Day. Rollie Hemond, like a terminal patient going through denial, said, "You know, some of your best streaks start after games like this." Also some of your worst.

Lots of bad teams win on Opening Day. Didn't the awful Mets teams of the mid-'70s have a great Opening Day record? From 1975 to 1983 the Mets hadn't lost an Opener, and a lot of those teams were terrible. So were the Orioles.

They lost another game to Milwaukee, 3–1, two days later. Then they went to Cleveland for a four-game series. After losing the opener, 3–0, the Orioles succumbed to a 12–1 drubbing. "I don't know which was worse, watching this game or playing in it," confessed Terry Kennedy. Mike Boddicker balked home two of the Indians' dozen runs. Mark Williamson would make a pick-off attempt at first by tossing the ball into center field. The Orioles dropped the remaining two games in the series, 6–3 and 7–2. Over the first six games of the season they had been outscored 53–7.

Williams and Hemond had seen enough. On the same day that he was pleading guilty to a February third DWI charge, Cal Ripken, Sr., was replaced by Frank Robinson. "I wasn't seeing signs of positive progress," said Hemond. He also admitted that if Robinson had turned down the job offer, he would have left Ripken in place for a while longer.

For Ripken the turn of events came as a surprise. He told *The New York Times,* "There was no indication it was coming. I was in uniform, I was at my desk getting ready to write the lineup. Roland called me to his office and told me I was being relieved." He had lost 36 of his last 47 regular-season games as the Orioles manager.

♦

For Robinson it was his third tour of duty as the only black manager in baseball. He had been saddled with bad teams in Cleveland and San Francisco and had had some success in turning them around. He didn't believe that the 1988 Orioles were a bad team. "We're going to try to get to .500 as soon as possible and then go from there," he said that day.

Robinson knew what his first job would be, to soothe Cal Junior and Billy. "I thought it very important to do that as quick as possible," he would say later. "I wanted them to know I was not upstairs rooting against Cal."

Like the veteran ballplayer that he is, Cal Junior was circumspect in his public reaction. "I've never played for Frank as a manager," he told *The Washington Post*. I have a great deal of respect for him as a baseball man. I'm sure he'll do a good job." Asked whether he thought his father got a fair shake, he said that as a player it was not for him to say. "Do I have an opinion? Again, I'm a player. I don't have an opinion on that. As a son I'll keep my opinions to myself."

Billy "wears his emotions out front," says Jon Miller. "He took it the hardest. You could tell that it affected his play for a while. He's one of these intensely loyal kind of people. If he'd been in the Old West and he had a brother who was a gunfighter in a John Wayne movie and got thrown in jail, Billy'd be the one who'd come in and break him out. It was real hard for Billy. Billy has a great feel for his dad anyway." He wore his father's number seven that night and would keep it for the remainder of the season.

Robinson would find himself under additional scrutiny because of his race. Not only was he, once again, the only black manager in baseball, but he was hired shortly after the furor that was aroused when Al Campanis remarked on ABC's *Nightline* program that blacks hadn't been named to managerial posts because "they lacked the necessities." The only necessities that black managerial candidates had lacked to that point was the old-crony ties that kept men like Dave Bristol (657–764 in eleven years managing in the majors, best finish: third) and Chuck Tanner (1,352–1,381, 19 years, one first-place finish) in the majors. Robinson had assembled those connections, and he had heard all the whispers and felt whatever pressure there was to be felt. "I don't think I ever felt the pressure of being in the position of being a black manager," he said. "I am aware of the pressure of the position, but I don't let it bother me."

It was nothing compared to the pressure he would feel over the next three weeks.

The Orioles dropped their next two games. At this point, for whatever consolation value it might have been worth, the Atlanta Braves were also 0–8. Robinson suggested to reporters that "interleague play could help us both, if we played one another." After the Orioles lost to the Royals, 9–3, for their eighth consecutive loss of the season, Robinson was interviewed by a Baltimore TV station. While waiting there he looked out the window and noticed a warehouse fire. "I looked closer and saw it was the Robinson Company," he noted. The Braves finally won after losing their tenth game; the Orioles would have to wait a while longer to extinguish the flames.

The losing streak continued. Another loss to the Royals made it nine in a row. Cleveland was coming to town, the only team that had finished behind the O's the previous year, the team that had swept them on the first road trip of the year. Someone asked Earl Weaver what he would have done to get the team out of their slump. Jon Miller recalls:

He said he hadn't been paying that close attention that he could make specific suggestions, "but the best way to stop a losing streak is for Dave McNally to go out and pitch a shutout." The funny thing is, the next night, Mike Morgan went out and pitched a shutout. He pitched it for ten innings and in the eleventh inning they lost 1–0. In fact, they gave up a run in the eleventh, then in the bottom of the inning, Cal Ripken hits a single and Eddie Murray hits one into the teeth of the wind to right field and misses a home run by a foot and a half. Gets a double, they've got second and third and they still don't score.

The Orioles fans and the Baltimore community began to pitch in with helpful ploys. Baltimore drivers left their headlights on all day. Disk jockey Bob Rivers pledged to stay on the air until the O's won one. Phone-in shows were filled with fans pledging loyalty. Couples vowed to abstain from sex until the first Oriole triumph. (Was there a significant drop in the Baltimore birthrate in the fall of 1988?) Another couple offered to "keep doing it" until that first victory, daunting for even the most prurient minded.

Robinson remained jovial in the face of disaster, perhaps surprising some who knew his well-deserved reputation for volatility. As the losing streak mounted, the press attention grew as well, and he was handling it with great aplomb.

Game thirteen was prefaced by Robinson predicting a lot of Oriole runs, "fifty, to be exact, we'll win 50–49." Amazingly, the Orioles broke out on top, 3–0, but Mark Thurmond got shelled by the Brewers for five runs in 1²/₃ innings. Cal Ripken, Jr., hitless in his last 29 at bats, finally broke out with a home run, but the Brewers got three more on three consecutive errors by the O's. Typical of the evening was a sequence in which Wade Rowdon was given the hit-and-run sign with Larry Sheets, no speedster, on first. Rowdon swung through the pitch, but Sheets missed the sign, so no damage was done. Robinson decided to tempt fate and flashed it again. This time Sheets got the sign and took off for second, but Rowdon missed it, taking the pitch, and Sheets was cut down easily. The 9–5 loss tied the major-league record of thirteen consecutive defeats to open a season, held by the 1920 Tigers.

At the opening of the Orioles' fourteenth game of the year, a banner was hung in center field: "0–162, THAT'S WHY THEY CALL THEM THE O's." On this night the sentiment wouldn't look so farfetched. Mike Boddicker gave up a two-run single to Jim Gantner, then hitting .147 with no ribbies, to secure an 8–6 loss, Boddicker's ninth straight defeat.

The next night it was Scott McGregor's turn. One of the winningest pitchers in the 1980s, he gave up six runs in 2²/₃ innings to the Brewers. His last victory had been almost two years before.

Loss number sixteen was prefaced by more nuttiness from radio personality Bob Rivers, who brought the Amazing Kreskin on his show to help channel the brain waves of listeners to the Orioles, instilling winning thoughts. The Royals, their opponents, were struggling through a more modest five-game losing streak, but by now any team that faced the Orioles would emerge looking like the '27 Yankees. Tonight would be no exception. Mike Morgan would start for the O's and would depart without retiring a single batter, giving up seven consecutive singles. Dave Schmidt would allow three more hits and by the time the inning ended, the Royals led 9–0. The final score was 13–1. For the first time in the season Robinson got angry. "It was the first time since I've been here that we were actually looking to lose," he seethed.

By now everyone was beginning to feel the pressure. Teams were afraid of losing to Baltimore. "If they were eight and eight, it would be just another game," George Brett told *Sports Illustrated.* And if they were 3–13, nobody would be paying attention to them. Jon Miller recalls:

> The general rule of thumb for a bad club is that you get ignored. You get ignored by your fans, you get ignored by other teams' fans when you travel, they get their smallest crowds when you're in. Nobody cares about you.
>
> The Orioles, it was the opposite. They were making history; the big problem was, it was not pleasant. A lot of the ballplayers were in such deep slumps, there were guys worried about their professional lives. That they could be sent out anytime soon. Or even a more basic worry, *Have I lost it?*
>
> I remember Frank Robinson telling a story during that slide about his worst slump. I think he'd gone 0-for-22 once when he was with Cincinnati. He said, during that stretch, 'cause it went on for five or six games where he did not get a hit, he started thinking to himself, *I've lost it. I'm never going to get a hit again.* It was in the back of his mind. No matter what he tried, nothing worked. He wasn't hitting the ball hard. He really had this basic fear, *I've lost it. I don't remember how to do this.* And here we had a whole team of players having that problem.
>
> It was the only time I ever saw Eddie Murray offer any kind of self-deprecating humor about his abilities as a player. It was a funny joke that he made about himself, something about hitting the ball to him as a sure way to get on base. He was trying to lighten the scenario, but I never heard Eddie before or since make a joke like that. Eddie was the consummate, complete clutch ballplayer. "Hit it to me," in a no-hitter. "I want to be at bat in a tie game in the ninth inning with men on." That's what he lived for. He was in a terrible slump [at the plate], he was in a fielding slump, he was getting booed.
>
> The amazing thing about Frank during all this is he was enter-

taining the media every night. It was like the World Series every
night, they had 250 people from the media covering the ball club by
then. Frank was sociable and humorous. He was courting the media,
after games too. He never shied away from them. It seemed like he
was doing everything possible to shield the ball club. These guys
were under the glare and didn't want to be. They were reduced to
"How come?" and "Why?" and their answers were "I don't know."
So Frank was handling all this stuff, but deep down it was killing
him.

The next night the Orioles would lose 4–3 on the kind of fluke
play that could only happen to a team that qualified for this book.
With the game tied at three in the ninth, Bo Jackson hit a high fly
ball, a ball that was so poorly hit, Jon Miller recalled, "that Bo
himself is upset about it; he throws away the bat and is jogging
toward first berating himself." Unfortunately, there was a 25-mile-
an-hour wind blowing toward right field. The ball hit the top of the
bullpen fence and Jackson ended up on third with a triple. "The
next guy rolls a single through the drawn-in infield and it's all
over," Miller sighed.

The next night's loss was infinitely more conventional, a six-
hitter by Bret Saberhagen beating the Birds 3–1. Loss number nineteen was more of the same, a pitchers' duel between Frank Viola
and Mike Morgan that the Twins won 4–2. It was the next game
that would be the heartbreaker.

Game number twenty was to be Scott McGregor's last game.
In fact, Hemond had already begun to move kids in from Rochester, the Orioles Triple-A farm team. Keith Hughes and Craig Worthington would both play in this game, and reliever Bill Scherrer
would have a leading role in the drama. McGregor didn't have
much and was cuffed about for four runs by the Twins, blowing a
three-run lead, but tonight the Birds wouldn't back down. Hughes
hit a two-out, two-run single in the first, Worthington homered in
the second. By the eighth the game was tied at four and Robinson
went to his bullpen for Scherrer, using the lefty to face Kent
Hrbek, hoping to keep the left-handed Hrbek in the park. Of
course, Hrbek homered. Tim Laudner followed with another ho-

mer. By the time the inning was over, the score was 7–4. Jon Miller retells the tale:

> All of a sudden, for the first time during the streak, they get this sizzling two-out rally going, Cal Ripken and Eddie Murray each drive in runs with two outs, now it's 7–6. Fred Lynn hits a hard grounder that Tommy Herr picks up and they end up losing 7–6. That was one of the hardest ones for Frank. He stayed back in his office until deep into the night. Richard Justice of *The Washington Post* was still in the ballpark writing late at night and he happened to go into the clubhouse for whatever reason, not expecting to find anyone there, and there was Frank back in his office, with his head buried in his hands.

With this, their twentieth loss, the Orioles had tied the American League record set by the 1916 Athletics. A certain gallows humor usually prevailed in the Orioles clubhouse during the streak. Cal Ripken, Jr., said to a reporter newly assigned to the Orioles' forced march, "Join the hostages." When President Reagan called and asked Robinson if there was something he could do to help, Robinson asked, "Can you play first base?" After this loss, however, he would be subdued with the press, accepting blame and responsibility for the decision to leave Scherrer in to face Laudner after Hrbek's blast. Even the press was beginning to realize, as Thomas Boswell's column the next day headlined, HEY, THIS ISN'T FUNNY! Larry Sheets was on the verge of tears in the clubhouse, massaging Eddie Murray's shoulders as he softly told Boswell, "It's just not to be right now."

"It was not pleasant to be around," Miller recalls. "And how they handled that stuff I don't know."

Oddly enough, Miller and his partner, Joe Angel, became lightning rods for the press, deflecting some of the attention away from the beleaguered players. He explains:

> There was such a sheer number of people from the media with us, needing to do stories, and the players didn't want to talk. After all, what were they going to talk about? After a while it was the same

story every day, it never changed. It wasn't like there was some new angle on it.

We came into Minnesota for a three-game series, started with a day off. We were there for four days when the streak had gone to 18. I started writing down every time I did an interview and in four days I did 53 of them. I felt like a rock star.

I couldn't even leave the room. One morning the phone rang at six A.M. As soon as I'd finish with one, I'd hang up the phone and it would ring again. I'd do four in a row like that, I'd hang up the phone and the [message] light would be on. I'd call down for the messages and there'd be seven messages. I'd hang up from retrieving the messages and the phone would ring. I went from six A.M. to about 12:30 P.M. sitting on my bed doing interviews. I finally hung it up, threw some clothes on, and sneaked down a stairway from the 27th floor and snuck out a back exit to get outside and take a run. There were cameras in the lobby, writers sitting around the lobby.

It was a funny thing; this was the worst thing that ever happened in Orioles history and it's the best thing that's ever happened to me.

Back in Baltimore, DJ Bob Rivers was completing his two hundredth consecutive hour on the air. *The New York Times* reported that "according to locals [he] is becoming somewhat cranky." For the city this wasn't too funny either. After all, when Bob Irsay snuck the Colts out of town under cover of darkness, the Orioles had stayed. Moreover, the city and state had committed themselves to building a new stadium. More than that, there was a real and deep affection for the Orioles in Baltimore.

On April 28 the Orioles completed their visit to Minnesota by losing to the Twins, 4–2. It was their twenty-first consecutive loss, Mike Boddicker's tenth in a row, a new team record. Boddicker walked six and hit three batters. Rollie Hemond had shown up at the stadium wearing the same gray suit he had worn when his 1983 White Sox had clinched their divisional title. The suit, which had not had the champagne washed out of it, had been hanging in a hallway at Comiskey Park, but Eddie Einhorn and Jerry Reinsdorf, the Sox' current owners, had shipped it to him that day. He put it on in the eighth inning. It must have been too late.

The agony was almost over. When it ended, it was almost anticlimactic. As Jon Miller says, "They dismantled the White

Sox, and they did it swiftly and suddenly." Beginning with an Eddie Murray homer, the O's pounded four Chisox hurlers for nine runs, their biggest scoring outburst of the season. Rollie had worn his magic suit again and this time it had worked.

Understandably, the Orioles were reluctant to celebrate. Mark Williamson, the winning pitcher, put it in perspective. "I'm relieved," he said. "It's not like we won the seventh game of the World Series. Maybe we won't be so much of a household name now."

That was the way Jon Miller felt when it ended too. He recalls the sensation vividly and remembers how he handled the victory on the air.

> When it ended, I basically described the scene, because it was quite a scene. The game ended, they won 9–0, there wasn't any drama. If they'd had a 3–2 lead and held on to win it, it would have been exciting, but it wasn't exciting. What was intriguing was that all of a sudden, all of these media people began flooding onto the field and within a minute of the game being over, after the Orioles had congratulated one another, there's all these impromptu interviews and press conferences going on all over the field. Down by the dugout there's Frank Robinson surrounded by a hundred people with all these lights on and there's different players handling interviews, all right out on the field. So I just described the final out and described all that. That's all I did.
>
> This was not a victory celebration they were having, except in the sense that the feeling of prevailing that the survivors of the *Titanic* probably had when they were taken out of their lifeboats by another ship. They weren't popping any champagne corks. Then they went on with their lives, trying to forget about the horrors they had just endured. That was always my response to people who asked, "What's it like being with the Orioles?" I said, "It's like being in a lifeboat in the North Atlantic, having seen my ship sink and we've got a 12-person lifeboat with 25 people in it."

The *Titanic* struck an iceberg. What happened to the Orioles? Mike Boddicker said after the streak, "If we took a college team and put it out there for 21 games, even they'd win a couple." A team isn't supposed to go into a collective slump that lasts for over three weeks. It defies the law of averages, especially when you go down the roster of this ball club. But it happened. In April the 1988 Orioles hit .203, with only twelve home runs. In the first twelve games of the streak the O's scored eighteen runs, hit .186, slugged .247 with an on-base percentage of .247.

More important, as sabermetrician Don Malcolm points out, after game thirteen the pitching went south. In the final nine games of the streak Orioles opponents hit .337, slugged .539, and had an on-base percentage of .394.

Now there could be no doubt. This team couldn't be saved with Band-Aids. Radical surgery was necessary. Hemond and Melvin began to operate even during the streak, bringing in kids from Rochester. Over the course of the season Oriole rookies would account for an AL-high 674 at bats. Robinson would use a total of 108 different starting combinations, by far the highest total in the majors. He would also use 15 different starting pitchers.

The worst was finally over on the field, but there were greater tragedies to be borne. Edward Bennett Williams, the team's owner, had been fighting a losing battle with cancer and finally succumbed on August 12. In late May he had effectively turned control of the team over to one of his law partners, Larry Lucchino, who had found a buyer willing to keep the team in Baltimore. Longtime trainer Ralph Salvon also died during the season.

The rest of the season was comparatively uneventful. After their first win of the season in game 22, Baltimore would drop thirteen of the next eighteen. Jon Miller says, "It's like they started off historically bad and then went into a slump." After that, Hemond and Melvin dismantled much of the remaining old team. Mike Boddicker was traded to Boston, where, to his delight, he found himself in the midst of a pennant race. Fred Lynn was sent to Detroit, where he fell victim to one last battle with the Baltimore gremlins. Lynn negotiated too long on the buyout passage of his no-trade contract and the private jet carrying him to Chicago to join the Tigers didn't make contact with the tower at O'Hare until 12:10 A.M. on September 1, so he wouldn't have been eligible for postseason play, had the Tigers made the play-offs.

The Orioles finished the year 54–107, their worst record ever.

They became only the fourth team in major-league history to post a worse record in each of five successive years. They lost sixteen of their final nineteen games and failed to win a game in fifteen series. No Oriole pitcher won ten games. Their twenty road victories was the lowest total in 36 years, their .238 batting average the lowest in the AL in six. With the huge dip in Larry Sheets's production—down to .230, ten homers, 47 RBIs—there was no one to protect Ripken and Murray in the order, and the results were readily apparent: between them they had 51 one homers and 165 RBIs, good, but not up to their standards.

The foundations of a new team were slowly put in place. Outfielder Brady Anderson came over from the Red Sox for Mike Boddicker. Steve Finley was the International League's Rookie of the Year, Craig Worthington its MVP. Young arms like those belonging to Jeff Ballard, Gregg Olson, and Pete Harnisch would serve to anchor a pitching staff. Phil Bradley came in a three-way swap with the Phils and Dodgers, Randy Milligan for a song from the Pirates. Bob Melvin was obtained for Terry Kennedy from San Francisco. Mickey Tettleton, who had been picked up during the 1988 season, would become the everyday catcher, with Melvin as his backup. Eddie Murray was sent to Los Angeles for Brian Holton, a pitcher, and minor-league shortstop Juan Bell (brother of George). Cal Ripken, Sr., was restored to the third-base coach's box.

From spring training it would be obvious that something was very different about the new Orioles. From Day One, Frank Robinson told his players, "Listen, they lost 107 games last year, they had a 21-game losing streak, that's history. We can't change it, but it's irrelevant to you guys. You're going to be asked about it constantly. We're not thinking about anything but today's game. All our goal is, and all we tell the media about setting goals is, that our goal is to play as hard as we can play today and to win today's game through that effort."

The change was apparent in spring training, where the O's went 14–15, a 147-point improvement over the previous spring. All through spring training they had been taunted by *Boston Globe* sportswriter Dan Shaughnessy. Jon Miller recalls:

Shaughnessy wrote a column saying, "Here's a prediction for Opening Day, Clemens will pitch a no-hitter against the Orioles." And he printed the possible lineup for the Orioles and said, "See what I'm saying? Name the guy in that lineup who's most likely to get a hit." The Orioles put that up in the clubhouse during spring training and somebody wrote on it, "Bullshit!" Somebody else wrote, "Only if he has a really good day." Shaughnessy kept writing this every week, "Only fourteen days to Clemens's Opening Day no-hitter."

But they beat Clemens. Late in the game he had a 3–1 lead but they came back and tied it and went ahead. They finally won it in extra innings against the bullpen. They played a hell of a game with a sellout crowd and the crowd went nuts. Of course, the questions were "No 21-game losing streak this year?"

They set the tone for a lot of things that day. Steve Finley made an incredible catch up against the wall on a ball hit by [Nick] Esasky. He caught it, slammed into the wall, dislocated his shoulder. It set the tone for the day and season. Everybody in the park knows that ball doesn't get caught last year, somebody's waiting to play the carom and hold the guy to a double last year. This is a new ball club. And it was a fearless, courageous kind of play by Finley. He could have shied away at the last, because the wall is waiting to tear his arm off.

That was the tone for the entire season, and the Orioles, having rebuilt around defense and young pitching, were in the pennant race until the last weeks of the season. In fact, they were in first place for 117 days and only relinquished the lead on August 31. How did they do it?

Bill James likens the 1989 Orioles to the 1960 edition, which climbed from a sixth-place finish in 1959 to second. "What they did was almost the same as what they did in 1960, and that was what was eerie about it. The Orioles in 1960 and again in 1989 collected those guys who were trapped in Triple-A who were pretty good ballplayers and gave them a chance to play, guys like Mike Devereaux and Randy Milligan and Steve Finley and Brady Anderson, who had just been there waiting. And those guys played."

They played so well that the Orioles went from seventh place,

54–107, to second place, 87–75. The improvement was the fourth best in major-league history, tied with the 1936 Braves.

The 1989 Orioles justified their late owner's faith in Rollie Hemond, Frank Robinson, and Doug Melvin, and the city of Baltimore's commitment to keeping them in town. Was the 1989 team the foundation of another Orioles dynasty? It's impossible to say at this point. If nothing else, the Orioles set a standard for future bad teams to strive to live up to.

1988 Baltimore Orioles Roster

Player	POS	G	AB	R	H	2B	3B	HR	RBI	SB	BA
Brady Anderson	OF	53	177	17	35	8	1	1	9	6	.198
Butch Davis	OF-DH	13	25	2	6	1	0	0	0	1	.240
Jim Dwyer	DH	35	53	3	12	1	0	2	15	0	.226
Ken Gerhart	OF-DH	103	262	27	51	10	1	9	23	7	.195
Rene Gonzales	3B	92	237	13	51	6	0	2	15	2	.215
Keith Hughes	OF	41	108	10	21	4	2	2	14	1	.194
Terry Kennedy	C	85	265	20	60	10	0	3	16	0	.226
Tito Landrum	OF	13	24	2	3	0	1	0	2	0	.125
Fred Lynn	OF	87	301	37	76	13	1	18	37	2	.252
Eddie Murray	1B	161	603	75	171	27	2	28	84	5	.284
Carl Nichols	C-OF	18	47	2	9	1	0	0	1	0	.191
Joe Orsulak	OF	125	379	48	109	21	3	8	27	9	.288
Billy Ripken	2B	150	512	52	106	18	1	2	34	8	.207
Cal Ripken	SS	161	575	87	152	25	1	23	81	2	.264
Wade Rowdon	3B-OF	20	30	1	3	0	0	0	0	1	.100
Rick Schu	3B	89	270	22	69	9	4	4	20	6	.256
Larry Sheets	OF-DH	136	452	38	104	19	1	10	47	1	.230
Pete Stanicek	2B-OF	83	261	29	60	7	1	4	17	12	.230
Jeff Stone	OF	26	61	4	10	1	0	0	1	4	.164
Mickey Tettleton	C	86	283	31	74	11	1	11	37	0	.261
Jim Traber	1B-DH	103	352	25	78	6	0	10	45	1	.222
Craig Worthington	3B	26	81	5	15	2	0	2	4	1	.185

Figures include games played with Baltimore only.

Pitcher	G	IP	H	ERA	ShO	SV	SO	BB	W	L
Don Aase	35	47	40	4.05	0	0	28	37	0	0
Jeff Ballard	25	153	167	4.40	1	0	41	42	8	12

Pitcher	G	IP	H	ERA	ShO	SV	SO	BB	W	L
Jose Bautista	33	172	171	4.30	0	0	76	45	6	15
Mike Boddicker	21	147	149	3.86	0	0	100	51	6	12
Gordon Dillard	2	3	3	6.00	0	0	2	4	0	0
John Habyan	7	15	22	4.30	0	0	4	4	1	0
Pete Harnisch	2	13	13	5.54	0	0	10	9	0	2
Scott McGregor	4	17	27	8.83	0	0	10	7	0	3
Bob Milacki	3	25	9	0.72	1	0	18	9	2	0
Mike Morgan	22	71	70	5.43	0	1	29	23	1	6
Tom Niedenfuer	52	59	59	3.51	0	18	40	19	3	4
Dickie Noles	2	3	11	24.30	0	0	1	0	0	2
Gregg Olson	10	11	10	3.27	0	0	9	10	1	1
Oswaldo Peraza	19	86	98	5.55	0	0	61	37	5	7
Bill Scherrer	4	4	8	13.50	0	0	3	3	0	1
Curt Schilling	4	15	22	9.82	0	0	4	10	0	3
Dave Schmidt	41	130	129	3.40	0	2	67	38	8	5
Doug Sisk	52	94	109	3.72	0	0	26	45	3	3
Mark Thurmond	43	75	80	4.58	0	3	29	27	1	8
Jay Tibbs	30	159	184	5.39	0	0	82	63	4	15
Mark Williamson	37	118	125	4.90	0	2	69	40	5	8

Figures include games played with Baltimore only.